D0444972

Praise for Mink River

✦ Editor's Choice Prize for Fiction, *Foreword Reviews*' Book of the Year Awards

✦ An *Oregonian* Top Ten Northwest Book

"Award-winning essayist Doyle writes with an inventive and seductive style that echoes that of ancient storytellers. This lyrical mix of natural history, poetry, and Salish and Celtic lore offers crime, heartaches, celebrations, healing, and death. Readers who appreciate modern classics like Sherwood Anderson's *Winesburg, Ohio* or William Faulkner's *As I Lay Dying* will find much to savor here. Enthusiastically recommended." —*Library Journal* (starred review)

"[An] original, postmodern, shimmering tapestry of smalltown life ..." —*Publishers Weekly*

"The strength of the novel lies in Doyle's ability to convey the delicious vibrancy of people and the quirky whorls that make life a complex tapestry. He is absolutely enchanted by stories, with the zeal and talent to enchant others ... The greatest gift of *Mink River* is that it provides every reason in the world to see your own village, neighborhood and life in a deeper, more nuanced and connected way." —*The Oregonian*

"Doyle's language is rich, lush, equal to the verdant landscape he describes, and his narrative ricochets with a wondrous blending of the real and magical from character to character as he tracks the intersecting lives of Neawanaka oe summer." —Greg Sarris, *San Francisco Chronicle*

"Doyle explores the inner workings of a community and delivers a timeless story of survival, transcendence, and good cheer." —Tim McNulty, *The Seattle Times*

"This is a story to get lost in, as stories upon stories unfold in this tiny town on the Oregon coast. *Mink River* is flat-out fabulous." —Sheryl Cotleur, Book Passage, Corte Madera, California

Mink River

a novel

Brian Doyle

Oregon State University Press
Corvallis

Map and spot drawings by Mary Miller Doyle

Library of Congress Cataloging-in-Publication Data
Doyle, Brian, 1956 Nov. 6–2017 May 27
  Mink river : a novel / by Brian Doyle.
    p. cm.
  ISBN 978-0-87071-585-3 (alk. paper)
  1. City and town life--Oregon--Fiction. 2. Oregon--Fiction. I. Title.
  PS3604.O9547M56 2010
  813'.6--dc22

                          2010007210

∞ This paper meets the requirements of ANSI/NISO Z39.48-1992
  (Permanence of Paper).

First published in 2010 by Oregon State University Press
Twelfth printing 2021
Printed in the United States of America

 Oregon State University
OSU Press

Oregon State University Press
121 The Valley Library
Corvallis OR 97331-4501
541-737-3166 • fax 541-737-3170
www.osupress.oregonstate.edu

For Mary

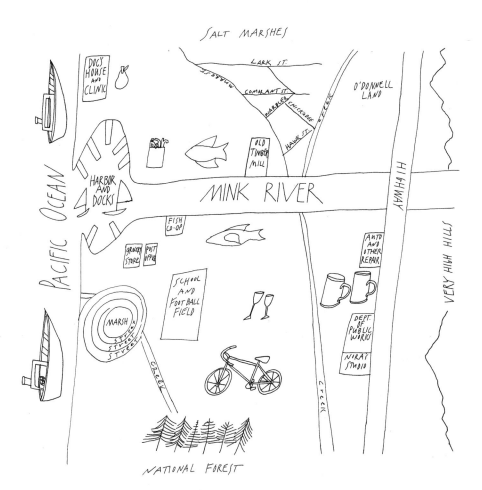

The only music I can compose is that of little things.
　　　　　　　　　　　　　　　　　　—Giacomo Puccini

*The past has not passed away but is eternally preserved somewhere
　　or other and continues to be real and really influential
　　… everybody and everything is so closely interwoven that
　　separation is only approximate …*
　　　　　　　　　　　　　　　　　　—Pavel Florensky

*Animals, as they pass through the landscape, leave their tracks
　　behind. Stories are the tracks we leave.*
　　　　　　　　　　　　　　　　　　—Salman Rushdie

I

1.

A town not big not small.

In the hills in Oregon on the coast.

Bounded by four waters: one muscular river, two shy little creeks, one ocean.

End of May—the first salmonberries are *just* ripe.

Not an especially stunning town, stunningtownwise—there are no ancient stone houses perched at impossible angles over eye-popping vistas with little old ladies in black shawls selling goat cheese in the piazza while you hear Puccini faintly in the background sung by a stunning raven-haired teenage girl who doesn't yet know the power and poetry of her voice not to mention her everything else.

No houses crying out to be the cover of a magazine that no one actually reads anyway and the magazine ends up in the bathroom and then is cut to ribbons for a fourth-grade collage project that uses a jar of rubber cement that was in the drawer by the back stairs by the old shoebox and the jar of rubber cement is so old that you wonder secretly if it fermented or a mouse died in it or *what*.

No buildings on the National Resister of Hysterical Places, though there are some old houses, the oldest of which finally collapses on page 141; *no* cheating ahead to watch it slump like ice cream at noon, please.

But there are some odd sweet corners here, and friendly houses and sheds and barns and a school and churches and shops, and certain rhythmic angles in the town where a road and a building and a line of trees intersect to make a sort of symmetrical geometric architectural textual physical music in the right light—the kind of juxtaposition of things that painters like to paint for inchoate inarticulate unconscious reasons they can't explain.

And the light itself—well, there's a certain *certainness* of light here, the way it shafts itself through and around things confidently, exuberantly, densely, substantively; it has something to do with the nearby ocean, maybe. Or the rain, which falls eight months a year. Or the sheer jungle energy of trees and plants here, where the flora release so many feminine ions that the light fractures into geometric patterns that are organized along magnetic lines coherent with the tides and sometimes visible to the naked eye.

Really and truly.

And some buildings here have a moist salty dignity even as they grow beards of stringy pale moss green as seasick old men; and long relaxed streets that arrive eventually where they are headed but don't get all fascist and linear and anal like highways do; and unusual fauna right *in* the town sometimes, like the young elk who ate a whole box of frozen hot dogs at a school picnic once, or the black bear who wandered through the recycling shed at the Department of Public Works and tore apart a pile of newspapers and was discovered reading the *New York Times* travel section, turning the pages daintily with her claws as big and sharp as steak knives.

Right now, for example, look up, right over there, see the eagle flying low and fast down Curlew Street? Watch: as he sails over the grocery store he whirls and *snatches* a whirling piece of cardboard, and he flapflopflaps down the street triumphantly, big as a tent, you can almost hear him thinking *I am one bad-ass flying machine, this weird flat brown bird didn't get away from* me, *no sir, nothing can elude my lightning deftness in the air …*

Not something you see every day, an eagle chortling over a beer box, eh?

And down the street goes the eagle, heading west, his capacious shadow sliding like a blanket over the elementary school, where a slim older woman with brown and silver hair and brown and green eyes is holding court over the unruly sixth grade, her eyes flashing;

and over her grandson Daniel age twelve with hair braided into three thick braids of different colors (red, black, brown) who is zooming on his bicycle just in front of a logging truck, giving the driver wiggy nightmares for a week;

and over a sturdy young woman named Grace in an open meadow high on a hill where she is slicing apart a small car with a blowtorch her muscular right arm pumping and flexing with the torque of the torch and the leap of her muscle making her tattoo flash like a neon sign *KISS* flash *MY* flash *ASS*;

and over a lithe woman called No Horses in her studio crammed with carving tools as she is staring thoughtfully at a slab of oak twice as big as she is which isn't very big at all;

and over a man named Owen Cooney who is humming in his shop crammed with automobile parts and assorted related ephemera as his pet crow sits quietly on an old Oregon State University football helmet watching;

and over a grocer grocering a priest priesting a doctor doctoring teachers teaching two cooks cooking a man beating his son an insurer insuring a woman vomiting in a creek a banker banking an old nun's heart faltering in her room on the top floor of the hotel a man telling a lie in court a teenage couple coupling on *top* of the blankets in the downstairs bedroom of her parents' house so as to be sure that no rumpled sheets will tell tales of their vigorous unclothedness;

and so many more stories, all changing by the minute, all swirling and braiding and weaving and spinning and stitching themselves one to another and to the stories of creatures in that place, both the quick sharp-eyed ones and the rooted green ones and the ones underground and the ones too small to see, and to stories that used to be here, and still *are* here in ways that you can sense sometimes if you listen with your belly, and the first green shoots of stories that will be told in years to come—so many stories braided and woven and interstitched and leading one to another like spider strands or synapses or creeks that you could listen patiently for a hundred years and never hardly catch more than shards and shreds of the incalculable ocean of stories just in this one town, not big, not small, bounded by four waters, in the hills, by the coast, end of May, first salmonberries *just* ripe. But you sure can *try* to catch a few, yes?

At the west end of the main street, where it begins to slide off precipitously toward the ocean, there's a long low building faced all around with cedar shakes. Right over this sprawling structure the eagle turns south toward his nest, and as he wheels against the noon light his capacious shadow slides over two elderly men at a rickety alder table in front of the long low building, and they look up right quick.

That thing big as a tent, says the taller of the two.

Adult male, says the shorter man.

How can you tell from here?

Can see his ego. The angle of his dangle.

They grin.

Actually I can tell it's a male, continues the shorter man, because you notice that he's carrying a piece of cardboard, which is foolish, so there you go.

Gratuitous slur on our gender, says the taller man.

Men: the final frontier, answers his companion. As your lovely bride says.

The two men are drinking beer and eating salmonberries. Between them is one empty beer bottle; they split a beer every day at lunch. They work together in the long low building behind them. They are, collectively, the Department of Public Works. They have publicworked together for more than forty years, in various jobs. They are the best of friends. They are in their late sixties, they think. They are not totally sure about their ages because neither of them is in possession of a real actual birth certificate for reasons they were too young to learn at the time.

The salmonberries are the first of the season and the two men are eating them very slowly, tasting every bittersweetorangeyellowacidic drop and then slowly sipping the beer a tongueful a thimbleful at a time.

Yum, says the taller of the two men.

Yup, says the other.

Not everyone likes salmonberries.

Vulgarians.

I am told they are an acquired taste.

Vulgarians?

Salmonberries.

Yeh. Listen, this afternoon we have to get back to work on the Oral History Project. We promised that we would get back to work on it the day after the rains stopped and the rains stopped last night and we have got to get to work. We are behind something awful on the Oral History Project.

One of our best ideas absolutely. Whose idea was that?

Yours.

Was it?

You were going on interminably one day about how one way to defeat Time is by recording every story possible. Not only from people but from everything living.

For Every Thing that lives is Holy, says Blake.

Yeh, you said that. Also you said that with the Project we could build an impregnable bulwark against entropy. I remember you saying that because you hardly ever hear the word entropy. Excellent word.

Or impregnable, says the taller man thoughtfully. Unable to be made pregnant? I have to confess, says the taller man, that I was under the impression you invented the Project as part of your vast and overweening ambition.

Nope. Your idea. It fits the expanded public works idea beautifully though. What a resource, eh? Here is what I want to do this afternoon. I want to record osprey calls along the river—those high screams, you know? Piercing sound. On a May day as they are finishing their nests. I wonder if they are speaking in a different tone now than midsummer or early fall. These are the things to know. Let's add that to the list of Things to Know. Thank God for computers. Remember when the Things to Know was on paper? My god, we had to buy that barn just to keep the reams of Things to Know. That was crazy.

Listen, says the taller man. I've been thinking …

Did it hurt?

Listen, my friend, says the taller man, holding on to his line of talk like a rope, did you ever consider that maybe the scope of public works as we have conceived it is too big altogether? I mean other towns and cities use their departments just to fix roads and sewer lines and streambeds and such.

We do those things.

But we also are prey to what I might call a vast and overweening ambition. I mean, really, to preserve history, collect stories, repair marriages, prevent crime, augment economic status, promote chess, manage insect populations, run sports leagues, isn't that a bit much? We even give haircuts.

Are we doing insects? Did I know that?

I'm teasing. But we try to do everything.

Not everything.

I think maybe too much.

I think not enough, says the shorter man.

Don't you ever think we could be wrong? asks the tall man.

Billy, says the shorter man, *this* is why people call you Worried Man.

Cedar, my friend, says the taller man, not smiling, I worry we are arrogant.

Cedar leans over the table and stares his friend in the eye.

Billy, he says quietly. Billy. We heal things. That's what we do. That's why we're here. We've always agreed on that. Right from the start. We do as well as we can. We fail a lot but we keep after it. What else can we do? We have brains that still work so we have to apply them to pain. Brains against pain. That's the motto. That's the work. That's what we do. Soon enough we will not have brains that work, so therefore.

We could stop interfering, says the tall man. Who are we to talk to that young woman, for example? Grace?

Who else would say anything to her?

Her family.

What family? Her mother's gone, her brothers are donkeys, and the father … isn't much in the way of a moral compass, let's put it that way. Look, Billy, what good are we to anyone if we are not ambitious to make a difference? If we don't use our brains we are just two old men fixing potholes. Are potholes enough, my friend? I think not.

I watched that girl's face as we talked to her, says Worried Man. She was humiliated. You know it and I know it. Her face stays with me. Was that right? Did we have the right to sting her like that? Is that the purview of the public works department, to embarrass the public?

To speak to her honestly about her behavior is to care about her, Billy. In a way it is to love her.

Is it?

Isn't it?

Is it?

They drain the last thick dense bitter drops of their beer.

Owen says today is Joan of Arc's feast day, says Cedar, standing up to go.

Her name wasn't Joan, says Worried Man, also rising. It was Jeanne. Jeanne La Pucelle of Domrémy.

Brave child by any name, says Cedar.

She was a meddler too and look what happened to her, poor thing, says Worried Man.

She changed the face of history, says Cedar.

She was roasted to death one morning and her ashes were thrown in the river and the men who murdered her also managed to murder her real name throughout history, says Worried Man.

They bow and part: Cedar to visit a client, as he says, and then to the river to record osprey calls, and Worried Man to his office in the Department to record an answer to this question from his grandson Daniel: *How did my mother get her name?*

2.

This is me, Worried Man, making a tape for my grandson Daniel, about how his mother, who is my daughter, got her name.

Well, No Horses got her name because our people were the best horse stealers *ever*. By our people I mean the People, capital P—we who have lived here in the coast hills longer than even our stories remember.

We were terrific horse stealers. We were *awesome*. No one could steal horses like us. And stealing a horse is *hard*. I mean, the creature weighs half a ton, and they're skittery, and they're smart, some of them, and they know they're not supposed to hustle off quietly into the bushes in the middle of the night; they're supposed to stand drowsily in the milky dew until the morning when they get to eat again. Horses just want to eat. Anyway, you have to get to the scene silently, sometimes slipping past sentries and sentinels, and then you establish an immediate rapport with the horse, silently of course, and then detach all ropes and hobbles and such, and then you calm the horse, and lead him away, past the sentinels again, and the fact is that slipping past a sharp-eared sentinel with a confused fat half-ton animal is no easy matter, as you can imagine.

Well, if you got caught they'd slice your throat.

I'm always hearing about counting coup in battle in the old days, where a guy at great risk to life and limb touches his enemy with a coup stick, escaping with great acclaim and all, but what's the point? I mean, you touched a guy with a stick. Big deal. I'd rather risk life and limb and come out of the fray with a *horse*. Now *that's* an accomplishment. You got something to show for your labors.

Well, one time we were berrying in the valleys east of here, boiling berries into cakes, cooling the cakes in the creeks, and packing down horses with enough berry cakes to choke a small whale—an orca maybe. Though they'd eat anything. Coyotes of the ocean.

Of course to carry the cakes back here to Neawanaka we needed horses, because this was before everyone and their aunt had a truck. We had a lot of horses. These were fine animals absolutely, and they needed to be guarded carefully by stalwart sentinels with sharp ears and sharp eyes. I was chosen as sentinel, being then young and sinewy and in the fullness of my itchy first strength. But I was also in the fullness of my first cocky stupidity, and I had boasted that I could pick more berries than any other man or woman, and also be a sharp-eared and sharp-eyed sentinel, and it turns out I was wrong. On the third night I was so tired and sore that I fell asleep, and that's when horse thieves from the valley made their move.

They slipped up on me and under my horse blanket they affixed four long thin poles of red cedar, willowy whippy things, and then ever so gently ever so daintily they lifted me on the blanket and propped up the poles so that they could gently urge the fat fool horse out from under me, which they did, and left me propped up in the air sound asleep. Then they unhobbled our horses and silently made away with all of them—a dozen of the finest horses you ever saw.

The next morning was difficult.

We all walked home, of course, a very long walk, all my former friends jeering and cursing, and all of us carrying those damn berry cakes, and when we got to Neawanaka everyone was hooting and jeering and telling the story of how I fell asleep, and I have to say that there was a lot of embroidering going on. I know a little about embroidering stories myself, as you know, but this was wholesale embroidering, all sorts of exaggeration, really not suitable at all to the occasion.

My young pregnant wife Maple Head was waiting for me in the little cedar cabin we'd been given by her parents, where we live still, as you know, and when I came in to see her she swung her legs over the side of the bed and stood up and asked about all the hooting and hollering and jeering and embroidering, and I felt that I had better tell her the story myself, so she would get a fairly accurate version of a very unusual event.

So I did.

She laughed, snorted, chortled, wept with laughter, rolled on the floor, guffawed, howled, and etcetera absolutely. She laughed so hard, in short, my little thimbleberry, that she went into labor on the spot, and a few minutes later your mother was born, and that is how your mother received her name, which is, as you know, No Horses. And that is the end of that story.

3.

Neawanaka has been a settlement of one size or another for perhaps five thousand years. Human beings lived here for all the normal reasons you can name: it is well watered, with small but persistent creeks to the north and south, a small but serious river running right smack through town, and an Ocean. There are trout in the creeks, salmon and steelhead run up the river and creeks seasonally, and perch and halibut and cod and such swim not too far offshore; there are so many fish of so many kinds in and around the town that for perhaps five thousand years the name of the town was So Many Fish in the native tongue spoken here. There are deer and elk in the spruce and cedar forests. It hardly ever snows in winter and hardly ever bakes in summer. It does get an unbelievable amount of rain (nearly two hundred inches one year, according to Cedar, who measures such things), and the rain starts in November and doesn't really end, as a continuous moist narrative, until July, but then those next four months are crisp and sunny and extraordinary times, when every living creature, from the pale cloudberry close to the ground to the eagles the size of tents floating overhead, is grinning and exuberant.

And there is of course an amazing amount of wood growing here— spruce and alder mostly, although there's some big cedar and hemlock still in the more remote ravines where loggers couldn't and still can't easily log. And there are more bushes and plants than you can shake a shrub at, most of them providing some sort of food or use, and there are grouse in the spruce thickets also, and a little quail with a topknot that makes really good eating if only you can catch it, so all in all there is enough food to get by, and enough material to easily build shelter, and weather that doesn't set out grimly to kill you, as Cedar says of some other weathers he has known, so people have lived here probably from the first couple of days after the glaciers slid away muttering, or from the first day that a little boat filled with exhausted people from Elsewhere landed on the beach or in the mouth of the Mink River.

Howsoever the first people arrived in this little green cupped hand of a place, they stayed, and like all people everywhere, when eventually they encountered other groups of people, and the other people wanted to know what the people living in the cupped green hand called themselves, the cupped green hand people looked at each other's faces, and cleared their throats uncertainly, and met briefly to confer, and then emerged from their confab, harrumphed, rattled their weapons, and said, why, we are, well, of course, what else would we be, The People.

4.

This is me, Worried Man, making another tape for Daniel, about how I met my friend Cedar.

Well, about forty years ago Maple Head and I were courting on the Mink River. We were way up in the hills near its source to the east. East in rivers of bliss. Blake.

We were pretending to be fishing but really we were learning how to make love. We were trying all sorts of ways of making love to see how we fit together as bodies and companions without family and friends around to shape us with their emotions and expectations, and seeing what ways of making love made us deeper with each other and what ways were just acrobatics or showing off. We were trying to make love absolutely with every muscle and every shred of our attention.

Maybe, thinking about it now, we were trying to figure out how to make love in such a way as to make time not matter at all, or defeat it for a while. Which we did for a while.

I'll say no more.

Hand in hand wandering terrified of each other's beauty. Blake.

Well, we were there by the Mink, and we *were* actually fishing that afternoon, and we were sore and tired and happy, and to be honest neither of us planned on fishing very long at all, and as I remember your grandmother and I were already casting eyes at each other more than we were casting for fish, but then I noticed a person's body going past me in the river, and everything changed absolutely from that moment.

I waded in fast and grabbed that body.

For a not very big body it seemed awfully heavy and I couldn't tell if it was an alive body or a dead body. But I was young and strong then and not afraid of dead things, which are only cousins to living things, so I hauled with all my might and got it up on the riverbank through the ferns. Sword fern, I think. Maybe bracken.

The body was naked and brown and face down in the grass and I flipped it over and it turned out to be a man, who turned out to be Cedar, who turned out to be alive, although awfully waterlogged. We didn't know he was Cedar right at that moment of course, and of course neither did *he* know he was Cedar right then, because he had been in the river a long time and was nearly completely drowned. I'd say he was about ninety percent drowned. He was awfully full of river. Which is probably why Cedar has such a thing for rivers and rain. Heck, he lived *inside* the river for a while, which you can't say about many people, especially living ones.

Anyway when Maple Head saw me haul Cedar out of the river she came sprinting through the fern like a deer, a lovely sight absolutely, that woman could bound and float like a swallow and still does when she walks, if you pay close attention.

She knelt down and looked into Cedar's face, and he had just opened his eyes and seen me and realized that he wasn't drowned, and when he saw her face he smiled, and she smiled, and he said *I like your face better than his*, and we all laughed, although then I decided to throw him back in the river.

But I didn't, which was a good thing, because he turned out to be Cedar. We brought him home and he recovered pretty quickly, but he never could remember how he got to be in the river or where his clothes were or anything at all from before we fished him out. All he could remember was that his name was Cedar. He knew that much.

So that's how Cedar didn't drown.

Lately I have been absorbed by bicycle repair and so I must conclude this tape. I have repaired seventeen bicycles in the past month during which time I have become fascinated by spokes, which are really wires, and now I am utterly into wires—weight-bearing capacity, elegance, metaphor. They are so thin and taut and lithe like your grandmother. I have some very interesting ideas about wiring and strength and the webbing of time, the structural basics of time, you understand, and they must be pursued apace, life being short but not brutish, so I must go. That is the end of this story.

5.

There are halibut as big as doors in the ocean down below the town, flapskimming on the murky ocean floor with vast skates and rays and purple crabs and black cod large as logs, and sea lions slashing through the whip-forests of bull kelp and eelgrass and sugar wrack, and seals in the rockweed and giant perennial kelp and iridescent kelp and iridescent fish and luminous shrimp too small to see with the naked eye but billions of which feed the gray whales which slide hugely slowly by like rubbery zeppelins twice a year, north in spring and south in fall.

Salmonberries, thimbleberries, black raspberries, gooseberries, bearberries, snowberries, salal berries, elderberries, blackberries along the road and by the seasonal salt marshes north and south.

The ground squirrels burrow along the dirt banks of the back roads, their warren of mysterious holes, the thick scatter of fine brown soil before their doorsteps, the flash of silver-gray on their back fur as they rocket into the bushes; the bucks and does and fawns in the road in the morning, their springy step as they slip away from the flower gardens they have been eating; the bobcat seen once, at dusk, its haunches jacked up like a teenager's hot-rodding car; the rumor of cougar in the hills; the coyotes who use the old fire road in the hills; the tiny mice and bats one sometimes finds long dead and leathery like ancient brown paper; the little frenetic testy chittering skittering cheeky testy chickaree squirrels in the spruces and pines—Douglas squirrels, they are, their very name remembering that young gentleman botanist who wandered near these hills centuries ago.

The herons in marshes and sinks and creeks and streams and on the beach sometimes at dusk; and the cormorants and pelicans and sea scoters and murres (poor things so often dead young on the beach after the late-spring fledging) and jays and crows and quorking haunted ravens (moaning *Poe! Poe!* at dusk) especially over the wooded hills, and the goldfinches mobbing thistles in the meadowed hills, and sometimes a falcon rocketing by like a gleeful murderous dream, and osprey of all sizes all along the Mink like an osprey police lineup, and the herring gulls and Caspian terns and arctic terns, and the varied thrushes in wet corners of thickets, and the ruffed grouse in the spruce by the road, and the quail sometimes, and red-tailed hawks floating floating floating; from below they look like kites soaring brownly against the piercing blue sky, which itself is a vast creature bluer by the month as summer deepens into crisp cold fall.

6.

Maple Head is in the sixth-grade classroom at the school. She is the teacher. The school is on the west side of town at the edge of the spruce forest. She is standing by the chalkboard. The school building was once a barn. She is a slim brown woman with long rich curling silver hair with brown leaping in it. The children call her Teacher. The lesson this afternoon is geometry: radius, diameter, circumference. Her eyes are brown and green and when she is angry the green parts of her eyes flash like fish leaping in a river. Barn swallows still nest in the school. She is glaring at the O Donnell boys who are as usual causing a ruckus. They are 16 and 14 and are guests in class today because of general recklessness and boneheadery and lazitude and punishness and detentionery. O Donnells have lived in Neawanaka for more than a century. They were among the Irish Catholics who came after the Hunger and rooted here because the land was no good for farming so nobody wanted to steal it from the People or shove the gaunt ragged foreigners off it. Green fish are leaping furiously in her eyes. The O Donnells were fishing people mostly. Maple Head is a very good teacher and a kind woman through and through but at the moment she is entertaining fishy green thoughts about the O Donnell twins and their motley clan in general and she contemplates her heavy ruler made of hemlock and the mule heads of the O Donnells and the closet with the lock in the basement of the school where one might, if one were so inclined, cram two O Donnells, but she doesn't, although fish are leaping all over the place in her eyes.

Her grandson Daniel should be in her class but instead he is in his father's shop. He was sent over with a school typewriter to be repaired and he is lingering in the shop. He loves the inky oily smells there. He is a round boy with hair in three long braids of three different colors (red, black, brown) like his hero the legendary Irish warrior Cú Chulainn. Daniel's eyes are brown with green flashes. He sits in the third row third seat. He is twelve years old. He likes to play basketball and read and ride his bike. He makes friends easily because he likes to listen and he is almost always cheerful, even with girls. He thinks about girls all the time. He likes to ride his bike in the woods as fast as he can go. Girls are beginning to think about him. A month ago he began to write poems and observations in a small black notebook that he hides in his closet. Two girls in particular think about him a lot but don't say anything to anyone about their thoughts. He is ashamed of hiding his book but he cannot imagine showing it to his parents. He would be horrified if they read what he wrote. He is writing about himself.

No Horses is in her studio at the Department of Public Works, the long low-slung building with the cedar shakes on the east side of town, where the hillside falls away to moist meadows down below. The meadows are brown and green and her eyes are brown and green. Her studio is at the south end of the building to get the most light. Her husband Owen built a little deck at that end and cut a door to it and cut a door-sized piece of glass for it. He's good with his hands that way. The door is shaped like No Horses, a little humorous touch of Owen's. He's good with his head that way. There are two chairs on the deck and a little round table and a hummingbird feeder. Often from the deck she sees elk in the meadows, and hovering buzzards, occasionally a bald eagle. Once a young bear. Once a red-tailed hawk with a snake in its mouth—an image so immediately arresting that she ran from the window to her workbench and started a sculpture in sandstone that isn't working yet though she has hopes.

7.

The doctor is in his office at the north end of town where the hill dives gently down toward the dunes. He has three patients left to see. They are waiting in his waiting room. One is coughing so hard that the second has a vision of him coughing his organs onto the floor one at a time: spleen, kidneys, liver, gallbladder in a steaming pile on the rug. The doctor is a small neat dark man with eyeglasses. The third patient sells boxes and containers of all sizes. The doctor has stepped out back to smoke a cigarette. The third patient likes to say that he sells air with boundaries. The doctor is on the tenth of his twelve daily cigarettes, "one for each apostle," as he says. The third patient has a raging pain in his belly that will kill him in about three weeks. The third patient privately suspects that something is fatally wrong inside him but he has said nothing to anyone. The doctor is unmarried but he has private hopes. The third patient has thought seriously of telling his daughter about his fears but he has refrained. No one is sure of the doctor's age; he is the sort of lean leathery man who could be forty or sixty. The third patient has refrained from telling his daughter about his pain, although he feels closer to her than to anyone else in the world, because she has just fallen in love with a boy, and she just lost her virginity to him, and she's pretty proud now of being a woman, but the boyfriend is sleeping with another girl also, which he hasn't told the third patient's daughter. The doctor will confirm the third patient's fears in about thirty minutes.

The third patient's daughter will find out that her boyfriend is a liar in about three weeks.

8.

Grace O Donnell is in the barn on her parents' farm, patching tractor tires and cursing in new and interesting ways to make her brothers laugh. She spent the morning cutting apart a car with a blowtorch, and she is due out on a fishing boat in another hour, but she swore, so to speak, that she would get to the tires today because her father is now in his seventies and while he is still healthy and still mean he can no longer easily bend over and pick up heavy tools although he never admits or tells anyone that because he is Red Hugh, hard of hand and head, chief of the clan, asking no help or quarter, quick to lash fools and children with his long white rod, *an slath ban*, although he doesn't dare lash Grace or Declan anymore, because of Grace's cold eyes on him when he loses his temper and reaches for the stick and because Declan told his father one afternoon in the meadow that if ever you raise that fecking stick at me again I'll yank it out of your fecking hand and cram it down your fecking throat, you hear me, old man? you hear me?

Grace notices that Red Hugh can no longer easily bend over and pick up heavy tools so she patches the tires.

She gets three tires patched before she notices that the first tire she patched is already flat again and this sets her going on a fit of cursing that even for her is inspired stuff, and she has been swearing like a cuckolded sailor since she was seven years old. It is a skill she learned in part from Red Hugh, a master curser who starts cursing even before he gets out of bed, and Hugh still can get a good burst going, given the right conditions, although he can't sustain an hour's worth of snarling invective like he could in the old days, not that any of his children miss his bile, which is now directed wholly at his wife, who isn't there to hear it, because she packed a suitcase two years ago and walked out the door without a word. The suitcase was enormous. It was far too big for her to carry. The sound of it being dragged down the gravel driveway will stay with Grace and her brothers for ever and ever and ever.

9.

Owen and his pet crow Moses are in his shop at the south end of town, where the highway is. Officially his shop is called **AUTO & OTHER REPAIR** but Other Repair is the greater part by far of his business. The shop is split into two large rooms, one oily and fragrant and filled with many pieces of cars, and the other filled mostly with tables and shelves on which sit several thousand things and pieces of things, among them Moses, who likes to sit on an old football helmet over the long bench where Owen works.

It is a heroic clutter. It is the clutter's dream of clutter. Close your eyes for a minute and think of all the closets you have ever crammed with stuff, and all the basement workbenches asprawl with tools, and the shelves crowded with fishing gear and sports equipment and paintbrushes and furnace filters and nails and eyelets and grommets and washers and such, and merge them all in your mind, not haphazardly but with a general sense of order, a relaxed and affectionate organizational sense, such that you would have a pretty good rough idea where something might be if you needed to find it, and when you went to look for it you would find it in less than a minute, and even when something took more than a minute to find, you would find something else that you'd been looking for not desperately but assiduously; then think of all the rich dark male smells you have ever liked, the smells that remind you of your dad, your grandfather, your uncle, your older brother. Paint in cans that have been imperfectly sealed so a touch of the smell leaks out, and flat whippy paint-stirring sticks half-coated in dried paint atop the cans, and if you are really good with the Nerves of the Expansive Nostrils, as Blake says, you could maybe distinguish the color of the paint from the smells— the vanilla smell of white paint and the fragrant-baby smell of blue, the loud smell of red like a car backfiring, the library smell of brown. And the smells of sawn cedar and maple and fir boards. Ashes. Varnish. Plywood. Cigars. Somewhere on a shelf a redolent piece of redwood. Sweat. Boots. Oil. A hint of gasoline as if it had been spilled quite a long time ago and cleaned up meticulously but the room remembers when it happened. Rubber. The cold impersonal greedy smell of metal. Sawdust. The handled smell of tools. Liniment. Coffee. The brown smell of boxes and cardboard. Beer. The vacation-cabin smell of pine. Oiled saws. Old newspapers. Woodsmoke. The burnt-wire smell of old radio and television tubes. Turpentine. The grandmotherly smell of old upholstery rising warmly from the sagging couch in the corner. Apples. Wet clothes. Bread. Crow.

Its stew of smells and sense of ragged order was the very essence of Owen's shop; children loved it on first sight and old men felt so comfortable there that they would bring Owen things to fix that he knew and they knew didn't need fixing, although he charged a flat fee of ten dollars per job for such things, which the old men paid happily, figuring that ten dollars was the fair cost of an afternoon spent poking around Other Repair, which they also loved because Owen let them poke around freely, without rebuff or boundaries, although he politely declined their inevitable requests to actually repair things, though unanimously they offered to work for nothing, and many of them had offered to pay for the privilege.

Owen's son Daniel recently began a list of the things in this room: watches, alarm clocks, toasters, tape recorders, tape decks, microwave ovens, lawnmowers, half a boat, telephones, computers, kitchen clocks, chairs, tables, televisions, screws, bolts, an alarm system for a boat, answering machines, global positioning devices, fishfinders, fishing reels, hedge clippers, scissors, shears, trowels, the bottom half of an ancient cotton gin, a Beretta pistol, welding tools, hammers, pliers of every conceivable size (Owen maintains that the pliers is the greatest tool ever invented), saws, screwdrivers, an anvil, winches in three sizes, Moses, and taxidermy tools, which is where Daniel stopped recording what he saw, because the tools were being applied to the top half of a huge beaver and Daniel wanted to help, which he did, to the quiet pleasure of his father.

10.

Cedar pays a visit to the man who beats his son. The man works at the fish co-op. His son is in the eighth grade. They live alone. They moved here a year ago from away, the man and the boy. The father beats the son only inside the house. The son no longer cries when he is beaten but tries to make his mind soar out of his body like a bird while the father back on earth is punching and kicking him in the chest and ribs. When the father loses his temper he swings at his son's face and once he has begun swinging he cannot stop although he shifts his punches to the boy's chest and ribs so as not to leave marks and when the boy falls to the floor and curls up the father kicks him with his work boots. The son lifts weights three times a day. When the father is exhausted from beating the boy he goes out on the porch and sobs with great silent wracking sobs and the boy goes to the freezer where he has ice packs arranged by size and a fishing vest he has stuffed with ice. The boy explains his bruises in the gym by saying that he also lifts at home and is clumsy with the weights. The father feels twisted and foul. The boy has run away twice. The father beats the son two or three times a week. The second time the boy ran away Michael the cop found him sleeping in a cave on the beach in a sleeping bag made of old jackets wrapped with duct tape. Michael told Cedar about the boy. Cedar stands outside the back door of the co-op.

Tell me the thoughts of man that have been hid of old, he thinks. Blake.

He steps into the co-op. The father is cleaning a catch of scallops at a long table. The air inside the co-op is bone cold. Weathervane scallops, Cedar notes, the Public Works computer in his head automatically gauging their size. The man is sweating as he wields the shucking knife flick flick flick. The nuggets of scallop meat fly from the knife into a steel bowl.

You will keep your hands off that boy, says Cedar quietly, and the man's head snaps up but his knife keeps shucking flick flick flick.

When the rage comes you will walk out of the house with your hands in your pockets, says Cedar, and the knife stops flicking and there is no sound at all in the room.

Your love for him will heal you, says Cedar, and the man drops the knife and whirls around but Cedar pins the man's arms to his sides with a grip of stone and doom and he leans in closer and says, Your love will heal your boy also.

The man spits a huge gob of spit in Cedar's face and Cedar puts his dripping nose against the man's scarlet nose and says very quietly, If you hit that boy again I will break your fucking wrists like fucking twigs, and the man says nothing and there is no sound at all in the room except the two men breathing hard and the refrigeration unit chuffing.

11.

That is one honking huge beaver, dad.

Tis.

Where's it from?

The Mink River. Grace found it drowned.

Must weigh fifty pounds.

You know prehistoric beavers weighed maybe five hundred pounds. Or more. They were the size of cars.

Really?

Really really. And they were smart. Imagine a really really smart beaver the size of a car.

Yikes.

Imagine you're in the river waist deep fooling around and you see coming toward you a furry car that's thinking maybe you are getting a little too close to its lodge. Which is itself the size of a city. You'd pee so fast you'd raise the river.

You make me laugh.

You know, I love this, when we work together.

Yeh.

I do really.

Me too.

Soon you'll be off to college.

Not for years, dad. And who knows what will happen then?

You sound like my dad. He was always leery of the future.

Why?

Hmm. Good question. Well, he was leery of the present and past too, come to think of it. He was a leery guy. Guy Leery—sounds like a movie star.

Leery of what?

Hmm. Of what would happen, I guess. Or not happen.

Was he paralnoid?

Pa Ra Noid. Not really, no. He was a tough man, very brave in his way. He was just … worried. It was always in his face. A worried man. So to speak. Should have called *him* Worried Man and not your other grandpa. My dad never trusted that things would work his way, is the best way to put it. So they never did.

You're cutting the beaver's ear off.

Ah, so I am. Shit on a stick. Damn my eyes. Never talk and work. The work suffers.

You were saying.

Well, my dad had a hard life, Danno. He was a child of the Hunger, in a way, *an bhuchaill gorta*, and he never found work he really wanted to do, and I think he was lonely all his life.

Until he met Grandmother.

Well. He was lonely after that too.

Tell me.

Let's finish the beaver first.

You should tell your dad's story for the Project.

I could, that. Your grandpa Billy would like that.

Grandpa is making tapes for me.

How so?

Answering questions I ask.

Like?

How Mom got her name, how he met Cedar.

Ask him how a young Irish fella from County Mud & Blood bamboozled his one extraordinary daughter off him. He'll laugh at that.

Grampa has a great laugh.

He does that. Ask him how a young fella with no prospects and education and hair black as the inside of a dog somehow against all odds and sense persuaded the stunning No Horses to marry him. Ask him was it some Celtic druidry or what that won me my wild wee wife.

How did you meet Mom?

Ah, there's a thousand tapes in that story, son.

Did you ask Mom to get married or did she ask you?

I sank to my knees, son, on the highest hill I could find, and I asked her it straight out, with my heart hammering and yammering and warbling and whistling like a water bird in my ribs, and she smiled that sideways smile and said *yes* and your daddy has been a capering fox every minute since with few exceptions absolutely, as your grandpa would say. And now to the beaver.

12.

No Horses in her studio is a study of alternating currents of motion and stillness; a river racing and resting; electric femininity waxing and waning. When her hands are in motion the rest of her is still and vice versa. Often she walks in circles like her father; around her work table, around the room, around the Department building when she's really frazzled and has to think out a piece of work, around the hills on which Neawanaka perches when she can't work at all and has to go burn off the throttled electricity.

At work in clay or wood or stone she stares, she breathes evenly, she is riveted, she is lost. No phone. Music gently. Bach when she is in stone, rock and roll in clay, jazz in wood.

This afternoon there is a slab of spruce on her work table weighing perhaps two hundred pounds, as tall and broad in the shoulders as a man.

Maybe it will *be* a man, she thinks.

She circles the table.

I *like* men, she thinks, smiling.

By God, she thinks. I'll *make* a man. I'll make one from scratch. My new man. Be fun to tell Owen.

She checks grinning to see if there is a knob in the right place to make a man. Keeps circling the table. She never touches a raw piece of clay or wood or stone until she gets a feeling about it, and once the feeling comes she chooses her tools carefully, balancing various chisels and gouges in her hands to see who wants to work today, choosing music carefully for pace.

She puts on Miles Davis and then reconsiders and puts on Chet Baker.

No genius today, she thinks. Just dreaming. Just the right music by which to make a man, she grins: and o how very *many* men have been made to the music of Chet Baker, hmmm?

Thinks about making love to Owen. His lips and hips arrowing into her.

Such bony relentless hips, she thinks.

In the rest of her studio are blocks and slabs and chunks of wood: maple, cedar, fir, more oak, walnut, alder, spruce, hemlock, cherry, ash, laurel, elm, myrtle, redwood. Sawdust and shavings and chips on the floor like tiny frozen leaves. There are tools everywhere: racks of chisels and gouges, mallets and mallet heads, planers, jointers, table saws, circular saws, chain saws, and bandsaws. There are routers, drills, sanders, clamps, glues, oils, finishes, a huge hydraulic hoist, and carving benches with attached wood vises. And sharpeners everywhere. There are more sharpeners than anything else in the room. Daniel counted them recently: thirty-nine, his mother's age.

13.

Cedar on the Mink River sitting and thinking. Watching the ripples. His recording equipment whirring in the fern of the riverbank. Ospreys rowing through the air above. Two adults two young. Mergansers, kingfishers, ouzel on the river. Water water river river talking talking. He hears the low bass booming of rocks being turned over by the river. Like a low mutter. Basso? Baritone?

He watches the ouzel and thinks of No Horses. Smiles; she is his goddaughter and the affection he felt for her during her childhood and adolescence has grown into a real respect for the woman she has become.

No Horses, she is one tough woman, he thinks. Lovely, strong, patient, talented, kind. My sweet little Nora.

But he thinks uneasily of the talk they had this morning in her studio, after he and Owen wrestled the spruce slab onto her carving table and Owen longlegged it back to his shop. A hard talk. A talk about holes. It began as a talk about carving holes in wood and then spun into holes in people, things missing; or as she said the feeling that something was missing that you'd never had and hadn't known you didn't have until suddenly you knew it.

He chews on that remark for a while, as the ospreys row in their floating lines up and down the river.

14.

Dad, says Daniel.

Yeh.

Tell me how you met Mom.

I should save it for a Project tape.

Tell me now?

It's a long story, son. Suitable for telling by the fire.

But Mom will be there.

Is that bad?

You'll look at her.

And?

You know what I mean—when she's in the room your eyes go there.

When she's in the room the temperature rises, boyo.

Dad. That's gross.

Good thing for you I love your mama and versa vice.

I love her too, dad, but sometimes.

Sometimes what?

Sometimes you pay more attention to her than you do to me.

I don't.

You do.

You don't mean that.

It's okay. I don't mind. Sometimes I mind.

Well, when you're married …

You pay too much attention to Mom.

What?

Does she pay that much attention to you?

Sure she does. Sure now.

15.

Moses the crow barks once and Daniel looks up at the seven clocks mounted above the workbench and says *gotta go dad* and hustles out of the shop and sails back to school on his bike his braids flying red black brown; he wants to be back in class just before school ends. Owen keeps rebuilding the beaver but now his mind is all awash and awander with No Horses. We met on this beach. Salt and sea. We were walking each alone me north she south. In the afternoon. The way she walks leaning forward her hair pouring out behind her like a river a comet's tail. O that hair as black as the back of midnight. *An chuilfhionn*, the maiden of the flowing locks. When we passed on the strand we paused and her eyes flashed and her hair whipped around her face *mbeal-ath-na-gar ata an staid-bhean bhreagh mhodhamhail* red ripening in her cheeks like a berry on a tree. Her graceful neck her lips like bruised fruit. I never saw anyone or anything like her ever. There was a zest in her eye. I wanted to say something courteous and memorable but out of my mouth to my utter surprise fell *chailin dheas mo chroidhe*, dear girl of my heart, because she had me all flustered there in the salty wind, and I was so surprised at myself I laughed, and she laughed, a sound like the peal of a silver bell, and she said what language is that? and I said O that's the old Irish, walk with me and I'll teach you a bit, I was surprised at my own boldness but *do mharaigh tu m'intinn*, she made my mind all feeble with her eyes.

I will walk with you, she said, and we walked along trading words in our old languages, me in the Irish and her in the Salish, and soon we were trading stories in American, and soon after that we were trading salty kisses in our own language her long hair whirling around us like the salty arms of the salty sea.

16.

Worried Man notes the hour—golden russet slanting light, the hour when the angle of the sun heading toward the ocean illuminates everything seemingly from inside, so that plants glow greenly with their bright green souls naked to the naked joyous eye.

Bright angelic wings bespangling every bough like stars. Blake.

And he sets off on his rounds.

Around the Department of Public Works building, one circumference, for luck and to check the mildewing southwest corner of the building where Cedar has his rain gauge.

Then up Hawk Street to the doctor's to collect the doctor.

Then Lark to Heron to Murre to Cormorant to Warbler to Chickadee, which has only the one resident, Mrs. L, who hands him berries or pears depending, whose pain is in her wrists and knees. He can feel her grinding soreness as they turn into Chickadee. When they get to her gate she hands him a little soft paper box of salmonberries, which he hands to the doctor. As the doctor asks her about her pills and such, Worried Man rubs her wrists.

His huge hands are beaver tails, maple leaves, baby halibut.

He notices that the berry box is deftly made of yesterday's newspapers.

From Mrs. L's they take the old sand quarry road, now half overgrown with young alder, to the other end of town, where the few houses huddle in a rough circle around a seasonal marsh, waist-deep in winter and dry in summer. Around the dell they go, on these streets that have no names, streets known by who lives on them, and then down the beach stairs to the water. By now the sun's nearly in the ocean and the tide's mostly out and they brisk along stride for stride, silent, meditative. This is the real edge of the town, this strand of sand and seawrack, the shells of Dungeness crabs, a sneaker here and there from a wreck at sea, a fishing float occasionally, a shard of wood, bones, sticks, logs. Sometimes a dead seal or sea lion or shark. Once a doe that maybe fell from a cliff. Once a humpback whale. Sometimes very much alive sea lions, who are really big and bark like dogs and move much faster than you might imagine. Once a dead man.

As they near the river they pass the keel of the *Carmarthen Castle*, which wrecked there more than half a century ago.

Welsh, says the doctor, not slowing.

Mm?

Wheat and timber, sailing from California to Oregon.

Why did it wreck?

The captain who was roaring drunk on an unbelievably foggy night turned into the Mink thinking it was the mighty Columbia River and discovered he was wrong. The whole load of lumber slid into the Mink. Some was teak. Note that the O Donnell barn has a lovely teak door. The only fatality: a rooster that had three times been around Cape Horn.

Worried Man stops suddenly.

You feel it? says the doctor quietly.

Mm.

The doctor stands silently for a minute while Worried Man casts about for the pain in the air. He has tried to explain to the doctor, and to Cedar, and to his wife, that he doesn't hear or smell or feel the aura of someone else's pain—he, just, well, catches it, sort of. I just am *apprised* of its existence, sort of, he says.

What does it feel like?

Like electricity, in a way, says Worried Man. But there's a sort of screaming or tearing in it. A chattering. It's hard to explain.

Where is it?

Nearby. Up.

Can you tell … ?

A woman.

The doctor, discreet, bows gently and heads back to his house. Worried Man, equally discreet, waits until the doctor turns the corner and then he heads uphill away from the ocean.

The night falls thick, he thinks, I go upon my watch. Blake.

17.

Daniel arrives, panting for dramatic emphasis, with only five minutes to go before the last bell rings. His grandmother glares at him but he is smart enough not to smile and then the bell rings and the class flutters and rustles and sprints and bustles off and Maple Head crooks her finger at Daniel to come to the desk and as he shuffles to the front of class he looks closely at her eyes under her thunderstorm eyebrows but sees no green fish leaping so he smiles.

I'm sorry, Gram.

I'll only be a half a minute, you said.

Sorry.

Hmf.

You know what Dad's shop is like, Gram.

O alright. You missed geometry.

I know it all. Test me.

Just do the questions after Chapter Five tonight. How's your dad?

Stuffing a beaver.

Sentence of the day. Where'd he get it?

Grace.

Walk home with me?

Okay, Gram.

He rides his bike slowly, standing up on the pedals, and she floats smoothly over the fresh-washed asphalt, her feet feathers and songs, the rising wind pours her hair into the air. Rained gently last night, just enough to wash the town clean, and then today a clean crisp fat spring day, the air redolent, the kind of green minty succulent air you'd bottle if you could and snort greedily on bleak wet January evenings when the streetlights *hzzzzt* on at four in the afternoon and all existence seems hopeless and sad.

Daniel watches his grandmother's hair stream behind her and he sees the brown fish leaping in the swirling silver river.

How'd you meet Grampa?

We met by the river.

Did you love him right away?

No.

No?

I was fascinated, though.

Was he fascinated too?

Yep.

How could you tell?

I could tell.

How?

I could tell. You'll see someday.

Was he in love?

He was ... fascinated.

Is that the same as love?

Better.

Better than love?

There is no real love without fascination.

Is he still fascinated?

I sure hope so.

Are you?

Yes indeedy.

Was Grampa skinny then too?

Skinny as a stick.

And funny like now?

Funny and kind like now.

What year was it when you met him?

A long time ago, Danno.

How old are you, Gram?

Old enough not to tell my impertinent grandson.

Why don't women say their ages?

Because people make assumptions.

How old is Grampa?

Older than dirt.

How old is Cedar?

No one knows. Not even Cedar.

Really?

He doesn't know what year he was born, love. Or where. Sometimes I think he is one of what your dad calls the ancient ones.

Daoine sidhe, the fairies.

He doesn't say fairies, does he?

Daoine maithe, the good people, he says. That's respectful.

You're getting good with the Gaelic.

Dad's teaching me a little. It's cool.

The good people are always found near water, right? Like Cedar.

Cedar's small and fast, too, like them.

He is that.

Wasn't he ever married?

Not that I know of.

Was he married before you met him?

I don't know, love. I don't think so.

Didn't you ever ask about when he was a boy?

He doesn't remember, Daniel. He was nearly dead when your grampa pulled him out of the river, and being in the water that long can hurt your brain.

It didn't hurt his, did it?

No. It did drown his memory, though.

I think he's really smart.

He's a great man in many ways.

If Grampa died would you marry Cedar?

Your grandfather is too fascinated with this world to leave it. Trust me.

But if he did die would you marry Cedar?

I see you want Chapter Six for homework also?

Daniel grins and pedals off like a rocket and Maple Head floats along through the fallen leaves smiling, her eyes flashing with fish.

18.

Owen at work on the beaver grins remembering the afternoon he gave No Horses her first lesson in the Irish language. They met on the windy beach again and walked hand in hand down to the cave at the south end and sat there facing each other in the brilliant sand.

Okay then, he says.

Okay then, she says, smiling.

We'll start simple.

We'll start simple.

They grin.

I'll give you the Irish and you repeat it.

Okay.

That way it will slip into you gently.

Okay.

Like music does.

Okay.

Not like school.

Enough already. Let's start.

Okay then.

Okay.

Ta an thathnona go brea.

Ta an thathnona go brea.

That means good afternoon.

Ta an thathnona go brea.

Good. Now: *conas ta tu?*

Conas ta tu.

Good. That means how are you?

Conas ta tu?

Good. Now *cen t-ainm ata ort?*

Cen t-ainm ata ort?

Excellent. That means what is your name?

Cen t-ainm ata ort?

What actually *is* your name?

Cen t-ainm ata ort?

No no, I mean what is your name really?

Sometime I'll tell you.

Now is a good time.

Some other time.

He thinks: who *is* this woman?

Okay then, he says.

Okay.

We'll start simple.

Okay.

I'll give you the Irish and you repeat it.

No.

No?

No. This time you just say it and I will listen. I like the music of it. I like watching your mouth form the words. You have a good voice. I won't understand a word of it but it'll slip into me gently. Like music.

What should I say?

Say anything you want. I won't know.

Okay then.

Don't be rude.

No no. Well, *ta gruaig dhubh ag an mbeirt againn.*

What did that mean?

We both have black hair.

That sounds sweet. Okay. I'll stop asking what it means. You just talk now.

Okay. *Is capall fain I an fharraige inniu* [The sea is a wild horse today]. *Creatur fiain, alainn is ea tusa freisin* [You are a wild lovely creature also]. *Bhi blas salainn ort nuair a phogamar a cheile inne* [You tasted like salt when we kissed yesterday]. *Ba mhaith liom pog a thabhairt duit aris inniu* [I would like to kiss you again today]. *Chun an fhirinne a ra, ba mhaith liom do do phogadh an oiche go leir* [I would like to kiss you all night long in fact]. *Ba mhaith liom do chiocha teanna a phogadh freisin* [I would like to kiss your firm breasts also]. *Ba mhaith liom do dhidi a phogadh go dti go seasfaidh said suas cosuil le saighdiurini* [I would like to kiss your nipples until they stand up straight like little soldiers]. *Ba mhaith liom unfairt leat ar an ngaineamh lom laithreach agus muid inar craiceann dearg* [I would like to roll in the sand naked with you right now]. *Isteach linn san uaimh seo 's bauilimis an craiceann go mall reidh ar feadh seachtainne* [Let's go in this cave and make love slowly for a week]. *Aithrimis an t-abhar I dtreo go bhfeadfainn seasamh faoi dheoidh* [Let's change the subject so that I will be able to stand up eventually]. *Ta do shuile chomh fiain agus chomh tarraingeach leis an bhfarraige* [Your eyes are as wild and alluring as the sea]. *Silim go bhfuilim ag titim I ngra leat* [I think I am falling in love with you]. *Nil d'ainm fiu amhain agam* [I don't even know your name]. *Is bean iontach thu* [You are extraordinary]. *Ce faoin speir ata ionat?* [Who *are* you?]

19.

Owen grinning finishes the beaver and stands back to get a good eyeful of his work. The trick with stuffing a beaver is to make it the imposing animal that it is alive, but not to force the issue of aggression; to reflect, in the now-frozen carriage of the creature, its diligence and muscularity, its sturdy urge to relentless work, not the fact that it could bite your pecker off with bright-orange choppers the size of playing cards. So

Owen has placed beaver-bitten alder sticks in its rubbery black hands, and mounted the animal half-risen, alert to danger but unafraid—a burly worker absorbed in the business at hand but attentive to and ready for trouble if it shambled into view.

Very deftly done, says the crow.

Thank you, says Owen.

It looks alive. I'm scared.

Liar. If it was alive you'd be teasing it.

Grace will be pleased.

Hope so.

A most interesting young lady.

Owen turns to regard the bird carefully. Moses, who had been taught to speak by a shy nun who found him broken in the mud, is intricately courteous and circumspect; also he has a dry humor and a corvidian cast of mind, as he likes to say, that combine to make his remarks intriguing. Owen enjoys the play of Moses' mind. They have been friends, he and Moses, since the nun brought the bird in to be repaired, years ago now.

What do you mean?

Just that. A most interesting young lady.

How so?

Well, this morning I noticed her cutting apart a car with a blowtorch, for one thing. And you notice she chopped all her hair off.

I assume she had reasons for these things.

I think she likes you.

So she cut up a car?

Who can understand the ways of human beings?

I am a joyously married man.

Which has nothing to do with it.

I'm not available.

Which is not the point.

It *is* the point. She knows I'm married.

Yet she likes you.

How do you know?

I can tell.

Tell me. I'm curious.

The way she carries her body when you are near.

I think you're wrong.

I have been wrong before.

Let's go home, says Owen.

Okay, says Moses.

Keep an eye out for Daniel on the way home.

Okay. Not hard to spot him. Always speeding, that boy.

And all that hair.

And all that hair.

Moses floats over the town: over the grocery and the church, the pub and the bowling alley, the clinic and the school, the barber on his porch with a cigar, the cop car behind the liquor store, the teenage boys smoking dope behind the rec center, the father beating his son again, the teenage couple in a dark fringe of woods near her house, kissing gently, their lips bruised and hot, their empty bellies churning, his pecker sore, her breasts sore from his sucking them all afternoon, her mother just coming through the screen door and opening her mouth to call *O Rachel where are you where are you?*

Moses floats over the old hotel where the nun is dying in the last light, the very nun who taught him to speak. She sees him from her bed but he doesn't see her and she can no longer cry out to catch his ear, nor whistle, she can no longer speak at all, but she stares at him wheeling, and a hundred yards away he feels her hot glance like a whisper in his feathers.

The mother on the porch calls: *Rachel? Rachel?*

Moses sees the doctor on his porch and Grace at sea smoking a cigarette and Worried Man climbing uphill through salal bushes and Maple Head loping over the maple leaves and Owen shuffling longleggedly home and the teenage couple kissing gently in the trees near her house; but he doesn't see Daniel.

20.

Worried Man pushes through the salal thickets, gets halfway up the hill, and has to stop and sit down. This has happened to him several times in recent weeks but he hasn't told Maple Head. It's like he hits a wall and his legs get so rubbery that he's afraid that if he doesn't sit down pronto he will fall down and he is old enough now to worry about broken hips and such.

Twilight.

He peers uphill, sees nothing but more salal, blackberry, elderberry, huckleberry, alder all grandfathered with moss; near the top of the hill an old spar tree from the logging days here before the war.

He stands up and closes his eyes and feels for her pain. It's straight uphill. He slogs ahead through the thickets, looking for deer trails. He's lived his whole life in these little dense green hills, and he's learned to cast about for the subtle trails that animals make and do not advertise, but this hill doesn't feel familiar at all, which is a puzzle: he knows the town like he knows his face, its crannies and pools and slopes and angles and corners and scars.

Up he goes.

21.

Cedar gathers up his recording equipment and goes back to the Department. As he passes under the lintel he sees the Mission Statement (BRAINS AGAINST PAINS!) pinned up there, and the photograph of the founder, George Christie. George had been a logger as a young man and wished to get out of the woods, having seen his partner decapitated by a falling fir limb. He went to the three-man County Planning Commission, two of whom were his cousins, and a day later he was appointed supervisor of the newly established Department of Public Works.

The county paid George half of what he had earned in the woods but he figured he'd live longer and he could find some wiggle room in the budget for himself and the family he dreamed of nightly in his room at the hotel. Soon afterward he fell in love with the grocer's daughter Anna, who loved him back, and they eventually had the family he had dreamed about and she hadn't: six daughters and two sons. Eventually Anna drank heavily and the family shivered and teetered for a while, but as families sometimes do it turned its collective energies to caring for Anna.

George ran the Department for thirty years, the last five with Cedar's assistance, and when he retired he appointed Cedar supervisor. Cedar immediately appointed Worried Man co-supervisor, much as Captains Lewis and Clark were co-captains of their Corps of Discovery (which had been on the beach not far north of the town, many years ago, and in fact Worried Man's greatgrandfather had met and conversed with Captain William Clark of the United States Army, whom he found to be a pleasant and efficient man, although a little obsessed with salt, and weary of eating elk, which they had eaten for seventy days in a row at that point, I hope to never see let alone partake of elk ever again in this blessed life, said Captain Clark, a line that Billy's greatgrandfather found endlessly amusing).

Just before George retired, he and Cedar drafted the Department's Mission Statement and posted it publicly, as required by the county, and although the Planning Commission had fervently ignored it, Cedar kept it posted by the door and referred to it often. Below the firm pithy headline it read: This Department, will be responsible for, the construction and maintenance, of all necessary roads, paths, passageways, and trails, within the boundaries of the town, without regard to species of resident; e.g., deer and rabbit trails will be maintained at public expense, as well as waterways, of all sorts, heretofore established, or to be established at any time, in the future, in any way, shape, or form. Also the Department will record and advocate the recording of history, in every way, shape, and form, in all extant media and via media to be invented in the future. Also the Department, and/or its assigns, will also at all times practicable offer its services to residents, of all species, in matters having to do with public assistance and education, under any conceivable, or to be conceived, definition of public work. Questions? See the Director.

22.

Grace on the boat with her older brother Declan. Smoking cigarettes. Declan runs the boat and decides what to fish for: scallops sometimes, salmon sometimes, halibut sometimes. Depends.

Why'd you crop your top? asks Declan.

Felt like it.

Why?

Change.

You look like a broom.

Piss off.

And why'd you cut up mom's car?

Felt like it.

With my torch.

It's dad's torch.

Which means it's mine. *He's* not going to use it.

Leave him alone.

Why? You love him all the sudden?

Piss off.

The boat slides on through the twilight and as they pass the mouth of the Mink full dark drops over the ocean like a scene change in a theater. The boat rocks and slaps. Tide coming in. Their cigarette ends glow. The silence is rich. A small fast dark bird whips by the stern and Grace identifies it instantly: nighthawk.

They're not usually at sea, are they? she says.

Who?

Nighthawks.

Feck if I know, Grace.

Odd.

Tonight Declan has rigged the boat for halibut and when they are far enough off the beach they set the long lines and eat sandwiches and drink coffee and wait. After a while Declan squeezes into the little cabin to read by lamplight but Grace stays in the stern, staring into the dark. Declan knows her well enough, after two decades, to leave her alone. But he watches her face for a while, with its fringe of hacked black hair.

A *woman*, he thinks. Who knew. Was just a kid. Now look. Those shoulders. That fecking tattoo. Breasts. Mouth on her like a mean dog. Smart though. College smart. She'll never go. Should have gone. She'll marry some loser with refrigerator parts in his yard and ten mangy dogs and a huge tab at the pub. Waste. Should make her go to college. Dad should send her to college.

There's a joke. The old man doing something for someone else. Hell fecking freeze over.

23.

In the hotel the old nun thinks of Moses. She was young and strong when she found him. *Lithe, pliable, supple,* she thinks. She has been a teacher of reading and writing all her life and words swing and sing through her mind all the time in parades and poems. *Concatenation.* He had fallen from his nest in a maple tree and was huddled brokenboned groaning in the mud and leaf litter. *Moaning sobbing weeping.*

She'd crouched and stared.

A new crow is an awkward cake from the bakery of the Lord; all angles and bones, half naked still from the shell, hardly feathered at all.

She and Moses gaped at each other, each frightened; the nun of this angry little sudden bony goblin in her path and Moses of this giant billowing creature clearly leaning in to tear him to shreds.

It had been an unnerving day for Moses: strenuous escape from the shell, rush of smells and winds and Mother, and then lurching out of the nest and the hell-ride down through the whipping branches and slapping leaves and smashing to the ground pain pain pain and now this leering awful nightmare;

who cradles him in the lap of her white habit and brings him first to Owen, who builds a complex latticework of splints and slings (and paints them black for symmetry, detail being everything and the core of beauty as he says), and then to her room in the old hotel, where she reads aloud to the bird for weeks, Edmund Burke mostly, and painstakingly teaches him to speak. She starts with words she thinks will fit the shape of his mouth: *car, roar, raw.* Then when he has a hundred words in his vocabulary she teaches him to put them together in groups.

He realizes quickly that groups of words are more powerful than the individual words are and one bright summer afternoon when she is bent over her desk in the window he floats over from the top of the refrigerator to her desk and says to her *pain mud mother.* A sentence neither of them ever forgot.

24.

Worried Man reaches the spar tree near the lip of the hill and holds on for dear life. He's really dizzy now and he's worried.

He sits down.

He's lost the trail of the pain for a moment; his own pain shoved it out of his head.

Room for only one pain at a time, he thinks. Well. There's a lesson. Take a note, Billy. Get that down on tape. His head spins. He stretches out on the ground. Fern. Bracken? The base of large trees, he has noticed over the years, are often draped in fern. Wonder why. Like skirts. Fern skirts girdle female trees? Huge wooden women. Like Anna Christie. Huge wooden woman. *Not* wooden, turns out. Fascinating woman. Not pretty but *what* grace and dignity. Not pretty but beautiful. And what a singer. And what a drunk. A *howling* drunk. Felt her pain all the way across town. What a voice. Her pain had something to do with her voice, he remembers; he remembers that her pain quivered in a curious way. Quavered. Some women have a pulsing energy almost too sharp and salty to endure and when they are in pain their pain is ferocious and shatters all over the place. Her pain had wobbled his knees and by the time they got to the Christies' house Cedar had to help him hobble up the stairs. Where they found Anna screaming drunk that night and her family escaped to a motel. Broken glass everywhere. Broken dishes. Puke and blood. Music blasting. Opera. When I turned off the music I thought she would kick me to death. Her boots in my ribs. Cracking my bones. Cedar talked to her all that night, his voice like a cello. He and Anna sang in the dark. Songs with no words. The river sang too. Anna big as a bear. I couldn't sing. Her voice like a river. They sang by the river.

He sits up and draws a bead on the pain above him and gets it clear in his head again. It's a *young* woman, he realizes. The pain is raw, uncut by experience. Whoever she is hasn't felt pain of this sort ever before and it is flowing out of her like blood from a severed vein.

25.

I'll tell you a story about working in the woods, says George Christie to his daughter Cyra. They are sitting comfortably in their kitchen. We wore what we called tin pants, which were wool pants coated with paraffin to keep the rain off. Cyra and her twin Serena are the last of George and Anna's children. At the end of the day the guys would hang their wet socks and unmentionables and shirts around the stove in the middle of the bunkhouse and the smell had *hair* on it. This fall the girls go off to college. Sometimes there were sixteen of us fellas bunking in one shack all together and we had us *some* fun, I can tell you that. Cyra once found her mother passed out in the creek and for a long moment hesitated to pull her out. We played us a lotta cribbage, and fellas who could play harmonicas and fiddles, they were popular fellas. Cyra is frightened of college but thrilled that it's far away. We ate like bears, we did, pancakes and potatoes and bacon and steaks, as much as we could cram home, Cy, but we were none of us fat, as you burned it off so fast, and if ever you saw a fat man in the woods you knew there would be three accidents that day. Cyra thinks she might want to be an actress or maybe a filmmaker. It was more deadly than war, was your daddy's life then, and I saw fellas cut up in all sorts of ways, but when my friend Minor got killed that was the end of it. Cyra wonders how her dad can still love her mom after all the screaming. We had our own language there in the woods, words I don't hear anymore, and I miss 'em, Cy: *barberchair* and *bullbuck*, and *chaser* and *choker*, and *crummy* and *gyppo*, and *highballing* and *hooking*, and *kerf* and *peavey*. Cyra loves her dad best when he is just telling stories relaxed and grinning like this and not wearing his cold *I will endure* face as her twin sister calls it. Here's a word to describe your daddy, Cy: *jillpoked*, which is what you call an old log what's rooted in the ground at one end and all airy at the other. I'm all airy these days, waving in the wind. My feet are set good but my canopy's moving around something fierce.

26.

No Horses closes up shop. She sweeps the chips from the day's work into a pile under the work-table; it is her habit to leave the chips under the table as she is working on a piece, so that she will be able to tell at a glance how much work she's done.

A decent pile today. A good start. The hips are coming clear. Lean male hips. Men have hips like tea mugs, she thinks. Women have hips like spoons. A man's hipbones are handles for his woman's hands.

She leans the broom against the table and feels the hipbones of the oak man on the table. Good. That's right. So, she thinks, pubic bone here, and belly here, and navel here; she marks the lines with a pencil for tomorrow's work.

Who is this man coming out of the tree, she thinks. Being born. Seed from tree. She grins, remembering her father's remark when she told him she was working in oak:

Ah, the rough bark opens, he said. Blake.

She oils her chisels and puts them away, and checks her hammers for flaws and puts them away, and turns out the lights of the studio, and puts on her jacket, for while May days at the coast hint at summer the evenings are absolutely convinced still of winter. By the door she pauses—and then locks the door and goes back through the shadowy studio to the porch, through the door shaped like her, and there she sits down in the dark, under the dark bent knives of herring gulls floating inland to wherever it is they sleep,

and she begins to weep.

All day long she fended off this moment with the tools in her hands but now she cups her face in her hands and sobs and sobs and sobs.

27.

Daniel on his bike thinks of his family. He rushes downhill through the onrushing night. We're so weird. My dad is Irish and my mom is one of the People, which makes me an Irish-People-American. My dad works with a talking crow. My mom says that she finds out what wood and stone want to be when they grow up. My grandfather in Ireland died working on a road that doesn't go anywhere. My grandmother in Ireland lives on a hill that's she never left not once in her whole life and she says if she leaves the hill she will die for sure. My grandfather from here thinks about time all the time and walks around town every night feeling other people's pain in his head. My grandmother from here is the strictest teacher in the history of the world. Their best friend is a tough little old man named for a tree.

Is this a nutty family or what?

At the bottom of the hill there's a wide grassy meadow on either side of the river. Sometimes at dusk you can see elk. Tonight he sees a rack of antlers against the sunset and he stops quietly under a big spruce tree. Waits patiently. He has learned to wait patiently from his mother, who is patient. After a while he picks out the outline of the rest of the buck. Enormous. Then he sees one doe, feeding; then a second doe.

Then he sees the buck rear up and flail his front feet at the second doe and for a minute he thinks the buck is attacking the doe, but then the buck straddles his front feet around the doe's rump and mounts her. She quivers under his weight. Daniel is the most still silent person in the history of the galaxy. So silent and motionless and dazed under the deep-green skirt of the spruce as Moses floats overhead on his way home that not even Moses, who sees very well in the dark, sees the boy with the long braids in three colors: red, black, brown.

28.

In the cop car behind the liquor store there is a cop named Michael. He and his wife Sara have two small daughters. Michael does pushups with the girls sitting on his back giggling. He likes to make love to Sara in the first pearly light of morning, before the girls are awake. She prefers making love at night with candles and wine after the girls are asleep. He liked being a policeman when he first started but now he is burdened by the brokenness he sees every day. She wishes he would quit the force but feels she cannot comment on his profession as he is bringing in the money. He loves opera and his favorite opera of all is Puccini's *Tosca*, which he knows by heart and plays constantly in the car. She thinks secretly that he will leave her because she is not exciting. He has been on the force for sixteen years and has four more years to go before he earns his pension. She feels fat. He asks her questions sometimes just to hear the vibrato in her voice. She has been fish counter at a dam and a waitress. He is afraid he will not last four more years on the force but doesn't tell Sara because he doesn't want her to worry about financial stability. She discovered three months ago that she is pregnant but hasn't told him yet. His favorite parts of *Tosca* are the subtle ones: the shuffling old sacristan who prays at the sound of the Angelus, the cannon signaling the police, the sheep bells and church bells heard at the opening of the final act. She plans to tell him that she is pregnant every night after dinner but something always gets in the way. Their older daughter is hers and their younger daughter is theirs. He is a serious scholar of Puccini's life: how Puccini walked thirteen miles to Pisa to see Verdi's *Aida*, how Puccini once remarked that "the only music I can compose is that of little things," how Puccini left his opera *Turandot* unfinished at his death, only two scenes from completion, and how Arturo Toscanini, when *Turandot* had its premiere in Milan in 1926, lay down his baton out of respect for the composer when the production came to its truncated end, and would not finish with the scenes added by another man, the scenes that finish the opera to this day.

In the cop car behind the liquor store Michael is thinking of Sara and humming: *Non la sospiri la nostra casetta*, Puccini's song about a future rendezvous of lovers.

29.

As night falls Anna is sitting by a creek singing. Her husband George built a little bench there so that he and she and the children could watch the chinook salmon spawn every fall. Anna is trying to sing the baritone line that the creek is taking as it turns over rocks. Chinook are also called kings and tyees and hookbills and blacks and chubs and winter salmon here even though they don't come up the creek in winter. Anna still tests the highest register of her voice even though it is shredded beyond repair. Fishermen north of Neawanaka also call the chinook *tshawytscha*. After a while Anna stops trying to anticipate pattern in the water and she just sings alto above the baritone growling of the rocks in the creek. Young chinook might stay in their birth streams for a year or two. Anna rocks back and forth as she sings. Once young chinook do make their run to the ocean they may stay there as long as three years before returning home. Anna rocks and rocks. After the chinook spawn they die. Anna loses track of the time. The exhausted salmon wash into eddies and pools and logjams and dissolve and feed a thousand creatures among them their own children who then sprint to the sea. Anna rocks and rocks until her daughter Cyra emerges from the fern on the riverbank and gently touches her on the shoulder and walks her home for dinner.

30.

Worried Man is still sitting by the spar tree in the dark but now he is thinking of the first time he ever saw Maple Head. She was standing on the bank of the Mink River combing her wet hair with her fingers. She was lithe and supple and slim and her hair fell brown and curling and swirling past her shoulders and he couldn't take his eyes off her hair. Her fingers combed through her hair as the river quietly roared by and her hair looked like the river when salmon were whirling their way through it like living threads through living cloth. Her hair swirled under her fingers and she glared at him and he stood transfixed and all he wanted at that moment was to run his fingers through the cascading living water of her hair, the flashes of every other color in it depending on the angle of the light, her eyes like that too, flashing in green and brown, her hair and eyes rebellious and alive.

I took a step forward, and she took a step back, so I stepped back, to show her I didn't mean any harm, and then she stepped forward, and we both smiled, and that was that absolutely ever since.

Our first dance together.

Every thing has its own vortex. Blake.

Thinking of Maple Head cheers him right up, and he stands, gingerly, still holding onto the tree, and stares uphill into the darkness, and gets a clear bead on the pain again.

And climbs.

31.

Maple Head in the kitchen of her little cedar house is humming. This morning before she left for school she had whirled flour and water and yeast and salt into dough and set it to rise all day. It's risen so high during the day that the plate she put over it to keep out fruit flies and such is now perched helpless and teetering atop the bubbly mountain of dough. She scoops it out of the bowl and humming punches and hammers it down and sets it to rise again for a while and pours a glass of white wine. The night is warm and fragrant and she humming opens the kitchen window. She cleans sorrel and asparagus and puts lemon and wine and mustard on a piece of salmon and humming sets three plates on the table in the kitchen in case Cedar pops in for dinner.

She steps out on the porch to look for Worried Man but she is not worried—he is certainly finishing his walk and will be striding up the hill in a moment. Stares at the first stars, the last swifts chittering and swooping overhead, the first bats. Dreams. Sips wine. Thinks of Daniel's hair. Daniel's questions. Billy skinny as a stick. Tall. He stepped back politely. I liked that. His grave amused courtesy. His eyes. She sips the wine. Too early for owls. Swifts. Some of these are the new birds of the year, the fledglings. First flights. Scared and exhilarated.

Steps back into the kitchen, humming, and shapes the dough into two long thin loaves to bake, and slips the loaves in the oven, and then notices perhaps forty bright-orange salmonberries lined up in a long row on the windowsill, lined up by color, so the darkest are at one end and the brightest at the other. She smiles and says to the window *come in,* and Cedar's face appears smiling.

32.

Where's himself? asks Cedar.

Still walking. Come on in.

What's for dinner?

For you, salmonberries. For us, salmon.

I was hoping for salmon *with* salmonberries. The delightful symmetry.

Hope no more. Sit.

I like watching you from here.

You just like peering in windows.

No, no—it's seeing you in your kitchen. You fit.

Come sit down. Where were you today?

Recording osprey on the river.

Osprey have oral histories?

Sure they do. You could spend a whole lifetime studying them, May. The crook of their wings, the tuft of feathers by their eyes, the way their talons fold over to assure their grip on fish. Fascinating creatures. The construction of the nest, the tree they choose. They must pick certain trees for the angles of sight they provide to the river. The way they row through the air with their shoulders. The high-pitched cry, almost a scream. Like a hawk's scream but more eaglish. A fascinating people altogether, the osprey people.

Eaglish? she says grinning.

Does this mean I fail sixth grade?

Just the adjective part.

A new word in the world. I should copyright it.

Such a scholar.

I had an interesting talk with your daughter this morning.

Mm?

About holes.

Holes?

She kept talking about the feeling you have when you know something's missing in your life but you don't know what it is.

No Horses said that?

She did.

Hmm.

Is she okay, May?

I think so—she was here the other night with Daniel and she seemed fine.

She seemed troubled to me.

Did you tell Billy?

I haven't seen him all afternoon. He was going to make tapes for Daniel and then walk with the doctor. Figured I'd catch him here.

Now he *is* late, Cedar. Can you peek out and find him? This bread will be ready in a minute and then we will have salmon *with* salmonberries, and you, my dear, will eat with us.

I'm so honored. Have you ever invited me to dinner before?

Hmm: forty years times a hundred dinners a year adds up to, let's see, four thousand invitations. Or maybe eight thousand. And not one declined.

I never said no? Ever?

To *my* dinner?

He grins.

I'm off, he says.

And you *may* do the dishes tonight.

May I do the dishes, May?

You may.

Back in a minute.

Thank you. I'm sure he's coming up the hill but still.

Don't eat all the bread! he says his voice grinning and fading and she grins too but in the bottom of her belly she thinks of Billy.

33.

Moses, having paused in a hemlock to reconnoiter, commences to worry about Daniel and after a minute he jumps into the air and floats away black against the blackening night. Floats through a blizzard of gnats and snaps right and left to catch one as swifts and swallows do. Floats over spruce and cedar, the school, the church, the grocery. Ponders Daniel's usual routes through town. Floats over the old hotel. Hotel reminds him of the old nun. Her laugh like the peal of a bell. When she gave him a bath in the sink. Water everywhere. Shaking with laughter. My belly hurts from laughing so hard, Moses. My empty belly. The fruit of thy womb. Sometimes I wonder, Moses. My salty sea. A boat of a boy a gull of a girl. The way she dried him tenderly in a towel and oiled his feathers with olive oil. I will anoint you as your namesake was anointed, Moses. The way she lit four white candles in the corners of the tub when she bathed. The four holy directions, Moses. Her breasts never sucked by man nor babe rising out of the soapy water like islands. My spirit ponders, Moses. The way she cut her own hair. The way he held the mirror for her while she cut her hair. The way she twirled a lock of her hair with her right hand while she wrote letters and cards with her left.

The way she sang exuberantly in the tub. *My voice rises to God and He will hear me, Moses.* Her grave calm patience with her students. The way she said *why, I was hoping it was you!* whenever she opened her door for anyone at all. The worn tiny tattered creased photograph of her father she wore around her neck. *I will meditate with my heart, Moses.* The way she watched any and all storms as delighted and terrified as a child. *The clouds poured out water and His arrows flashed here and there, Moses.* The worn wooden prayer beads under her pillow. *My voice rises to Him, Moses.* The way she knocked on doors with both hands and wore only red hats and gave away books after she read them and wept at her desk sometimes for no reason he could see. *Surely in vain I have kept my heart pure, Moses, and washed my hands in innocence.* The way she counted carefully between thunderbolts so as to gauge their whereabouts. *There is thunder in His whirlwind and the deeps also tremble, Moses.* The way she finished each walk along the ocean by staring out to sea. *Our paths are in His mighty waters, Moses, and so are holy and hidden.*

34.

On the boat Declan unwraps sandwiches for himself and Grace and they eat silently. The grocer puts a handful of walnuts in his pocket for his little son who likes to crack them although he won't eat them. Moses in flight snaps at a mosquito to see what it feels like to be a swift eating such swift little meats. The priest sips red wine and opens his mail. Owen is chopping carrots and potatoes and onions. The man who has beaten his son twice today is sitting on his back stoop smoking a cigarette. Anna Christie is serving steaming plates of pasta with clam sauce to her husband and the twin girls Cyra and Serena but George notices that she has not filled a plate for herself. The boy who was beaten twice today is eating frozen waffles straight from the box as he stands in the kitchen with the refrigerator door open. No Horses is hunched over with her arms wrapped around her legs and her nose pressed into her jeans through which she smells her skin, which smells like as Owen says cinnamon and firelight. The old nun licks her top lip, the last time she will ever do so. Cedar finds three salmonberries in his pocket and pops two into his mouth. Maple Head eats three salmonberries from the windowsill. The banker sips his coffee as he drives home. Worried Man stepping through the last pair of trees on the top of the hill walks right into a spider-web and gets a strand in his mouth and tastes it smiling and looks up to see that he is under a deck or patio from which the pain is emanating. The O Donnell brothers and their father Red Hugh are eating steak that one of the brothers has overcooked because he never cooked steak before. Sara feeds her daughters grilled-cheese sandwiches and apples. The man who lied in court is drinking beer on the beach near the wreck of the *Carmarthen Castle*. Michael is rubbing salt and oregano into a chicken for dinner with Sara after the girls are in bed. Rachel is in the shower with her head back and her mouth open and the hot water cascading into her mouth and between her breasts. The two cooks at the diner are eating stew in the kitchen before the dinner rush. Rachel's boyfriend Timmy is eating his dinner, a chocolate bar. The woman who sells insurance during the day takes a salted roasted cashew from the bowl on the bar and chews it slowly. Daniel whizzing through the dark on his bicycle is chewing gum. The doctor finishes his last cigarette of the day on the porch and then stands at the cutting board in his kitchen and very slowly cuts a pear into small cubes and then very slowly eats each cube and then brushes his teeth and turns the heat down and checks the locks and turns out the lights and disrobes and gets into bed and takes off his spectacles and folds them carefully on his night-table and then he lies awake for hours with his eyes glinting in the murky dark.

35.

Daniel knows he is running late for dinner and he'd like to get home to change his clothes so he goes even faster than usual, which is astonishingly fast, and he also takes the dirt path through the woods rather than the road, because it'll save him at least three minutes depending on how fast he can go in the dark. It's full dark now and there's no moon. The first segment of the path in the woods is a straight shot, flat and padded with spruce needles, and he leans down and pumps his legs as fast as they can go, and it seems even to Daniel who is a connoisseur of speed in all forms that he has never gone faster in the whole long length of his whole entire life. The wind is seething behind him and the spruce trees are waving. His braids come loose from the exhausted rubber band he's been using to bind them and his hair flies out behind him like comets' tails red black brown. He goes so fast his backpack flaps and flaps against his back. At the end of the straight section of the path there's a tight turn to the left where the hill runs out of hill and there Daniel slows down a little, leery of missing the turn, which would mean a hell of a fall, and he puts both feet down to use his heels as rough brakes, and he makes the turn cleanly, skidding and skewing only a little in the needles, but just as he comes out of the turn and leans forward again to get back into overdrive for the last slightly uphill portion of the path his long red braid catches for maybe a tenth of a second on a prickly spruce branch, which is enough to make even Daniel lose his balance, and the uncontrolled front wheel of the bike skews to the left and Daniel skews to the right, and the bike slams shuddering to a stop and Daniel flies over the edge of the cliff with his backpack flapping and his braids going in three directions and his mouth open but no sound emerging whatsoever.

36.

Worried Man stares up at the porch, which looks vaguely familiar, but it's awfully dark.

Must be the utter and complete lack of moon that makes this hillside so strange, he thinks. The darkness dread & drear. Blake.

He gets a bead on the pain again, which is right above his head through the decking, and he thinks about calling up to her gently through the patio, but then considers that the young woman will have eleven heart attacks if suddenly a voice from beneath her feet asks about her stabbing pain.

I'll go around the house and knock, that's what I'll do.

He steps out quietly from under the deck, trusting that the blanketing night will hide him, and when he reaches the corner of the house he leans in to use his hands against the wall, so as to be sure of his steps. He feels a smooth tube attached to the wall, and then he feels the rough wood of the wall itself, but not until he edges along to the next corner does he realize that the tube is Cedar's rain gauge, that the wall is faced all around with cedar shakes, that his hands are upon the Department of Public Works, and that the young woman in throbbing pain on the deck is his daughter.

37.

Grace and Declan are back in port just after dawn. A good night's work. They've cleaned and iced the catch on the boat and they box it now in wooden crates and heave the boxes into Declan's truck.

Coming?

I need a drink.

Fecking seven in the morning, Grace.

I'm not tired.

She hops back on the boat to get her gear. Declan's itchy eyed and he stinks and his back hurts and all he wants is shower and sleep and he's worried about Grace and embarrassed by her and his temper rises.

You'll get drunk and screw some loser, he says.

So?

What for?

Feels good.

Come home and sleep.

I'm not tired.

Screwing drunks in their rathole rooms. Lovely.

She says nothing.

You'll get pregnant with some loser spawn and then what?

Then I'll be pregnant for a few hours and then I won't be.

Meanwhile half the town gets a crack at you.

So?

You're a cheap bus everybody gets to ride, Grace.

So?

You're my fecking *sister*.

So?

He guns the truck and rattles off. A spurt of yellow ice-melt slides off the truck. She walks down the street to the bar. The bar opens before dawn for the boats coming in. It's half-full of men. The only other woman is the bar maid, Stella. Grace gets a whiskey and gulps it, gets a second whiskey, sips it fast, and then gets coffee and a third whiskey. Takes her sweater off, tucks in her shirt, turns to survey the room. All but two of the men are looking at her. The faces of the men looking at her are greedy and masked. Several are smiling. She knows them all except the two not looking at her. Her throat is burning from the whiskey.

They must be from away, those two, she says to Stella.

I guess, says Stella.

Someone calls Grace from the other side of the room. She ignores the man calling her. She carries her coffee and whiskey to the table where the two men from away are eating eggs.

May I? she says, and the two men look up. She sits down next to the one who pulls out a chair for her.

38.

Of course there are many other people in Neawanaka. So very many. Old and young and tall and short and hale and broken and weary and exuberant. So very many it would take a million years to tell a millionth of their lives and we don't have the time, worse luck, for their stories are riveting and glorious and searing. But, ah, let us choose two, we'll go sidelong for a moment and peer in on, say, the young couple who were coupling on top of the bedclothes earlier in the day.

Their names are Timmy and Rachel. For Timmy's twentieth birthday Rachel has decided to give him herself. A friend from high school has a tiny family fishing cabin up in the hills near the source of the Mink and Rachel is going to borrow the cabin. She and the friend went up there this afternoon to arrange the cabin as a love nest as the friend says teasing but envious. They make up the bed with freshly ironed cotton sheets and set candles around the bathtub and Rachel sets a bowl of salmonberries by the bed.

What *are* you planning to do with those berries? says the friend.

Use your imagination, says Rachel and they laugh.

When they are done preparing the cabin they sit on the front step watching two tiny mud-brown wrens skittering and stuttering in the tangled brush around the door. The wrens have a burbling whirring wheedle like a sung question: *rrrrrrrrr?*

What kind of bird is that? says the friend.

Winter wren, says Rachel. Hear the rising note at the end of the call? And they flit around low to the ground like mice, that's a sign of winter wrens. My mom loves them though she says the males mate with several females in a season.

Men! snorts the friend and they laugh.

The wrens find something in the brush and get all excited *rrrrrr!*

House wrens are different, says Rachel raising her voice a little over the excited wrens, once they get together they stay together.

Rrrrr! say the wrens.

You want to marry him? says the friend.

No, says Rachel. I haven't thought that far. I don't want to think ahead. I don't want to think at all. I just want to be with him now.

He seems a little … raw, says the friend.

Rrrrr! say the wrens, hopping about.

He's cute, says Rachel, and he's gentle with me.

What does *he* want? says the friend.

He wants to *rrrrrrrr* me all day long, says Rachel, and both young women laugh, and they stand up to go, and the frightened wrens leap away into the brush chattering *kipkip kipkip.*

Rachel's friend locks the cabin door and gives Rachel the key and they drive home imitating the wrens *rrrrrrrrrr* and laughing but each thinks the other is laughing a little too hard.

39.

Owen Cooney taping at home here. I am telling stories for my son Daniel. They are sad stories some of them but we are made of joy and woe both. So. My greatgrandfather was Timmy Cooney who worked on a road that goes nowhere and there is a story in that. This was during Bliain na Sciedan, the years of small potatoes. The road is built of stones. The stones were carried by hungry men. The men were paid with one piece of bread a day. The bread wasn't enough and most of the men died. Some men fell right on the road and other men fell to the side into the grass and nettles and bushes. Timmy Cooney fell to the side of the road into the bushes and he crawled on his belly through the ditch looking for *caisearbhan*, which is dandelions, and *samhadh*, which is sorrel, and other herbs and weeds. His mouth was green from the weeds he ate. He was there in that ditch for two days and one night. On the second day he saw a man fall on the road above him where they were working and the man was too weak to stand up anymore and the other men working were too weak to carry him off the road, so they put their stones over him where he lay and they went on down the road.

My greatgrandfather remembered that place because there was a holly tree there.

After two days my greatgrandfather could stand up and he walked across a field to a little house. There was an oak tree there by that house. There was a man and woman and a dead girl there. The girl was about twelve years old. She was naked and my greatgrandfather covered her with half of his shirt because she was just beginning to grow breasts and no man's eyes should see that. Her father and mother were too weak to bury her so my greatgrandfather carried her out behind the little house to the edge of a little creek and folded her arms across her chest and covered her as best he could with mud and grass. He cried he said like he never cried before and never did again in all his long life.

Then he came back into the little house and made a fire and boiled oak leaves and grass and made a soup. The father and the mother seemed stronger after the soup but in the morning when my greatgrandfather awoke he found them both dead with the man holding the woman's feet to his chest inside his raggedy shirt.

That man died trying to warm his wife's feet.

There are many other stories about my greatgrandfather Timmy Cooney, but I will tell just one more now.

Many years after that morning he came back to that place to mark the graves of that family. He found the little creek where he had buried the girl but there was no trace of the little house and no graves marked for anyone. My greatgrandfather was very old then but he took a spade and marked out three graves by the creek and then took his hat and brought water from the creek and gave them to drink of their own water, as he said, the pure water washing away their pain and sorrow.

My grandfather who was there that day told me that story.

40.

The front door of the Department of Public Works is never locked, Cedar and Worried Man being of the shared opinion that a public service project should never close, and over the years they have found many things when they opened the door in the morning, including once two babies the size of two fists.

Worried Man wrenches the door open and runs straight through the building, sure of his way in the dark, through the reading room and cavernous central shop and warren of little offices in the back, his fear rising *what is the matter with Nora?* and he reaches her studio door and wrenches at it and just as he does he feels a stab of her pain like a train running right through his head and he wavers there by the door, his grip loosened for a second as he feels blindly for the source of the pain— *my child! Nora!*—and he wrenches ferociously at the door again but it's locked! *shit! shit!* and he hammers on the door with all his might which is considerable even in his later years he having been all his life a sinewy and passionate man and he yells *Nora! Nora!* and then suddenly the door gapes open and she stands there sobbing and he half steps half stumbles into the studio the half a wooden man looming on her table in the dark and she leans into her father and he bends down and folds his daughter into his arms hunching over her longleggedly like a heron and she tucks her head under his chin and weeps and weeps and he doesn't say a word but keeps his mouth buried in the black river of her hair and they stand like this for so long that her tears soak twin circles into his shirt and those circles never actually do wash out of his shirt and eventually the shirt fades away to rags and ribbons but the circles remain inviolate and one morning he joins them together reverently and folds them into his prayer bundle where there are many things like that.

As she cries into him he makes deep wet sounds in his throat.

Finally he says into her hair *talk to me talk to me* but she can't speak and he leads her to the porch and she puts her face on his long knees and cries again his long hands stroking her black hair he says *what? what?* with the front of his mind frantic for Nora and the back of his mind feeling for the pain he felt at the door, and that's how they are when Moses floats up to land *plop* on the railing and yells

Daniel is hurt! come! come!

She leaps up and takes two quick steps and sails right over the railing like a deer.

Worried Man shouts *run! run!*

Moses with two terrific strokes of his wings like twin black tents is away over the tops of the trees below him No Horses flies down the path her hair a river of black in the black night between the twin lines of black trees her heart black black.

41.

Owen Cooney here at home telling stories for my son Daniel.

I will continue with stories of Timmy Cooney.

Timmy Cooney was fifteen years old when the Hunger came. It came one night in late summer. When the family went to bed the potato plants were healthy and in the morning the plants were black and withered. The people went from field to field amazed. They dug up the potatoes but the potatoes were black and withered too.

That was how *an Gorta* began, the Hunger.

Soon there was no food at all and people stole from each other and knocked each other down when a cauldron for gruel and broth was set up in the town. *Bhi an t-ocras comh mor sin agus nach rabh trocaire in aon duine leis a-duine eile*, my grandfather would say, no one had mercy for anyone else.

With the Hunger came the fever and very many people died. Old people and babies died first, then children, then men, and finally women. They always died that way when the Hunger came to a town.

In my greatgrandfather's family there was a mother, a father, three girls, and himself. They suffered but lived because they would gather grains from stooks of rye and wheat and boil them, and they kept a few turnips in their garden, and my greatgrandfather caught what fish he could in the sea, and also he stole four sheep from a neighbor.

He regretted those four thefts all the rest of his days he said even though they maybe kept his sisters alive.

Finally his sister Cait died of the fever that howled after the Hunger came. She was ten when the Hunger began and fifteen when she died.

She loved to dance and had hair as black as the inside of a dog. She could leap and spin like a bird. She was the fastest runner of anyone. She could remember any story that was told to her and many was the cold wet night when around the fire she would tell stories, saying the voices of the characters in the stories so eerily perfectly that you'd swear the characters were in the room and the stories utterly alive, and people came from miles around to hear her tell her stories, children especially. When she finished telling her stories there would be a roar of laughter you could hear far away. Sometimes then when the mood was upon her she would dance by the fire, her hair whipping and flying, and such a sight you never saw, a girl so slight and light whirling faster than the eye could see, whirling so fast that you thought it entirely possible that if you blinked your eye she would vanish utterly and never be seen again on this grand grim green earth.

Mharbh an gorta achan rud, the Hunger killed everything, my greatgrandfather said.

42.

Cedar leans his head back to pop a salmonberry into his mouth as he walks down the dark road wondering

where is old Billy he should have come home by now the old goat out there smelling pain in town a good thing he does that because the fact is that he smells out half the work of the department without his nose we'd be out of a job ho ho so really his nose is the most important piece of equipment we have I'll have to get it insured can you imagine Billy noseless I mean what kind of public works department would go noseless not us that's for sure we are up to the minute with the latest nasal and otolaryngological technology I wonder how much we can insure it for we'll have to get a doctor's statement I can't wait to pitch this to the doctor this'll be hilarious and o the look on May's face o this will be delicious

when suddenly Moses' shadow flickers across his face

and from the crow's sheer speed and arrowing flight Cedar immediately smells bad trouble

and he spins on his heel to keep Moses in view against the dense dark sky and just as he does a woman runs by him so fast that he feels her tailwind rather than actually sees her

but he immediately recognizes her hair flowing behind her a river of black against the dense dark sky as she sprints away

and he begins to run after her but after one leaping step

he slams on the brakes and stands there quivering like a wire thinking

shit. shit. okay. all right. shit. don't run. think. moses must be leading her. nora's fast. she'll get there fast. someone hurt. billy? broke his hip. shit. in the woods. okay. shit. gotta get him out. need a truck. need a doctor. nose. noseless. get a truck. get the doctor. first the doctor. okay. doctor. go.

and he goes as fast as he can go toward the sea

where in his house by the sea in his room in his bed in the murky dark the doctor is awake his eyes glinting.

43.

One living being saw Daniel fly over the edge of the cliff and sail end over end into the thicket of spruce trees below the path: a young female bear on her early evening rounds, the same young bear who read the *New York Times* at the Department of Public Works. She is three years old this spring. Her name in the dark tongue of bears means *eats salt,* for her habit of scouring the beach for food. Today she has eaten six young ground squirrels, their mother, several dozen beetles, several hundred salmonberries, and a dead jay. The young squirrels were delicious. Later this evening she will eat two fledgling murres on the beach. She likes to sharpen her claws on cedar trees and will walk miles to find the right tree for sharpening her claws. She has eaten shark, skate, ray, halibut, perch, cod, cormorant, pelican, gull, duck, heron, salmon, steelhead, tern, sea lion, seal, and gray whale. She has eaten bat, beaver, bullfrog, deer, dove, rabbit, raccoon, and robin. She will mate for the first time in about a month, with a bear whose name means *only one.* They will be together for three nights and four days. She will give birth to female twins. He will never see the twins. She and the cubs will leave him in the pearly dawn while he is sleeping. He has never walked on the beach because he believes the roaring ocean is a bear of incomprehensible size. He got his name because his mother had never had a cub before him and never had one afterwards. His mother died a week after he learned to forage for himself. He grew so thin the year after his mother died that two loggers who saw him on a ridge one day thought he was a dog.

44.

Owen Cooney here telling stories for my boy Daniel.

I will continue the story of Timmy Cooney.

He saw and heard many things during the years of the Hunger, and he never forgot any of them, and he told those stories until the day he died. *Is mo lau nad muir n-oited imma-rau,* it is many a day since I sailed on the sea of youth, he would say, and *ad-ciu form bratt brothrach n-ais,* I see on myself the shaggy cloak of age, but I remember those who vanished and I will sing them.

So he would tell us about the two strong young brothers in his town whose shoulders were bent all the rest of their lives from carrying the coffins, and about the old man who ate a painting of food he was so mad from the Hunger, and about the way little children would ram their hands into a cauldron of boiling broth desperate for scraps of meat in the soup, and about the mother who killed her daughter to save her from the Hunger, and about the father who died and when the doctor opened him afterwards they found he'd eaten nothing but bits of skins of potatoes for months, giving all the potatoes to his wife and children.

There were a thousand thousand thousand stories like those stories, he said.

One time my greatgrandfather was cutting wheat when a man came walking down the road. He was carrying a load on his back. He stopped to rest by the field where Timmy Cooney was. It was late in the afternoon. The larks were whistling. Scanlan was the man's name. It was his dead wife he was carrying. He was taking her to the graveyard of the town where she had been a girl. She had died of the Hunger. He could have buried her where they lived but he knew that she wanted to be in the soil of the town where she had been a girl. She was sitting in a *sugan* on his shoulders, a carrying-chair made of rope and knotted tightly to his back. Their little son was walking with him. The wife was wearing a blue cloak and hood just as she did when she was alive. My greatgrandfather got some milk to give to Scanlan, but Scanlan wouldn't take the milk. He said it would overcome him because he had not eaten anything in days and he needed to keep what strength he had so he could bury his wife before dark.

The little boy drank the milk and off went the boy and his father down the road.

Char chlaon a pairt, my greatgrandfather said of that man: his love did not waver.

45.

Everyone is kneeling.

For an instant, for a split second, every knee everywhere touches down, into mud, wood, stone, linoleum, water, leaf litter, sand.

Grace is on her knees in a bed. No Horses is on her knees in the woods in the dark by her unconscious son who is face-down his shattered knees wet with blood and mud. Maple Head is on her knees in her kitchen looking for a broiling pan. The doctor is on his knees in his closet looking for his mudding boots. The man who lied in court is kneeling on the beach praying. Cedar is on his knees in the doctor's tool shed looking for rope. Worried Man is on his knees on the porch of the Department of Public Works praying. Rachel is on her knees in the tub of the cabin up in the hills. Her boyfriend Timmy is on his knees facing her. Michael the cop is on his knees in his living room with a daughter laughing on each shoulder as he snorts and whirls. He is a bear with two baby eagles on his shoulders and then he is a whale with two baby seals on his shoulders. His wife Sara is kneeling in the bathtub washing her hair under the faucet. The child inside her is kneeling on her bladder. The man who pulled out a chair for Grace in the bar is on his knees in the bed behind Grace. Stella the bartender is on her knees mopping vomit in the bathroom of the bar. Red Hugh O Donnell is on his knees where he has fallen after swinging his white stick at his sons and missing them altogether and the two sons Niall and Peadar are on their knees mocking him. The priest is on his knees by the bed of the old nun who just died. A moment ago he touched her knees with oil and whispered *bless you for all those hours in prayer for us.* Owen Cooney having finished making tapes is on his knees in his kitchen scrubbing the floor with oil soap; his wife and son are absent and it would be a poor steaming burro of a man who wouldn't take advantage of a little slippage in time to get the damned floor smiling shiny and ah the song on Nora's face when she sees this floor. The man who beats his son is on his knees by his bed praying. His head is bent to touch his blanket. His son is on his knees by the dryer in the basement pulling out clothes to fold there is a pile of his folded clothes by his left knee and a pile of his father's folded clothes by his right knee. Grace's brother Declan is on his knees in his bed sound asleep with three blankets pulled over him like three tents red black brown. Anna Christie is on her knees in the shallow water at the edge of the river. Her head is bent to touch the river. Her daughter Cyra has just knelt to wrap her mother in a blanket. As the blanket settles onto her mother's shoulders so do Cyra's long thin hands like birds landing gently and Cyra's long thin fingers probe gently tenderly into the tight taut muscles of her mother's big shoulders to draw out all the screaming there.

The river whirls and sings and Anna rises and sings and as she begins to sing all knees rise all at once from the mud the floors the beds the tubs all over,

except Daniel's.

46.

Moses wheels sharply and drops like a stone when he is directly over Daniel's body, to show No Horses the exact spot. He plummets, he falls. He is blacker than the black night. When he lands *plop* on Daniel's backpack No Horses throws herself over the edge of the path feetfirst and scrabbles wildly down the slope through salal and blackberry bushes. Moses shouts and she aims for his ragged voice. The bushes grab her angrily as she slams through them. Moses spins in a tight circle shouting. She stumbles over Daniel's mangled bike. Moses shouts *here here here.* She falls to her knees by her son's body his braids askew red black brown. Moses leaps back into the air. No Horses feels for Daniel's pulse. Moses whirls up up up. She feels Daniel's heart hammering

hammering hammering and she sobs and runs her hands over him tip to toe. Moses in the air sees Cedar and the doctor at the edge of the path. The doctor has a lantern. Daniel's legs are blood and splintered bones. Moses shouts to Cedar *go go go*. Cedar flings himself over the edge of the path feetfirst. No Horses is curled over her boy her black hair a black tent in the black night. Moses whirls and lands *plop* next to the doctor. Cedar lands on his knees next to No Horses and Daniel. The doctor says to Moses *is he alive?* And Moses says *yes but his legs are smashed*. No Horses holds Cedar's flashlight on Daniel's body. The doctor calculates miles and minutes to the hospital. Cedar skims his hands over Daniel tip to toe. Moses leaps back into the air and whirls toward town. The doctor feels in his jacket for his cigarettes. Cedar looks up from Daniel and peers into the thicket of spruce trees. No Horses starts to shiver. The doctor finds his cigarettes but doesn't light one. The flashlight wobbles. Cedar and the doctor brace Daniel's legs with thin shimmies of wood and tape the splints together so nothing moves, and they gently work a thin narrow sheet of wood under Daniel, and the doctor checks the boy's pulse and eyes and neck and spine again and again and again, and then Cedar stands up, but when No Horses crouches to pick up the top half of the litter Cedar says *Nora no* and he turns to the trees and says three words in a language she does not know and the young female bear steps out of the thicket of spruce trees and picks up the litter in her huge dark arms and walks with it upright uphill to where the doctor is waiting.

47.

The bear is confused and excited and angry. She cradles the boy in her huge dark arms and rumbles uphill right through the bushes. This animal is broken, she thinks. It smells bloody. The blood makes her hungry. She remembers the ground squirrels. The word for ground squirrel in the language of bears is *meat in holes*. The night is as black as she can ever remember. Daniel's braids flop and swing. She has never touched a human being before although she has seen and smelled many of them, all different flavors and sizes. In the dark language of bears the word for human being is *killer brother*. Not one killer brother smells like another one. Her thighs ache from walking upright. Once she smelled a dead killer brother on the beach. The word for dead is *no longer eats*. From fifty yards away she smells the doctor's cigarettes in his jacket pocket. She smells the sweat and salt of his boots. She smells the smears of jelly in Daniel's backpack. She smells the oil No Horses used to clean her chisels and gouges. She smells the oil Daniel used on his bicycle chain. She smells the bread Maple Head was baking when Cedar left the house. She smells rage and fish and ice on Cedar. She smells drowned beaver on Daniel. The word for beaver is *meat in water holes*. She smells pear and iodine on the doctor's hands. The word for pear in bear is the same as the word for apple. Daniel slides awake but his face is pressed so firmly into thick sour dirty dense black sweaty bear hair that he can neither see nor hear nor speak. The word for dirt is *mother below us*. The doctor hears the bear crashing toward him through the salmonberry bushes. The word for salmonberry is *eye of spring*.

48.

Maple Head reaches into the oven and taps her loaves of bread with her knuckles and each makes the right hollow sound and she slides them out gently onto a rack to cool. Eats another salmonberry from the windowsill. She's worried and not worried: her husband is liable to long winged arrows of thought as he says Blake says and often he loses himself utterly in some project to the point where he loses track of time altogether and she strolls down to the Department to find him late at night. Recently it's been bicycles. His hair all askew and his eyes lit up and his face lit up. She brings bread and wine and they sit at his rickety work table. His eyes flashing in the cavernous dark central workspace of the building where the truck and tools are. She keeps candles and wine glasses on a shelf there for when this happens. May, I've had the most astonishing thoughts. He whirls a stool into place for her. Now, May, sit right here you lovely sinuous creature and listen to *this*. His big hands swirling in the air. If time is a progressive thing, May, proceeding relentlessly forward on its unique plane, though capable of being stopped briefly, or of being *perceived* as having stopped briefly, then a study of all machines that progress along whatever plane or planes, but which can be stopped briefly, or *perceived* as having stopped briefly, will be useful to our work. Clearly then an exploration of the simplest propulsive machines is in order. Remembering that nature yearns always for the simple. Now here is a bicycle. The bicycle, May, is a creation of wondrous simplicity and clean design. The taut wiring alone is fascinating but we can discuss that later. Let's first consider the *premise* of a bicycle. Energy applied *here* is translated to a gear mechanism *here* and then to the chain *there*, and is then further translated to the rear wheel, which then creates an ordered propulsion of remarkable speed and grace, masterable even by a child such as our grandson who whizzes through town like an arrow with hair. Let's think of the bicycle as a *narrative*. Energy translated into story. And *time* of course is also an energetic story. Ceaseless, relentless, progressive. Most analyses of time, May, fixate on basic engineering problems such as where does the propulsive energy come from, or what happens at the end of time? Both of which are riveting questions. But unanswerable in this plane or planes. Of far greater interest is the *conduct* of time, not its source or ultimate destination. Its *behavior* is what you want to enjoy. Consider the river where as lovers we were born dripping. The *behavior* of the river is more interesting than how it begins or ends. Indeed the behavior of the river *is* the river, isn't it? Similarly love. In a sense we don't actually really *have* a past or future as lovers. As a river in a real sense isn't its birth or its destination. We have our behavior, our conduct. We have *stories* of how we as lovers were born by the river, yes, you running your fingers through your hair and me taking a step and what a step that was, and we have *dreams* of how we might be lovers in the future, but as boats joined on a river we really have just *now*, you smiling at me and your bread steaming and your wine glass glittering, and I am talking way too much again aren't I?

49.

In the last few minutes before the old nun died in her bed on the top floor of the old hotel she thought of Moses and everything she loved about him—the way he craned his head to peer at her, the way he landed with a *plop*, the way he crouched like a small black feathered weightlifter before jumping into the air, the ornate cast of his mind, his affection for the psalms, his interest in all languages, the way he would give her the bigger piece of fish when they split a fish for dinner, the way he dusted tables and windows with his wings, the way he snorted nasally when he laughed, the time he drank a glass of wine and ended up on his back on the grass both of them giggling helplessly, the way he woke her with a kiss on the forehead, the way he hilariously tried to learn to use a fork, the way he held himself motionless and nervous when she trimmed his toenails, the way he wormed himself into blankets by the fireplace so that only his eyes and beak could be seen, the way he never ceased trying to catch insects on the wing on the theory that he was every bit as talented as any piss-ant nighthawk or swift or swallow, the way he attacked hawks furiously and called them dirty names in all his languages and crowed ribaldly about it afterwards with his friends, the way he befriended children gravely, the way he waited by the library door and hopped in hurriedly when someone came in or out until the librarian cut a little pet door for him, the way he painted himself white once for her birthday, the way he would shout *awake harp and lyre! I will awaken the dawn!* to make her laugh when they were eating breakfast, the way he daintily collected berries in an old baseball cap, the way he posed as a stuffed crow when her mother superior made her annual site visit to her room in the old hotel, the way he tried to teach pigeons to speak before concluding that stones were smarter than pigeons, the way he studied fishing with herons and skimmers and ouzels and cormorants and grebes and pelicans, the way he flipped over and fell dramatically into the ocean pelican-like just to hear her peal of laughter whenever they walked the beach, the way he formally greeted all crows known or unknown to him with the words *peace be to you*, the way they both wept bitter tears in the kitchen when she told him one morning haltingly that she wanted him to leave, and would not tell him why, until his grave persistence finally got to her, and she told him that the doctor had told her that she was ill unto death, and she didn't want him to see her shrivel, she wanted to remain always lively and vibrant and herself in his heart, and he must go, and never see her again, and that way they would always have each other, always have this bronze morning, the bronze triangles of toast between them, the bowl of bronze berries, her right hand on his left foot, his eyes closed, her body shivering, the burble of pigeons on the fire escape the only sound in the room.

II

1.

Michael the policeman and his wife Sara are in the kitchen finishing the dishes after putting their two daughters to bed. Michael is washing and Sara is drying. Michael is humming Puccini's song *Recondita armonia* in which a painter compares the lovely features of the woman in his painting to the lovely features of his lover. Sara wants to tell him about the baby the size of his thumb who just fell asleep inside her but just as she dries her hands and screws up her courage to say

Michael,

he turns and with his hands all wet takes her gently by the waist and whirls her across the kitchen singing *ma nel ritrar costei il mio solo pensier, Sara tu sei!* and she can't help laughing, her arms and the towel caught in his embrace, and the moment is lost again.

Sing it in English, she says, her heart all confused and happy.

I have vowed my love to you, Sara, to you! he sings, and he leans in to kiss her but she ducks her head into his chest so his lips arrive in her hair.

Michael, she says into his shirt,

but just as she says his name he says tenderly, *E tanto ell'era infervorata nella sua preghiera ch'io ne pinsi, non visto, il bel sembiante,* she was so lost to all around her that she never saw me all the time I was painting her lovely features, that's what Mario the painter says about Tosca right in the beginning, Sara.

Does he love her? says Sara into his shirt.

O yes, head over heels, but she's a difficult woman.

And she loves him?

She adores him but she can't figure him out easily.

I know the feeling, Mario.

O, I am easily figured out, Tosca. *Tu sei!*

And this time she leans her face back to accept his kiss and they kiss gently, she floating in his long arms, the towel floating in the soapy water, the girl floating inside Sara.

2.

In bed that night Sara is restless and affectionate and as a gift to Michael she asks him to tell her about Puccini and he rises to the question like a fish to a fly.

O a riveting fellow altogether, cruel and generous, petulant and sweet, a fool and a genius, says Michael, his hands carving the air like swifts and swallows. He had seven sisters and their names are a poem in Italian: Otilia, Tomaide, Temi, Maria, Iginia, Ramelde, and Macrina. You wonder what effect seven sisters must have on a boy. His dad died when he was only five years old and his poor mom was left with all those young children and she was only thirty or so. What a woman. Albina was her name. If we ever have another girl we could name her Albina and then she'd have some of the muscle of Puccini's mama, don't you think? Because names matter. They do have power and magic somehow, don't you think? Let's have another baby so we can name her Albina. Anyway Puccini was a rotten student, he kept getting expelled from school, he ran around crazy in the hills. He had energy coming out his ears and he couldn't sit still for ten seconds straight. His mom made him take music lessons and he was terrible. There was a music contest when he was seventeen and he finished dead last. Last! Puccini! But he chased after songs even though it seemed crazy and his mom kept telling him that he would be an unbelievably great musician. Finally he wrote a symphony and then an opera, and so his career was started, but his mom died a week after his opera was performed in Milan. She was only fifty years old or so. The last time she saw Giacomo she gave him the ring from her finger. *There's* a scene from an opera, eh? What a woman.

Sara?

But Sara is asleep, her hands still, her bookmark propped precariously between her chin and her breasts, her reading glasses awry, her right knee thrown over Michael's left thigh. He props himself on one elbow and watches her: the sweet country of her face, her lace eyelashes, her lean high cheekbones, her breasts rising and falling under her slip, the circle on her right shoulder where she was vaccinated for polio as a girl, the burst of freckles in the russet sky of her back, the taut leap of her neck, the tiny hidden hollow at the base of her throat. Sometimes when they are making love he slides his tongue along her collarbone and into that tiny hollow which sometimes gives her a wet electric shiver in her belly but sometimes makes her twist away from his tickling tongue and neither of them knows what will happen when he does it sometimes she grabs his hair and arches wildly under him but sometimes she wrenches away trying with all her might to escape.

3.

Worried Man kneeling on the deck of the Department of Public Works in the black night after No Horses sprinted madly down the hill between the twin lines of black trees with Moses a black arrow above her discovers when he tries to rise that his knees have locked and he has to laugh. What a piece of work am I all rags and splinters. He uses his long arms as levers and hoists himself up along the railing and pauses there for a moment stretching his legs and sending his mind out over the railing into the velvet night feeling for the chattering cables of pain from his daughter and his grandson.

He finds Nora and he feels gently along the spine of her electric pain. A shadow of what it was, that's good, but her fear is so strong he can taste ashes in his mouth. O Nora. He feels anxiously for Daniel and there tearing through the dark air is the ragged burning screaming pain of the boy, o poor child poor child he'll have to get to the clinic I'll get the truck must tell May poor poor Daniel.

He feels a dozen other pains yammering and chattering at him in the moist ancient air, they are almost musical tones in his head: the shrill faint note of Mrs. L's arthritic wrists, like a flute high and away; the deep thrumming tone of Anna Christie singing and rocking by the creek; the jangled halting basso of the man who beats his son, rage and guilt and fear and exhaustion all twisted together in that poor man. Poor man poor man.

He opens his eyes and clears his mind and takes a deep breath and thinks truck keys May and notices that he is shivering night's not that cold hmm and he steps inside and closes the glass door gently and walks thinking of Daniel poor child through the studio past the wooden man but just as he reaches for the studio door a savage raging pain explodes in his chest so suddenly and cruelly that it knocks him to his knees and only by shooting his arms out blindly and landing on his hands does he avoid smashing his face on the floor.

O May he thinks faintly from far far away.

He can't breathe uh uh uh uh uh uh gasping uh uh uh uh but desperately raggedly he gains a half a breath uh uh uh and gulping uh uh a whole one uh uh then another uh and greedily aah he fills aaah his lungs as deeply as he can aaaah he would eat all the air in the room if he could aaaaah he would suck it dry the blessed air aaaaah and somehow the friendly air aaaaah forces the fire in his chest down aaahh and the rage retreats snarling aaah and he kneels there by the wooden man aaaah breathing aaah his shoulders shaking aah his knees throbbing ah his sweat dripping freely to the floor ah his mind whispering May o May o May.

4.

In the last few minutes before dawn when the world is a muted pearl moist and poised Sara's hands warm and eager draw Michael into her and they kiss gently and he slides into her gently and they make love gently her eyes closed and his open and then they lay cupped facing east so Sara can watch the curtain rise on the world. His arm a blanket on her arm gently.

Tell me more about your man Puccini, she says into her pillow.

Really?

Yes really.

Hmm. Well, his sister Iginia …

Shh. Whisper.

His sister Iginia, he whispers, entered a convent when she was nine years old and lived the rest of her life cloistered at the foot of a mountain, but they were very close and they loved each other dearly and when Giacomo was rich and famous he would come to visit her and hand her his wallet and she would take whatever she thought the convent needed. That story always stayed in my mind. He hands over the wallet without a second thought. He was a lout sometimes but never with his sisters.

That's sweet.

And Iginia told him stories too one of which he turned into a piece of music, about a beautiful nun who dies young.

What was her name?

Angelica. Isn't that lovely?

Shhh.

If we have another girl we can name her Angelica.

Or Albina, for Puccini's mother.

You remembered! I thought you were asleep.

Shh. What would you name a boy?

Giacomo?

No.

No?

No.

James?

Shh.

Giacomo is James in Italian.

Okay.

James?

James or Albina.

Deal.

Deal.

Do we need to be so sure about names right this very minute?

Yes.

5.

Maple Head looks at the clock again and decides enough is enough. She takes one loaf of bread and puts it on the windowsill with a note for Cedar and takes the other loaf and a bottle of wine and floats down to the Department of Public Works. The night is velvet and still. An owl wheedles in the woods. She floats over the path. The owl floats silently overhead. She worries. The owl lands in a big cedar. She decides not to worry. The owl hunkers and fluffs. She floats over the path. The owl is still. The wine bottle bumps against the bread against her back as she floats over the path.

She slips in the front door of the shaggy dark building.

Billy?

She floats through the cavernous dark central workspace of the building where the truck and tools are where she keeps wine glasses and candles for when Billy is working late.

Cedar?

She slips into the warren of little offices in the rear of the building.

Nora?

Sees the wooden man half made and half darker than the dark.

Billy?

Sees her husband on the floor sitting smiling in the dark.

Billy!

O May o May.

What happened?

I had … an adventure.

She is on her knees cupping his face in her hands.

Your heart?

Yeh.

Bad?

Yuh.

Still? Now?

No, no. It's gone now. I couldn't catch my breath there for a long while though.

She runs her hands through his hair and feels the sweat his fear hatched.

That was scary, May. To not be able to draw a breath. Wow.

She feels his neck and wrist for the throb of his pulse.

Your pulse feels raggedy.

What say we have a glass of wine, you lovely creature?

Let's get you to the doctor, love.

There are wine glasses in the shop, you know.

She has to smile and suddenly she's exhausted.

You are so … *you*, she says.

I'll take that as a compliment.

You almost died.

But I didn't die and you're with me and I smell fresh bread.

You almost died alone.

Never alone, May. Never.

She closes her eyes and he folds her in his long arms like wings and for a long moment they sit there together wordlessly in the dark the wooden man half made in the dark above them.

I'm scared to be old, she says into his chest.

Mm.

Are you scared too?

Yes.

I'm afraid we'll lose each other.

Never.

We're always on the lip of lost, Billy.

Now he cups her face in his hands huge as oars.

No matter what happens, May, no matter what, we will *always* have each other. We'll *always* be in each other. I don't know how but I know we will. Some bright morning everything will change. I see it sometimes in a dream. In my dream the morning is bright and silent. The colors are white and blue. Everything has a shining edge like it was cut from the most amazing ice. In my dream we go on journeys. I go one way and you go another. But we never come apart. We never lose each other. I can't explain it. We are always braided together. I can't explain it. That's just how we are. That's just how it is.

Pause.

You are a very strange and fascinating man.

I'll take that as a compliment.

I love you very much.

Then I am the envy of all men absolutely.

She opens her eyes and smiles.

What say we open that wine and talk it over? he says.

And they do, on the floor, in the dark, without a word.

6.

The instant after Grace's eyes open in the murky green dark of the trailer she is out of bed furious and silent and within seconds she is outside struggling into her jeans and sweater. Can't find her shirt. She stuffs her boots in her gear bag and spits twice furiously on the trailer and swings her bag to her shoulder and pads away barefoot. Just past dawn. She trips over a little fake knee-high picket fence and realizes she's in the trailer park near the highway. Spits furiously on the fence. Her mouth is sour and dry. When she is out of sight of the trailers she slips into a thicket of alder and pees and pulls her boots on and considers. Sunlight hits the tips of the trees. She brushes her hair what's left of it what was I thinking stupid me. Listens: robins, a thrush, a woodpecker, an ouzel, the silver plink plink of a hammer on metal. Stretches. Swings her bag to her shoulder, walks through the trees, and there in an opening in the woods through a bright yellow window in the warming morning she sees Owen Cooney hammering away at something in his shop. He's shirtless and sweating and looks like a painting of the ancient god Vulcan in his forge. Mom read that book to me a thousand times, gods and heroes and warrior queens. Vulcan's hard muscles and jet-black hair and relentless hammer. A book in the morning and a story at night. Thor and Hercules and Cú Chulainn of the three-colored hair red black brown. A book to wake and a story to sleep. The warrior queen Meadhbh the intoxicating one who started battles. Mom's hands turning the pages. The warrior queen Grace the brave one who slept with the hawsers of her ships tied to her bed. Mom's tiny hands the color of nutmeg and cinnamon. The princess Caer the wise one who could turn into a swan. Mom murmuring stories in the dark. The warrior queen Aife who fought Cú Chulainn and then slept with him. Mom wetting her forefinger with her tongue quick as a cat before turning the page. The princess Deidre of the gray eyes desired by all men but her heart open to only the one. Mom's fingers tracing Vulcan's rippled back as she told his fire and fury.

Grace steps forward and knocks on Owen's window.

7.

Owen's hammer pauses in mid-blow when he hears the rap of knuckles on his shop window and he turns to see who is knocking and sees Grace and she sees the startle in his face and her belly leaps and tumbles.

Grace. Come in.

Sorry to bother you so early.

Is it early then?

I think so.

I've been ... busy.

What's that?

Daniel's bicycle.

What happened to it?

He crashed, Grace. He went off a cliff. His legs are all smashed.

O God.

They operated for hours. His legs are all smashed. His knees are all smashed. My little boy. His bike is all smashed. My little boy. I have to fix his bike. He'll want his bike. My little boy. He's all smashed.

O God.

Everything's all smashed, Grace.

The shop is broiling hot and Owen is sweating profusely and he sits down heavily on his work-stool and bows his head so Grace can't see his face but only the roil of his hair black as the inside of a dog and the hammer huge and steel-blue in his hand.

She doesn't know what to say. She reaches out and puts her hand in his wet hair and he begins to weep and she reaches out her other hand and touches his rough jawline. His face is all wet with tears and sweat and her hand gets all wet. She steps forward and brings his wet face into her loose sweater below her breasts and he weeps and weeps his shoulders shaking and shuddering. Her belly roils and tumbles. She doesn't know what to say. The shop is broiling hot. She wants to say something but doesn't know what to say so she says nothing and he weeps and her hand sifts through his hair.

8.

Worried Man here telling stories to my poor grandson as he sleeps with his broken legs. I think my voice crawls into him and heals him some so I will tell him some stories of the People. We have been here from before even our stories remember, my sweet boy. We lived by the mouths of rivers. We had magic numbers. Five was the magic number for men and four was magic for women. We had brothers and sisters far to the north, into the ice. Sometimes their boats appeared here out of the mist and we would talk to them. We built big houses of cedar and often several families would live together in the same house. Some of our houses were a thousand feet long. We ate flounder, herring, smelt, seals, sea lions, whales, salmon, elk, deer, bear, and *yetska* roots from the marshes. In winter we wore waterproof hats and robes of woven cedar. We used cedar for diapers, canoes, masks, drums, arrows, paddles, cradles, harpoons, rakes, weirs, looms, nets, rattles, rope, bowls, horns, whistles, blankets, and baskets. When we fought we wore armor made of dried elk leather and we painted our faces red and black. We made hats woven of spruce roots. We liked to drink sea lion oil. We ate salmonberries, thimbleberries, gooseberries, bearberries, shotberries. When one of our children died we left her toys and dishes out in the rain to bleach and fade. The greatest people among us were those who gave everything away. Our names were earned by deeds or dreams. Sometimes our old people would hand over their tired names to their children and take fresh names with which to die. We told stories sometimes for ten hours at a time. We could sing for ten hours at a time for days and days. We went to the mountains to see clearly when that was necessary but we were a people of rivers and the sea. Our houses faced the river or the sea. Sometimes our best storytellers would be the mayors of the town. There were two mayors for each river. In winter we would dance and sing and pray the world back into balance. We made blankets and baskets. We made the best canoes there ever were and our infants slept in cradles shaped like canoes and our dead slept in canoes that we would hoist into *asayahal*, the south wind. South Wind had many adventures. He lives in a cave now. No one knows where the cave is but Cedar and I have an idea. Ice was *gecla* in the old language, and the winter surf was *xilgo*, wild woman, and thunder was *nixixunu*, powerful but kind. Everything had a story, Daniel. Beaver liked to be alone. Blue Jay was a gossip. Crane carried people over rivers with his long legs. Eagle you could trust. Muskrat was a brave little man. So many stories. And those stories had a certain flavor in the old language, a shape in your mouth, a taste. Sometimes when I am half asleep I hear the old words in my ears. I hear my grandfather saying *quoatseha tetlewap leluk*, goodbye you sweet boy. He would say that as he hugged me into his chest, as strong and hairy as a bear, so I never heard those words without his arms around me and his smell like salt and smoke. Sometimes I whisper those words to myself and they make me sad and warm at once. I whisper *quoatseha* to you now, my boy. Don't you be afraid. Crane will carry you over this dark river, his wings strong and fierce.

9.

Owen gets a grip on himself after a few minutes and stands up embarrassed and Grace steps back and dries her hands on her jeans. Her sweater sticks to her belly where his tears and sweat have soaked it through.

Sorry about your sweater, he says.

Not a problem. Really.

Can I lend you a shirt then?

No no. It'll dry off.

Got a clean shirt right here.

No no. Thanks though.

A cup of coffee then?

I don't want to keep you, Owen.

No no. It's good to talk. Good to be distracted.

I'm awful sorry about Daniel.

Yeh.

He'll be fine, I'm sure of it.

Yeh. Thanks.

He's a sweet boy.

Yeh.

I see him zooming around town every day.

Yeh.

He'll be fine, Owen. I know it.

Yeh. Thanks.

He makes coffee and gives Grace the clean mug and he takes Moses' mug in which the crow likes to store snail shells. Owen empties out the snail shells. She looks at his hands so as not to look at his body. He begins to sit on his stool again and then realizes that she's standing and he's shirtless and he pops up and offers her the stool but she declines. He hurriedly puts his shirt on but he doesn't want to sit down again so they stand there, coffee steaming. He looks at her closely. Hasn't actually noticed her for years, really. She was a kid. A strong girl good with tools and boats and such. Not a girl anymore. A young woman. A woman.

How's your brother Declan king of the sea? he says.

Good. Good catches lately.

Halibut?

Yeh. Price is down a little but the catch is good.

That's good.

Yeh.

And your family?

Good.

I can never remember your brothers' names.

They all look alike. Like puppies.

They both grin.

Do you ever hear from your mom?

No.

Sorry.

No no. It's okay.

More coffee then?

No no. I should be going. Got to get some sleep today. We're out again tonight after halibut.

Supposed to be a wild wind tonight.

We only go out a couple miles.

Is aicher in gaith innocht, fu-fuasna fairrge findfholt, says Owen. Bitter is the wind tonight, it tosses the sea's white tresses.

That's lovely.

Yeh. The old Irish sang in every sentence.

I don't know hardly any of it. All I know is curses from Red Hugh.

I'll teach you sometime.

I'd like that.

All right then.

I'd best be off.

Luck on the sea's white tresses.

Thanks. And thanks for the coffee.

Any old time.

I'll be here every day at dawn then.

They smile.

Daniel will be okay, Owen. I feel it.

Yeh.

Courage.

Yeh.

Say hi to No Horses for me.

I will.

But he doesn't. He is exhausted and riven with worry and after hammering Daniel's bike back into a rough semblance of what it was he goes home and sleeps for two hours and then he spends the rest of the day sitting at Daniel's bedside praying and staring so that night when he and No Horses crawl into bed blind with exhaustion and the hollow residue of fear they do not trade tales as they usually do but they fall asleep instantly curled back to front like spoons like hands like petals of a flower long and lean his arm a blanket on her arm gently.

10.

Owen Cooney here in my son Daniel's hospital room. He is here with two broken legs. I'll tell stories as he sleeps. Maybe the stories will help him. He has slept for two days. The last time he was awake he was falling through the air. He must have fallen fifty feet through the air. I keep thinking of him falling through the air. My sweet little boy. God help me. God heal my boy. God help my sweet Nora asleep on the floor. I will tell a story. I must tell a story. My greatgrandfather Timmy Cooney told stories. He walked and told stories. That's what he did all his life. He couldn't stop walking after the Hunger. He walked and walked. There are stories in the air as thick as birds around me, he would say. I will save those stories from starving, he would say. I have a great hunger for stories, he would say. He always walked west. That was his way. To the west was *Tir na nOg*, the Country of the Young, the Country of the Blessed, where no one ever grew old and no one ever was hungry. It was near to you when you heard bells, he would say. Some people said it was under a lake and some said a river but Timmy Cooney said it was under the great ocean to the west. Sometimes he saw it shimmering there. He would stand *ar chostai*, on the shore, and sing and tell stories. He said you could reach that country on the back of a white horse. You could live there for a hundred years and it would be the blink of an eye here. You could come back but woe to you if your foot touched the ground. You had to stay on the white horse. That horse would take you from one country to the other. It was a very good horse. There are more holy horses and holy countries than we will ever know, he would say. The way to find those countries is by telling stories. You can eat stories if you have to, he would say. A good story is a very good thing to eat. If you have a true story and some good water you will be all right, he would say. He would sit and listen to people for a long time without moving. He wanted to hear their true stories, he would say. He would never close his eyes. He was afraid of sleeping. Sometimes he wouldn't eat anything for days and days. He would just sing and tell stories. There are stories as thick in the air as birds around me, he would say. If people die young their stories haven't been told enough and there is no rest for them, he would say. Their stories are too hungry. I will save those stories from starving, he would say. Sometimes he would tell stories about stories. The stories of children are green, he would say, and the stories of women are blue, and the stories of men are red. You can walk right through a story on the road or in the woods and only hear one word from it, he would say. Or you can sit down inside a story and hear the whole story. Then the story is inside you. You can eat an infinite number of stories. No one can ever eat too many stories. When you have saved enough stories from starving then you will see *Tir na nOg*, the Country of the Blessed, where no one ever grows old and no one ever is hungry. *Geabhaedh tu an sonas aer pighin*, he would say, in that country you will find joys as common as pennies, as thick in the air as birds around you.

11.

Worried Man here at Daniel's bedside again telling stories as he sleeps.

I will tell more stories of our People.

We built all sorts of canoes, from tiny ones for duck hunting to enormous ones for the ocean. We could fit fifty or sixty people in a big canoe. Sometimes we would sail the big canoes north or south after whales or seals. Sometimes those big canoes would be at sea for days. Sometimes the canoe would come back without the people in it. My grandfather's sister disappeared this way. She went to live in the sea. Her name was Neshukulaylu. She was very strong in her body. She didn't marry anybody. She loved to fish for halibut. She loved salmonberries. She could really sing. She loved to hear stories over and over again. You couldn't tell a story too many times for Neshukulaylu! Her favorite story was the story where a man goes up the Mink River to spear steelhead but every time he finds a good pool for fishing, Thunder roars and pours down hailstones on the man's head, and the man can't catch any fish, and finally he loses his temper and curses at Thunder, and Thunder appears, a huge giant, and makes the man come with him to his huge house in the mountains. Neshukulaylu loved that story! She would laugh and laugh when she heard that story. She had red hair. When she was a baby her mother bound a bag of swan feathers to her head for a whole year and she had a swan forehead the rest of her life. When her canoe came back from the sea without her in it my grandfather and his three brothers burned it and rubbed the ashes all over their bodies. Then they made a red funeral canoe for her. It was cedar soaked in berry juice. They loaded it with fish and berries and told stories into it and put it *netaat*, near the water, in a spruce tree. It was still there when I was a boy but then the ocean came one wild winter and Neshukulaylu took her red canoe back to her new home in the sea. Her youngest brother would never tell stories about Thunder ever again. He wouldn't tell any stories about his sister either. He would get up and leave the house when people started to tell stories about her. But my grandfather liked to tell stories about her. He said that once you had a sister you always had a sister. He said where she lived there were halibut as big as houses and salmon bigger than the biggest canoe. He said that where she lived there were always berries, as many as you could eat, no matter how many you picked. He said that where she lived you could never be sick. He said that we little children would meet her someday. He said we

would know her right away from all the other people because she was
very strong and she had red hair and she would be laughing.

12.

When the old nun died on the top floor of the old hotel she felt her self
leave her body and drift up toward the ceiling, as she had half expected
might happen, but quite unexpectedly whatever she was now snagged
on the ceiling fan, which had been broken for years, and there she
stayed, stuck fast. Her body lay beneath her, composed and still. After a
while the night maid came in and found her body. The maid called the
priest, who anointed the body: forehead, eyes, ears, nose, mouth, knees,
feet. Then the priest called the hotel manager, who had much admired
the old nun, and the manager came up from his office on the first floor
and stood there at her bedside with the priest.

A great woman, said the manager.

She was that, said the priest.

None like her.

None before none again.

Forty years a teacher.

A thousand children.

Never lost her temper.

Twice she did, remember?

They smile, remembering.

Her face is peaceful.

She didn't suffer.

She just fell asleep.

Who will tell the crow?

I'll call the doctor.

The priest left and the manager, who had much admired the old
nun, knelt for a moment at her bedside, and then he left too, locking
the door behind him, and the room was still again. The old nun, or
whatever she was now, had seen and heard all this, indeed she could
see and hear far better than she could when she was alive, everything in
the room now unbearably clear, everything its absolute self, everything
rimmed with light like frozen dew rims twigs and leaves, the toaster

shining, the refrigerator magnets shining, her coffee cup shining, the painting of Moses shining, her to-do list with *fix fan!* on it shining, and she could hear for miles and miles, every sound crackling and distinct, every sound announcing its origin in a way she had never heard before. She heard owls, girls, trees, radios, fish, a fist landing hollowly on the chest of a boy, the suck of a baby at a breast. She heard a thousand thousand thousand sounds she had never heard before and would never have been able to identify before but now she knew them and loved them and had always known them and they were delicious and holy and necessary.

Beneath her the door to her room opened again and two burly men entered and examined her body minutely. Neither was the doctor. She wondered where the doctor was. She and the doctor had been good friends. One of the men below her signed a death certificate and the other man signed it too. Then they gently zipped her into a green plastic bag and the second man lifted her body gently and carried her out of the room in his arms. The first man made her bed carefully and turned out the lights and closed the door and locked it behind him and the old nun or whatever she was now hung in the fan in the dark listening and listening.

13.

Many times the priest had anointed the sick and the dying and the dead. He had anointed men and women and children and infants. He had anointed a boy one day old. He had anointed a boy one hour old. He had anointed three infants he was sure were dead but he couldn't bear to refuse to anoint them before the broken parents. He had anointed a newborn girl with no arms or legs. He had anointed a newborn girl whose heart stopped the minute his voice did. He had anointed a miscarried fetus in the arms of its young mother in a muddy berry field. He had anointed a man who was more than a hundred years old. He had anointed that man's wife a week later. He had anointed two fellow priests. He had anointed an actress in her dressing room. He had anointed a boy who hung himself in his basement. He had anointed a huge bishop who had a heart attack in an airport and died by the luggage carousel. He had anointed a basketball player who died at midcourt and who gripped the priest with his long strong hands so powerfully that the team trainer had to quietly break the boy's death grip as the doctor screened them from the boy's mother whose anguished howls echoed throughout the packed silent gym. He had anointed a logger decapitated by a falling fir limb. He had anointed people in wrecks on the highway. He had anointed the body of the man who washed up on the beach. You weren't supposed to anoint someone who was clearly and inarguably dead but he anointed them anyway and *ecclesia supplet*, let the church figure out the details, as the huge bishop used to say with a grin. The huge bishop had been his best friend. They had grown up together in farm country thick with oak and hickory trees. The bishop had a hickory walking stick that he carried everywhere. The stick was from the farm where he grew up. There was a stand of hickory so thick and dense there that deer and wild turkey and a red fox lived in it. When the bishop died by the luggage carousel his hickory stick clattered and rolled under the line of rental carts and a janitor found it late that night and brought it to the lost-and-found where the priest claimed it the next morning. *Per istam sanctum unctionem*, through this holy anointing, the priest had whispered to his dearest friend as he died in his arms, *et suam piissimam misericordiam adiuvet te Dominus*, may the Lord in his love and mercy help you, *gratia Spiritus Sancti*, with the grace of the Holy Spirit, and the bishop staring up at him tried to say *amen* but couldn't, and the priest whispered *ut a peccatis liberatum te salvet atque propitius allevet*, may He who frees you from sin save you and raise you up, and the bishop's eyes flashed and faded, and the priest rocked his friend in his arms for a long time as the luggage carousel went around and around and around.

14.

The doctor's house faces the sea. The front of the house is one long room with many windows all facing the sea. The room is filled with chairs and small tables. On one table there is a wooden carving of a sea lion, a gift from No Horses. There is a chess set and a wall of books about the sea at one end of the room and a telescope and a wall of maps of the sea at the other end. The maps are mounted in a massive hemlock frame, a gift from Owen. Along the back wall unobtrusively are two beds. When no one is in the beds the doctor uses them as couches. Usually there are people in the beds and in two or three of the chairs, for the doctor uses this room as a ward for those of his patients who cannot afford hospital or clinic fees, who have been discharged from the hospital but require his steady attention, who prefer for one reason or another not to recuperate in their own homes, or who have no homes. Today there are two people in the beds. Some patients are here for a day and some stay for weeks. One man stayed for months. He had been in the navy during the war and twice had been lost at sea. He would sit in his chair under the maps and tell stories of the sea. I was in the sea for days and days, he would say. The sea was in me for days and days. I still hear the sea in my head. Both times I was holding onto a big piece of wood and the sea kept licking me lap lap lap like a dog. This went on all night long. Those nights were so black. I said my rosary over and over, the joyful mysteries and the sorrowful mysteries and the glorious mysteries. I said them all because I couldn't remember what day it was. You say the joyfuls on Mondays and Thursdays and the sorrowfuls on Tuesdays and Fridays and the glorious on Wednesdays and Saturdays. My wife liked the joyfuls because they celebrated a woman's joys: Mary hearing the angel, Mary visiting her cousin, Mary having a baby, Mary getting the baby christened, Mary finding her lost child. My wife's name was Mary. She was the prettiest woman you ever saw. There was no one ever prettier than my Mary, not ever. I lost her a couple of years ago. She went to the sea in the sky. The first time I was lost at sea I was rescued by a fishing boat and the second time by a gunboat. The gunboat was also lost, isn't that funny? They were lost and I was found. After the second time I couldn't sleep anymore if I couldn't hear the sea lapping, so for the rest of the war I had to sleep on the beach, which was a problem, but the guys in my unit understood. They built me a little shelter on the beach, with a sand roof and a hidden door. Those guys could build anything. If you didn't know where that little shelter was you could never find it. I bet it's still there. Kids probably use it now as a secret fort or clubhouse or something. It was a real good place. You could hear the sea all night long there licking the land lap lap lap. I was there when the war ended. The guys came running to tell me that the war was over. I could hear their voices coming and their feet hitting the sand as they ran. Funny the things you remember: I remember their feet had exactly the same rhythm as the sea.

15.

No Horses in her studio is carving the oak man and thinking about men so as not to think about her boy. She wants to get lost in her head so she ticks off all the men she has ever kissed. That boy with the curly hair who stuck his tongue in my mouth. He was cute. He was shorter than me. We went steady for nine days. Eighth grade. The tall boy who gave me a ring. Tenth grade. He never said anything. He felt my breasts. I didn't have any breasts yet. I was so embarrassed. I was having my period too. He felt my pad. The boy who called himself Red who was in town for a weekend basketball tournament. Twelfth grade. Mm. The windy beach. The boy with the two dogs. I remember the dogs watching us as we made love in his truck. College freshman. He was sweet. He was a liar. He was sweet. The man with the long hair and the motorcycle. With the tattoo on his thing. The man from the library who just held me all night and wouldn't do anything. I liked him. There was something sweet about him not doing anything. I wonder if he couldn't. I fell asleep finally but he didn't. The quiet man from the canoe trip. We kissed that one night by the fire when everyone else was asleep and then he wrote me all those letters. Mm. He didn't tell me he was married. His wife found my letters to him. Mm. She wrote me a brave letter. Where is her letter? I saved it for the longest time. The strength of women. How could she forgive him? I couldn't forgive him. If Owen was with another woman. If I was with another man. He wouldn't forgive me. Would he? I wouldn't. He might. He wouldn't. Would I? I couldn't. Who would I go with? O stop. O just for a laugh who? Mm.

16.

Where and what is Neawanaka? Maple Head poses this question to her class. In one page or less explain our position, character, and/or unique properties. Extra credit for imagination. No copying. I'll give you ten minutes. Ready? Begin.

Answers: Neawanaka is a coastal village of approximately five hundred inhabitants. Neawanaka is a song sung by a wren in the rain. Neawanaka is a settlement at the mouth of the Mink River. Neawanaka is a seething melodrama of shocking proportions. Neawanaka is a town bordered to the north by a salt marsh to the south by a mountainous headland to the east by forested hills to the west by the Pacific Ocean. Neawanaka is what you call in geology a dingle or a dell, which is sort of a bowl in the earth. Neawanaka receives eighty inches of rain a year however there have been many years when rainfall exceeded one hundred inches the modern record for rainfall is two hundred and eleven inches; that was the year my cat drowned. Neawanaka is a town infested by Catholics who worship pieces of wood. Neawanaka is a brooding isolated rotten stump of a town where divorce is endemic depression is normal and alcoholism is all you can hope for, that's what my mom says. Neawanaka is the muddy fiefdom of two old men who have for many years manipulated county and state public works budget allocations to fund an endless series of foolhardy and very probably criminal enterprises, that's what my dad says. Neawanaka is a town invented by a Salish healer or holy man named Sisaxai or Sisaixi who lived a long time ago. Neawanaka is a small village on the coastal highway where weary travelers can pause to refuel and refresh. Neawanaka was from prehistoric times an aboriginal settlement of at least one hundred year-round inhabitants judging from the anthropological efforts of Poole and Callaway in 1913; see specifically their reports of gargantuan shell middens on either side of the river. Neawanaka is a moldy crummy scummy trap of a town that I can't wait to leave the minute I turn sixteen and can blow out of this wet hole for someplace where the sun shines more than ten minutes a year someplace like California where there are pretty girls not like here. Neawanaka was in former times a timber camp noted for the high grade of its cedar and spruce; indeed the phrase Neawanaka-quality is still heard wherever old loggers and millworkers gather to swap stories of the old days in the big woods. Neawanaka today offers one hotel of historic interest and bed-and-breakfast accommodations by inquiry at the colorful Stella Maris Pub, where fishermen and fisherwomen gather to talk shop and the ale is brewed on the premises by the cheerful proprietor herself. Neawanaka is still the home of a small fishing fleet that may be glimpsed heading to sea accompanied by the cries of gulls trailing the wakes of the picturesque boats. Neawanaka is the site of a working fish cooperative that last year according to statistics filed with the state processed more than a thousand tons of halibut, cod, perch, cabezon, rockfish, yelloweye, quillback, snapper, crab, sturgeon, salmon, rays, and trout (sea and river). Neawanaka is where I was born twelve years ago the seventh child born the seventh day of the seventh month. Neawanaka is the place where I am writing this exam paper for my teacher Mrs. Mann who is a really great teacher the best I ever had. Neawanaka is noted among birders for the variety of its bird population, which includes occasional appearances by pelagic species blown shoreward. Neawanaka is where my grandparents came from the old country seeking a new start in life. Neawanaka is a small coastal village of no particular economic, cultural, or scenic interest. However there is a public restroom adjacent to the grocery store.

17.

The boy in the south bed in the long room of the doctor's house facing the sea is asleep. In the north bed is the man who sells boxes and containers of all sizes. He is asleep also. Daniel's knees were shattered into more pieces than the surgeon at the hospital could count even with special magnifying lenses that made him look like a huge alien insect. The man who sells boxes and containers had a raging pain in his belly that turned out to be a tumor the size of a fist. The surgeon who put Daniel's knees back together told jokes as he worked and argued cheerfully with the nurses about what radio station to play and shook hands exhaustedly with them after they had finished working for him. The same surgeon was the man who cut open the man who sells boxes to get at his tumor the size of a fist and said only fuck fuck fuck when he saw the tumor's fingers and tendrils all woven intricately and relentlessly all through the middle of the man and he silently sewed him back together and none of the nurses in the operating room said anything when he was done. The man who sells boxes now has nineteen days left to live. Daniel now has nineteen pins and screws and bolts in his legs. The doctor used to smoke nineteen cigarettes a day, but then somehow he got himself down to fourteen, one for each apostle including the two apostles proposed to replace Judas after he hung himself, and then he managed somehow to quit the fourteenth cigarette, which he called Barsabbas or Justus, the names of the man who wasn't elected an apostle, poor fellow, and the doctor never actually smoked the thirteenth, which he called Judas, who for a handful of coins betrayed the man he loved, because the doctor couldn't bear to enjoy a cigarette named for the betrayer, not even once, and so he got right down to twelve, one for each of the eleven original apostles and the last for Matthias, the man elected to replace Judas, but there he stayed.

Despite a sincere and heartfelt desire to quit smoking altogether, for both personal and professional reasons, as a man fully cognizant of the subtle dangers of smoke and tar and nicotine inhaled into the tender pink tissues of the lungs, which are membranes as moist and vulnerable and innocent as the gates of a woman's desire, the doctor is stuck at twelve, for he is a man of great imagination, and each cigarette during the course of his day has taken on the flavor of the man for whom it is named. For example his first cigarette of the day, which is called Peter, is the foundation for all else to come, raw and headlong and rough and wonderful, and his fourth cigarette of the day is sweet John, gentle and best loved, inhaled peacefully right after lunch, and his seventh of the day is Thomas the Doubter, which he usually smokes late in the afternoon, when he is tired and riven with the pain of his patients, and fully aware, painfully aware, uncomfortably aware, that the specific assigned mission of the twelve apostles themselves, the real men who walked the earth long ago, fishermen and tax collectors and laborers and such, prickly and confused and exhilarated, was to cure and cleanse every disease and every illness, and drive out the demons in the minds of men and women and children, and accept no coin for their belts, nor sandals, nor walking sticks, but to be sheep in the midst of wolves, shrewd as serpents and simple as doves.

18.

Worried Man here by Daniel's bed, telling stories as he sleeps.

I will tell more stories of our People for my grandson.

We were the First People, you know. That's why other people called us Grandfather, because they came from us. If you were trading at Celilo, let's say, or you were at a potlatch up the coast where the grandfather of rivers, Nchiawana, meets the ocean and they fight all the time and make a wall of water, and you met someone from another people—Tenino, let's say, or even Nez Perce from the great mountains to the east—that person would call you Grandfather, because they knew right away you were one of the People. Now, some people wouldn't call us Grandfather, because they were absolutely sure they came from another people. Some people even maintained that they were the First People, and that we came from them. Like those Cheamhill people! They said that! Those crazy Cheamhills! They were a wild people absolutely. They had heads like stones. Once they got something into their heads you couldn't get it out again no matter what. In the old days we went to war with them all the time. That's when we would wear our elk-leather armor. We would fight them when we came to berry in their valley in summer or they would fight us when they came to the sea for fish in the fall. When we fought them we beat them like drums. We never did lose a fight with those wild Cheamhills. One time they got the Luckiamute people and the Tualatin people and a few of the Calapuyan people together and brought us a war, but we beat them all like drums. We had some help in that war, of course. We were a brave and strong people absolutely but not that strong. We flew in our canoes up and down the coast and got all the people of the sea together from the Clatsops and Kathlamets to the north, up by Nchiawana the grandfather of rivers, all the way to the Tututni and Chetco and Tolowa in the south. The Tolowas sent only one man but he was a great fighter, that man. There were so many languages in that fight! My grandfather said it was a wonderful thing to hear so many languages. There were more languages than there are fish in the sea, he said. My grandfather was in that fight and lost a finger off his south hand. A Cheamhill man swung a knife at him and he put his south hand up to fend off the blow and his last finger jumped off and ran away. My grandfather used to tell us to keep an eye out for that finger. I sure could use that finger back, he would say. It was a good finger and my other fingers tell stories about it at night. Sometimes they sing a song for its return. They sing very quietly. When you children are in bed tonight you listen and you might hear that song. The thumbs start singing in their deep voices and then the other fingers join them and finally the last finger on my north hand sings alone for its lover in the south to come home. It's a really sad and beautiful song. You listen closely and you just might hear that song.

19.

The doctor's spectacles are perched halfway down his nose and they are sliding ever so infinitesimally south. He is smoking his last cigarette of the day, the one called Matthias, while sitting at his table utterly absorbed in the Acts of the Apostles. The man who was numbered with us. Judas son of Iscariot. This man purchased a field with the reward of his iniquity. How very many fields have been purchased with blood money through history, mm? Judas falling headlong burst asunder in his midst and all his bowels gushed out. Intestines as a whole can be longer than one hundred linear feet in the adult male. That field is called *Aceldama*, that is to say, the field of blood. So many adult male fields of blood, mm? Cedar's stories of the war. Billy's stories of tribal wars. Owen's stories of the Hunger. The thirsty fields. Fields washed with blood. So many dead children. Grace's stories of her father. A hard man. Many men should never be fathers. The man who beats his son. But he loves that boy. At war with himself. Wars on land at sea in the air in the mind. Our stories are all of wars. We are all war stories. If violence is epidemic then it must be a disease. Must be curable. A good doctor could cure it. Violence a symptom of the human condition. Condition is chronic fear. Fear of the unknown. But everything is unknown. No one knows the hour. We are alone in the end. That sweet old nun dying alone in her room in the hotel. So we gather in circles against the darkness. Clans, tribes, families, nations, states, religions. Afraid to be alone. Afraid of time. Billy is right. Time the great silent enemy. We band together against time. Band together in circles. Circles enclose.

But circles also divide. Inside or outside the circle. So there is war. So there is violence. So the cure is to be alone. I am alone: therefore I am cured. He closes the bible and goes to his kitchen and very slowly cuts a pear into small cubes and then very slowly eats each cube and then brushes his teeth and turns the heat down and checks the locks and turns out the lights and disrobes and gets into bed and takes off his spectacles and folds them carefully on his night-table and then he lies awake for hours with his eyes glinting in the murky dark.

20.

Red Hugh O Donnell, father of Declan and Grace and Niall and Peadar, chief of the clan, hard of hand and head, who asks no help or quarter, quick to lash fools and children with his long white rod, *an slath ban*, is cursing as he drives along the river. He is on the road too late and he knows it. The milk should have been delivered this morning and those fecking sons of his were nowhere to be found. Useless rat bastards. The Mink River glints and swirls and loops sinuous and serpentine through the fringe of trees along the road. The sucker fringe, an old logger like George Christie would say, left there by loggers to give drivers the impression that the forest remains vast and impenetrable. Steel barrels of milk jostle and slam and jangle in the back of his truck. Sometimes they make a high ringing noise like faraway bells. Ahead of Red Hugh is a log truck loaded with fir logs. Douglas fir, named for some fecking British rat bastard. One log is as big around as Red Hugh himself who is as round as a fecking milk barrel but the rest of them are what an old logger like George Christie would call sticks and splinters. Red Hugh's white stick is in the passenger seat of the truck. Once Douglas firs grew fifty feet around, big as cabins and cottages. Red Hugh goes nowhere without his stick because as he says cursing some fecking fool will need it delivered to his fecking head for fecking sure. Once Douglas firs grew three hundred feet tall, taller than any church there ever was. Red Hugh needs his stick to lean on when he walks but he hides this need by cursing and brandishing the stick and calling everyone a fecking rat bastard. The Douglas fir has been judged variously a pine, a fir, a spruce, and a hemlock over the years but it is none of those things. Red Hugh has needed his stick to walk properly since he was twenty years old and was lost in the mountains for three days and lost both of his fecking big toes to frostbite. The Douglas fir has no family to speak of, being the only example of its species and the only species in its genus. The only person who ever knew that Red Hugh was crippled in his feet was his wife Maire who packed her fecking suitcase two years ago and walked out the door without a word. The Douglas fir is thousands of years old and was born in the time when ferns were dominant. The O Donnell clan is thousands of years old and was born in the time when the silent warriors called Tuatha de Danaan ruled the fecking world. The Douglas fir when young exhibits a remarkable pliability for a tree capable of such massive growth. Red Hugh when young was so exuberant and charismatic that his remote cousin Maire na Domhnaill fell in love with him and they ran away to America and married in the fecking mountains. One of the Douglas fir logs on the log truck in front of Red Hugh begins to work itself loose from its binding. Red Hugh curses his fecking useless rat bastard sons. The loose log waggles and shimmies its way out from among its brothers. Red Hugh curses the fecking milk cans. The log truck lurches and bounces. Red Hugh curses the fecking road. The loose log wriggles and skids. Red Hugh curses his fecking wife. The log truck hits a bump. Red Hugh curses his fecking daughter. The loose log flies into the air. Red Hugh curses the fecking darkness. The loose log slams through the windshield of Red Hugh's truck and hits his chest so hard that his heart and lungs and ribs and skin and spine and veins and arteries are instantly crushed to wet pulp and he dies in less than a second and his truck skews shuddering wildly into the river where it comes to rest with both front wheels in the rushing water and the loose log jutting out of the windshield like a huge brown arrow. As his truck settles burbling bubbling in the river Red Hugh's head sinks slowly toward the steering wheel and softly comes to rest and later when Michael the cop arrives it appears to him that Red Hugh O Donnell, hard of hand and head, who asked no help or quarter, quick to lash fools and children, is asleep.

21.

Red Hugh felt his self drift up into the air over his truck, as he had half expected would happen when he died, though he had not at all figured on dying in his truck. He had always figured he would die in his muddy field, a suitable death for a man mucking with cows, the death he expected, a heart attack pitching him face down in the mud that never dried not even in the hottest summer, not *his* fecking field, it was under some sort of fecking ancient water curse, as he had snarled many times to Grace and Declan, who themselves envisioned different ends for their father: that his hard cold cruel frozen hazelnut of a heart would finally rise up rebellious through his foul vulture throat and choke him to death (Grace's vision) or someone would beat the relentless life out of the old troll with that fecking stick (Declan's vision). Red Hugh however fully expected that his heart would stop on a howling wet day in his muddy field and he would pitch forward into a puddle and *drown* there, drowning in land, on land, his own land, his last breath, like his last penny and his last hope, buried in the sucking stinking mud of a field on a hill by the coast.

But no, here he was, or rather here what he was *now* was, drifting calmly up into the air above his truck settling bubbling into the river.

He sailed up slowly, eddying in the complicated air. He noticed all sorts of other creatures or former creatures or inexplicable beings or visions drifting up and around him. From them emanated all sorts of words and sounds. He didn't *hear* their languages and songs exactly but he *was* them in a way he could not have explained even if he still had a tongue. He was in and of and infused with all of the beings who floated with him and he spoke all of their languages and he had always known them and been most intimately their brother and they loved him and had always been his most intimate brother also. Some of these creatures or former creatures were undefined areas of mostly sound but some were still recognizable versions or bright shadows of what they had been when alive. The air was dense and shimmering with uncountable millions of them, all floating and swirling down to the sea. They rose from the land in numbers beyond calculation, steadily but calmly. A gust of wind sent an uncountable number of them whirling into the forest where some caught in the spruce branches and hung there smiling and others tumbled away calmly into the vast and impenetrable woods.

He looked down and saw his long white rod, *an slath ban*, float out of the passenger window of his truck and set off merrily down the river bobbing and whirling, a bright clean line against the swirling circles of the water. From sheer bodily instinct he reached for his stick but having no actual hand anymore nothing happened and he remained floating gently, turning this way and that in the freshening breeze. He had a memory of his body, and he retained the shape of his body, but he was no longer actually *in* his body, which felt peculiar and wonderful. He smiled.

My toes! he thought, and he looked down and there they were, and there they weren't, both things true at once, and he smiled again. He was also fat and old and young and thin and bitter and joyous all at once, which seemed wonderful.

Most of the beings or former beings floating above the river with him were too small to see and millions are or were infinitesimal insects but he could make out some familiar shapes amid the jostling beings: an enormous beaver, a sandhill crane, a rabbit, a blue jay. He saw a flotilla of tiny oval steel-blue creatures all floating together and it took him a minute before he recognized them. Mussels! he realized, smiling, and the instant he remembered them everything he ever knew or felt or thought about mussels hummed instantaneously through his mind as a chord or tone, and this tone was also a word, the word for what mussels are, for what they think of themselves as, and they sing it perpetually in voices almost too high to hear, *ataw ataw ataw!* they sing, a kind of a cheerful prayer or chant of musselness and musselhood, and the beaver sings himself, *tuqusu!,* in a gravelly baritone, and *gigiliw!* trills the smiling rabbit, and *aniza!* coughs the stately crane, and *waswas!!* shouts the jay again and again just as rough and exuberant as she'd been when alive, they sing themselves and their names in their languages, and Hugh finds that he too is singing chanting saying praying his song, his name in the old language, the language he was born into, *Aoidh! Aoidh!* he sings, smiling and turning slowly end over end as he rises through the lowering light with everything else that has recently died, all of them singing to the sea.

22.

Declan O Donnell wakes up in the very last minute of daylight and realizes with a start that he has slept for ten hours straight and he swings out of bed and the instant his feet touch the floor the sun drops into the sea. He showers and dresses for a night on the boat and wonders where everyone is. He wonders who took the milk to the co-op and where the old man is and where Grace is because they have to catch the tide. He checks the tide chart on the refrigerator and makes sandwiches and coffee and throws his gear in his truck and roars off.

Pokes his head into the bar by the dock just to check Grace isn't there. No reason for her to be there now, he thinks darkly, she's already caught her daily limit of loser, but he sees Stella the bartender whom he likes and she grins at him and he grins back and then he sees the boy whose father beats him whom he knows from playing basketball in the winter rec league. Good kid. Good ballplayer. Strong as a bear, that kid. Wouldn't shower with us because of the bruises. One time he had a bruise on his back the size of France. The old man must have hit him with a log or something. Some day that kid will hit back good and proper and there'll be a funeral.

Hey, he says to the kid.

Hey, says the kid.

Want a beer, Dec? says Stella the bartender.

Nah. Going out tonight. Just looking for Grace.

Grace the gracious, says a guy at the bar.

What? says Declan.

Give you the shirt off her back and her pants too.

Some guys laugh.

Give you the stars in her eyes and her full moon.

Some guys laugh again.

Fuck you, says Declan to the guy.

No, fuck *you*, says the guy, and he starts to stand up, but Declan catches him with a fist in the face just as he starts to stand up, and the guy's nose explodes and he falls backwards over the stool and knocks the next guy half off his stool, and then a friend of the first guy jumps on Declan's back and smashes his head against a table, but the boy whose father beats him grabs the friend of the guy off and shoves him to the floor like you would flick a piece of dust off your shirt, and then Stella comes running out of the kitchen and screams get *out!* get *out!* so they get out, Declan and the kid, everybody yelling.

Declan hoists his gear over his shoulder and heads darkly for the boat and the kid walks with him for lack of anything better to do.

Thanks for the help in there, says Declan.

Sure, says the kid.

Why'd you help me?

I don't know.

They walk in silence for a moment.

Ever been on a boat? says Declan.

Canoes and stuff.

Ever been on the ocean?

Nope.

Listen, come on out with us tonight.

Fishing?

Halibut.

Well … I don't know.

You doing anything tonight?

Just going home, I guess.

To your old man.

Yeh.

Come on out. We could use the help.

Can I help with the fishing?

Sure. You just need muscles.

I'd like to help with the fishing.

Okay then. All right.

They get to the boat and Declan throws his gear in and the crash of his gear wakes up Grace who is sleeping in the cabin.

Who the hell are *you?* she says to the kid.

He's coming out with us tonight, says Declan.

He's a kid.

I'm eighteen years old, says the kid. How old are you?

None of your business, and you didn't answer my question, says Grace.

My name is Nicholas, and you didn't answer *my* question.

Declan grins at the kid's brass.

You and Grace will get along just fine, he says.

I have to tell my father that I won't be home, says Nicholas.

We have to catch the tide, says Declan.

I don't want him to worry, says Nicholas.

I know you, says Grace. You're the kid whose dad beats him up.

Nicholas says nothing and Grace flushes.

I have to tell my dad. I don't want him to worry.

Five minutes and no more, says Declan.

I'll be back in four, says Nicholas and he takes off sprinting like a deer. Grace and Declan watch him go and then they pack their gear and bait up and sit silently as the boat rocks gently and just like that Nicholas is back on the dock not even winded. He climbs in and Declan guns the engine and off they go to the gate of the bay. Outside the bay big dark waves are leering and lurking.

Grace and Nicholas sit face to face in the stern.

My name is Grace and I am twenty-one years old, says Grace. Glad to have you aboard, Nicholas.

Glad to meet you, Grace.

Sorry about that crack back there.

It's okay.

I have a big mouth.

I don't believe it.

Believe it.

They grin and Declan shoots the boat through the gate of the bay and the waves reach hungrily for the boat and the wind howls and stars appear overhead and two cormorants hurry by intently like nervous commuters and a big seal pops his head out of the water looking for all the world like a cheerful bald bewhiskered grandfather floating peacefully in the vast and impenetrable sea.

23.

Worried Man here telling stories to Dan. He sleeps and sleeps, my little grandson, and I tell stories over him like blankets like prayers. He is my sweet little boy and we will heal him. All of us together. One morning he will wake up and all will be well.

I will tell stories of the way it used to be here. There is healing in these stories. They lived here for a very long time, these stories. They have seen many things and they forget nothing.

So.

My grandfather had two capes, one made from beaver and the other from deer, and three fur blankets, made from rabbit and bobcat and otter. He parted his hair in the middle and painted the part red and wore his hair in one braid. Women wore two braids and they also painted their parts red. Everyone wore earrings and some men wore nose rings but not my grandfather—he said he had things going into his nose all day long and there was no reason for a gatekeeper there. He said a lot of things that made you laugh if you listened carefully. And he told so many stories! He told me how when a baby was born its mother would stay awake for five days pressing her belly to make sure all the blood went home, and its father would stay awake for ten days praying, and the afterbirth would be left at the feet of a spruce sapling so the baby would grow as tall and strong as that fine tree. When a child's teeth came out one by one they were put by the same tree so the child's teeth would be straight and strong also. When a girl collected her first basket of berries or roots she would go around the houses and give them all away to the old people, and when a boy killed his first deer or seal he would go around and give all the meat to the old people. That's just how it was. When a girl or boy was ready to go find a name they went in the woods and walked and took baths. You might be out there three days or five days or ten days. You had to find your guardian spirit. You had to take a lot of cold baths! When you were ready to receive your spirit, there it was. If you weren't ready, it wouldn't show itself. If you saw a snake you would be a healer. If you saw a beaver or a woodpecker you would make canoes. If you saw a salmon you would be a fisherman. If you saw a wolverine you would be a warrior. If you saw a hawk you would be a hunter. That's just how it was.

When I was a boy I went walking to meet my guardian spirit and I walked for days. I lost track of the days after a while. I took a lot of cold baths! I walked all the way to the holy mountain, Wyeast. That was one long walk! I walked up the mountain as far as I could go and then I had to rest where the trees end. All things grew silent, even *asayahal*, the south wind, even the ravens who never stop telling jokes. I kept my eyes open. I was very tired but everything was so clear. Then I saw a huge bird coming toward me from the south. It was enormous! It saw me sitting there but it didn't veer away or anything. It kept coming toward me and getting bigger and bigger. I thought maybe it was Thunder coming to take me to his huge house! That bird flew right over me and he looked down and I looked up and our eyes started talking.

He said *I will take care of you now* and I said *thank you, Father.*

He said *now you must begin your work* and I said *what is my work?*

He said *you must see everything* and I said *I will see everything.*

He said *you can never rest* and I said *I will never rest.*

He said *your eyes are holy and burning* and I bowed and he flew on.

He flew up and over the top of the mountain. He got smaller and smaller as he rose up against the snow. Blue against white. Those have been my colors ever since. That was how I met Heron and we have been friends all these years since. I see herons all the time and whenever I meet a heron we have a good talk. A few herons just want to talk about fish and frogs but most of them have very interesting minds indeed. They have seen so many things and they forget nothing. That's just how they are. They are very quiet. Their eyes are restless and burning. They don't say much but when they do it is worth hearing. They say a lot of things that make you laugh if you listen carefully. That's just how they are.

24.

Daniel wakes up finally in the doctor's house facing the sea. He's been asleep for days in the hospital and here. The first thing he sees is the sea. The sea is green and blue and gray and white and purple. He stares at it for a long time. It shimmies and shivers and shines and shudders and shimmers and twitches and glitters and trembles and gleams. It stutters and whispers and moans and sighs. It snarls and roars and hammers the patient shore. It tosses its hair and rolls its shoulders and shuffles its feet. He can hear it singing from his bed. He can smell its impatient spice. He can smell storms and salt and seawrack. He can smell yearning and mourning. He is very tired. The room is silent. He tries to figure out where he is, exactly. The room is bright and filled with maps of the sea. All the windows are open. He is very cold. The air seems very clear. The sea sings. His eyes adjust to the room and he sees a chess set and a telescope and books everywhere and everywhere maps of the sea. By his left hand is a carved wooden sea lion. The sea lion is looking at him. The sea whispers. The room is very quiet. He stares at the sea lion. The sea murmurs. The sea lion has shoulders like brown hills and a trunk like a tree and flippers like oars. The sea grumbles. The sea lion looks at him steadily. The room is colder. He reaches out to touch the sea lion and his shoulder hurts something dreadful when he moves it but the sea lion wants to be touched. The sea hums deep in its ancient blue throat. Daniel tries to say something to the lion but his lips are dry as sand. His hand touches the lion's shoulder and the lion flinches slightly but doesn't pull away. The sea breathes in and out. The lion looks at him steadily. Daniel can feel the shiver of muscle under the lion's shimmering leathery skin. The room smells like kelp. The sea sings in a lost blue language. Daniel closes his eyes and drifts out to sea and sees halibut as big as houses and salmon bigger than the biggest canoe. He sees incomprehensible whales and canoes of every shape and size and color scattered on the bottom of the sea in numbers beyond counting. He sees lions above and below him and to each side and ahead and behind, lions of every size imaginable from tiny pups to hoary giants, lions in every imaginable shade of brown, lions swimming faster than the eye can see, lions looking at him steadily, lions speaking in a wet brown language he has always known, its words kelp and salt in his mouth, its verbs the whispers of the sea.

25.

Declan and Grace and Nicholas fish all night. The doctor stays up very late with Daniel who is awake but cloudy. Declan catches the biggest halibut he has ever seen. The doctor keeps Daniel awake as long as possible to check his responses and acuity. Grace catches an even bigger halibut, a fish the size of a door. At about two in the morning the doctor lets Daniel drift off to sleep. Grace's fish is so strong and desperate that all three of them haul it wriggling wrestling bucking into the boat. The doctor finds that he is not tired at all and he settles down at his kitchen table to read the Acts of the Apostles. The fishing is so good that Declan keeps their long lines out almost until dawn. The doctor cuts a pear into cubes and slowly eats each piece. Declan and Grace cut their sandwiches in thirds and each shares a third with Nicholas. The doctor's spectacles slide infinitesimally slowly down his nose. The wind changes north to south and the sea roughens. The harsh singing of the sea makes Daniel moan. Get in the cabin, Nicholas! shouts Grace. The doctor reads aloud to Daniel to soothe him back to sleep. Haul in and let's run home! shouts Declan. But there arose a tempestuous wind called Euroclydon, and when the ship was caught, and could not bear up into the wind, we let her drive, reads the doctor. Let her run on the wind! shouts Grace. And being exceedingly tossed by the tempest, we lightened the ship, and cast out with our own hands the tackling of the ship, reads the doctor. Cut the lines! shouts Declan. And when neither sun nor stars appeared, and no small tempest lay on us, all hope that we should be saved was then taken away, reads the doctor. Stay with the boat! shouts Grace. But there shall be no loss of life, for there stood by me this night a spirit, saying, fear not, and it shall be thus: you and all them that sail with thee are given life anew, reads the doctor. The river! the river! shouts Grace. And they sounded twenty fathoms, and then fifteen fathoms, reads the doctor. Hang on! shouts Declan. And they committed themselves unto the sea, and loosed the rudder, and made toward shore, and falling into a place where two seas met, they ran the ship aground, and so it came to pass, that they escaped all safe to land, reads the doctor. Grace and Declan stagger out of the water coughing. Daniel falls asleep. Declan stares at his battered boat dead on the shore. The doctor brushes his teeth and turns the heat down and checks the locks and turns out the lights and disrobes. Grace searches desperately for Nicholas. Daniel dreams of halibut as big as houses and salmon bigger than the biggest canoe. Declan searches desperately for Nicholas. The doctor gets into bed and takes off his spectacles and folds them carefully on his night-table. Daniel dreams of forests beneath the sea deeper and denser than any woods there ever were. Grace sinks to her knees laughing and shivering when she sees Nicholas walk out of the water with the two enormous fish on his shoulders. And so it came to pass that they escaped all safe to land, mutters the doctor to himself, and falls asleep.

26.

Michael the cop is waiting at the dock at dawn for Declan's boat to come in so he can break the news about Red Hugh O Donnell's death on the highway but when dawn reddens and fades with no sign of the boat and the weather still wild he gets the shivers and gets back in his car and heads along the beach road looking out to sea. In his car Tosca is singing her great aria near the end of Act Two: *con man furtiva quante miserie conobbi, alleviai*, sweet consolation I brought to those who are poor and unhappy! Michael sings along with her and the music swells and throbs bravely but he thinks darkly how often he has been the singer of death songs to people who find his presence on their doorstep no consolation at all. Many times he has delivered bad news to men and women and children and his news cut a ragged wound in them that would never heal all the rest of their lives and he knew it and they knew it. *Perche me ne rimuneri cosi*, Tosca implores God, why do you withdraw your hand from me? Michael has told a father that his son has drowned. He has told a child that his father has drowned. He has told a family gathered nervously for Christmas dinner that yes, the infant who wandered off into the woods has been found, but no, the child is no longer alive. He has told a wife that her husband has been imprisoned. He has told three children the oldest of them fifteen that their father has been imprisoned for life for reasons they all knew but did not say. He has told a mother that her son was killed by a drunk driver. The mother of the boy killed by a drunk driver had white hair and a face carved from white stone and she held her white front door with white knuckles and when he asked if he could come in she didn't say anything and when he asked a second time if he could come in she said no and they stood there silently face to face in the freezing morning for a long minute and then she said so quietly that he almost didn't hear her *which one is it?* which reduced him to tears then and still does whenever he thinks of it like right now near the end of Act Two so to be safe he pulls his cruiser over to the side of the road and dries his eyes with his sleeve as Tosca sings desperately *mi vuoi supplice a tuoi piedi,* on my knees I beg for mercy.

But you have many times delivered news of wonder and joy, he says to himself, and he thinks of the baby born on the hood of his car one warm spring night, and lost children found, and pets recovered, and thieves apprehended, and tires changed, and batteries resurrected, and property returned, and hunches borne out, and premonitions proven accurate, and crimes prevented, and the public protected, and hearts eased, but then Tosca plunges her dagger into Scarpia, shouting *that's the way Tosca kisses!* and Michael's heart lurches and he slams his cruiser into gear and roars down the road to the beach, because through the wild drumming rain he sees Declan's beached boat and Declan and Grace and Nicholas huddled next to it, and when he gets down there he bundles them into the blankets that he carries in his trunk, and bundles an exhausted Nicholas into the back seat with a thermos of coffee, but before he bundles Grace and Declan into the cruiser too he tells them quietly that Red Hugh O Donnell, chief of the clan, hard of hand and head, who asked no help or quarter, quick to lash fools and children with his long white rod, *an slath ban,* is dead, killed on the highway by a log the size of a boat. *Ah e morto or gli perdono,* says Tosca quietly, he's dead, now I forgive him, and she lights two candles and puts them by Scarpia's head, and lifts a crucifix off the wall and puts it on his chest, and kneels and blesses herself, and then rises and leaves and closes the door gently behind her, and so the curtain falls on Act Two.

27.

The old nun's funeral was held at dawn, in accordance with her specific wish that her life be celebrated as holy light was reborn in the world, and also at her direction the ceremony was held at the school, in the auditorium, where, as she had written in her meticulous mathematical handwriting in her will, she had spent so many thousands of hours in work and prayer and song, and where she wished, in a manner of speaking, to conclude her story. The Department of Public Works arranged all details of the event and the doctor quietly paid for coffee and rolls and fruit afterward.

The old nun had asked that the reading at her funeral be from the Acts of the Apostles, and she asked further that each reader read one sentence, so that many members of the community might thus weave their voices together in prayer for the unimaginable voyage of her spirit.

So they did.

And when the day was fully come, they were all with one accord in one place, said the priest.

And suddenly there came a sound from heaven as of a mighty rushing wind, and it filled the house where they were sitting, said the doctor.

And there appeared to them cloven tongues like as of fire, which sat upon each of them, said Maple Head.

And they were all filled with the spirit, and began to speak with other tongues, as the spirit gave them utterance, said Owen.

And they were confounded and they were all amazed and marveled, said No Horses.

And then they said to one another, what meaneth this?, said Worried Man.

Others mocking said, they are full of new wine, said Cedar.

And Moses the crow lifted up his voice and said unto them, There are wonders in heaven above, and signs in the earth, and she is raised up, and loosed are the pains of death, and therefore does my heart rejoice, and my tongue is glad, and I rest in hope. I am full in joy.

Now when they heard this they were pricked in their hearts, and they prayed and sang, and many wonders and signs were seen, and breaking rolls of all sorts and shapes even unto those stuffed with orange and red jam, they did eat with gladness and singleness of heart, and an acre of rolls and a sea of coffee disappeared with wonderful dispatch, and the school basement echoed with stories and laughter, and when finally they streamed forth from the school into the bright morning they walked in joy and peace, some to visit Daniel at the doctor's house, and some to work, and some to sea, and their thoughts were various and intricate beyond understanding, being composed of yearning and content and joy and despair in unequal measures, but each one, male and female alike, young and old, walked with an elevated spirit, and was memorious of the old nun, who had a laugh like the peal of a bell, and was unfailingly tender with everyone, and cut her own hair, and twirled a lock of her hair with her right hand while she wrote with her left, and sang exuberantly, and never buttoned the top button of her coat, and never lost her temper with her students, and loved to watch storms at sea, and carried her worn wooden prayer beads everywhere, and knocked on doors with both hands at once, and wore only red hats, and gave away books after she read them, and wept sometimes for no reason she knew, and loved to walk along the beach, and ended each walk along the beach by staring longingly out to sea, and was fond of saying to Moses, as she undid her coat after a walk and hung up her hat and set the teapot going on the stove, Our paths are in the mighty waters, Moses, and so are holy and hidden.

28.

No Horses and Maple Head stroll over to the doctor's to visit Daniel but when they get there he is asleep and so they sit by his bed and talk. Maple Head strokes the carving of a sea lion by Daniel's bed. A remarkable thing, she thinks. Almost alive. Sentient.

What wood is this? she asks.

Ironwood. Found it on the beach. Driftwood. It wanted to be something of the sea, I could tell.

You have an extraordinary talent, love.

If only it made me money.

At least you found your true work, Nora. Along with being a mother. And wife.

I suppose.

Is something wrong, love?

Tell me about the old days, Mom.

O those days are gone and gone, Nora, and I was a small girl only at the tail of them. These are new days and lovely ones too.

Sometimes I think that all people in all times must have had the same joys and sorrows, says Nora. Everyone thinks that the old days were better, or that they were harder, and that modern times are chaotic and complex, or easier all around, but I think people's hearts have always been the same, happy and sad, and that hasn't changed at all. It's just the shapes of lives that change, not lives themselves.

Maybe the old people had less time to be sad. Are you sad?

Tell me about the old people.

What about them?

What did they make from which wood?

O the artist's curiosity. Well, red cedar was for canoes, as you know.

Yes.

Yellow cedar was for bows.

A whippy strong wood. I use it to carve birds.

Yew was for harpoon shafts and such.

Hard to find now.

Hard then too. A shy tree.

And spruce?

Spruce and hemlock knotwood was good for fishing hooks. And red alder was for bowls and masks. That fellow Peter who had the library show of his masks used alder, I noticed. He respected the old ways. He said he's tried other woods but the alder was the right wood, he could feel it.

The wood will tell you what it wants to be.

How?

Hard to explain. You can feel it fighting the knife or easing into it.

How about maple?

Maple was for paddles.

Ironwood?

Needles and arrows.

Fir?

Caskets.

Pine?

Mostly we used the pine gum as a poultice for heart pain and rheumatism. I still make it for your dad and this reminds me to make some for Daniel's knees. He'll need it when he gets his casts off. Poor sweet boy.

Gram? says Daniel and the arms and hands of both mothers lift like startled birds and fly toward his pale drawn smiling face.

29.

It is night and the stars are cold in the sea and Owen is holding Daniel in his lap and the two of them are swathed in blankets and robes on the deck of the doctor's house and Owen is telling a story.

Well, son, my greatgrandfather Timmy Cooney walked and walked during the Hunger. He walked always west, to the sea. From miles away sometimes he said he could hear the voices of children crying from the Hunger. He saw children left at rich people's houses, on the steps or in the gardens. He saw houses bricked up and the people inside them dying from the Hunger. He saw people change their religion for a bit of soup. He saw people with the fever and they were as black as tar and all swollen up. He saw dead people being buried in bogs and trenches. He saw one house with a trapdoor in the kitchen where when one of the family died the others would put the body down the trapdoor. He saw a man carry his dead brother miles to the graveyard and then dig his brother's grave and then exhausted and sick he died himself and fell into the grave on top of his brother. That man's name was Conchubhar and his brother's name was Daithi. He saw a dog carrying a child's hand along the road. My greatgrandfather took the hand from the dog and buried it on a hill and put a stone over the grave. He buried a lot of people and put stones over their graves. All the rest of his life he wouldn't move a stone in a field for fear it would be a gravestone. He heard voices every night for years singing laments, *caoineadh*. He could hear them from miles away. He used to say he could hear laments and children's voices every night of his life until the day he died. He would sing a lament himself every night, stepping outside into the night and singing and then stepping back inside and banking the fire. He said there were more laments to be sung than any one man could sing in a lifetime but he was going to sing as many as he could anyway. He figured if he sang *caoineadh* every night of his whole life he might be able to lament all the children of a whole valley. That would be a good thing to do, he would say. So he would do that. After he got married to my greatgrandmother Maighread he got her to sing *caoineadh* with him every night too. They figured her laments might cover all the women in that valley. Then when my grandfather Martin was a boy they taught him to sing *caoineadh* also, the three of them stepping outside every night before bed and lifting up their voices to the trees and stars, and then stepping back inside. Timmy Cooney figured Martin's songs might cover all the dead men in the valley, especially since Martin was a boy and had many more years of singing in front of him than Timmy and Maighread. So they did that. That was a good thing to do.

30.

Daniel and the man who sells boxes are talking. They are both in chairs facing the night ocean. Daniel is wrapped in robes and blankets. All the windows are open. Gulls are pleading and wheeling. The man who sells boxes has seventeen days to live. Daniel has the statue of the sea lion in his lap. The man who sells boxes has a box of photographs in his lap. The photographs are of his wife and daughters and sons. He sifts through them and some make him grin and some make him wince and some make him hold them up in the light for a long time, staring.

Is that your family?

Yes. My wife and I have two daughters and two sons.

Tell me about them, says Daniel.

O there are too many stories to even know where to begin and I am no storyteller, says the man with a smile. You tell me about yourself first. What's your name?

Daniel Cooney, and I don't have much to tell yet, says Daniel. I'm twelve years old and my favorite thing in the world is my bicycle. Was my bicycle. And my family. Is my family.

You have brothers and sisters?

No, sir. But I have my mom and dad and my grandfather and grandmother live here and I am very close to them. My grandmother is actually my teacher in school.

You'll be back on that bike in no time, Daniel, says the man.

I'd like just to walk again, says Daniel.

The doctor says you will walk again and he never lies. He says you'll be running quick as a cat.

Have you known him a long time?

Long enough to trust him with my life. What's left of it.

Are you going to die soon?

In about two weeks. Give or take a day.

I'm very sorry.

Thank you.

I'll say prayers.

Thank you.

Daniel doesn't know what else to say and he is suddenly exhausted again and the man who sells boxes sees Daniel's eyes sag and he says, listen, son, you close your eyes and rest and I will tell you about my family, you just drift off while I talk, okay? and Daniel nods groggily and the man says, now here's a photograph of my wife taken when we first met. We were in a play, you see. There was a scene where I was supposed to open a closet and find her and at the first rehearsal I opened the closet and she stepped out and I forgot my lines. What a face! I couldn't take my eyes off her face. I loved her but she didn't love me, Dan. I waited a long time until she loved me back. Years. She loved other men during those years. Many men. That was a hard time. I wanted to love other women too, to stop feeling lonely, but I just couldn't work myself up to it. I tried hard but you just can't command yourself to fall in love. It doesn't work that way. Well, finally there came a time when she couldn't take her eyes off my face, either, and we fit together, we fit in good times and bad, we always stayed tender and kind with each other, which is a real deep thing in a love that wants to last, you know, and we had our children, lost one in there, we actually have five, I say four but really it's five, and now I have about two weeks to go before I go meet the missing one. Give or take a day. Her name was Laura. We called her Miss Laura Lee. It'll be good to see Miss Laura Lee again but I'll sure miss the other kids. They're all gone from the house now, even the youngest, she's down to college now, has her first boyfriend down there. I wanted to meet this boy but I don't suppose I will now. He wouldn't come up to see a dying man. I wouldn't either I guess. I'll tell you something, Dan. I'll miss her the most of all the kids. Her name is Gina. I love them all but that Gina has some zest, all right. She'll be a fierce woman, that one. It'll take a hell of a man to love her right. Be like living with a thunderstorm. Same as her mother. A fierce woman. Force of nature. The kind of woman you just hang on for the ride. The most exciting and the most heartbreaking woman you could ever meet. They don't know their own minds most of the time but their hearts are so damn big it hurts 'em inside. It's a lucky man who gets a woman like that. I don't suppose there are many women like that in this wide world. It'd be a wild world if there was, I'll tell you that. I've only met the two of them in all my born years. Married the one and watched the other come swimming out of my wife twenty years ago her eyes wide open from the start. Been a wild time with those two women, I can tell you that. Never a dull moment. Not one. A lot of tears and a lot of laughter. Wouldn't trade a minute of it. Even the bad times were deep, you know what I mean?

But Daniel is sound asleep now, the sea lion curled asleep in his lap, and the man who sells boxes grins, and quietly stands and slips a blanket off his own bed and wraps Daniel in it, and sits back down with his box of photographs, some of which make him grin and some of which make him wince and some of which make him hold them up to the light for a long time.

31.

Next day No Horses carves and chisels and whittles and slices and hammers and chips and snicks and shaves and slices the wooden man all the day and half the night and by that time there's hardly any wooden man left at all, he's mostly a pile of oak chips as high as her knees, and next day after that she starts all over again with a piece of spruce about as big as a goddamn car, as Owen mutters darkly after hauling and hefting the thing into the studio panting and sweating and cursing, and she works furiously all day and half the night making a new man, stopping only to run over to the doctor's house to see Daniel every few hours, and she doesn't stop to eat at all though Owen comes twice by with sandwiches and coffee. He leaves the sandwiches and thermos by her door. He doesn't knock. She doesn't eat the sandwiches or drink the coffee and Cedar quietly takes them away.

She reduces the spruce man to a pile of chips also, which makes her scream in frustration, so Owen and Cedar haul in a piece of cedar the size of a goddamn boat, and she reduces that to chips in less than a day this time, and she says nearly weeping that spruce and cedar are no good, she needs alder, and now Owen is both angry and worried, so he hauls in a piece of alder so big that he has to recruit not only Cedar but Worried Man and Declan and Nicholas, the younger men straining so hard that the veins in their necks bulge bizarrely and you can hear the cartilage in their knees and shoulders pop and the older men directing traffic feel sincere regret that they can no longer help with such crushing weight and they worry seriously about the weight-bearing capacity of the old oak floor.

Jesus, couldn't your woman be a weaver or something? says Declan.

Just pull.

They finally heave the goddamn log onto the work table, which groans and moans and they stand around for a moment getting their breathing back in order. Worried Man looks for the spot on the floor where he thought he was never going to actually get his breath back ever again. Declan chaffs Owen again about his uncontrollable wife. Nicholas grins at the chaff but doesn't say anything. Owen smiles too but his eyes wander outside to the hills where No Horses is walking furiously to calm the rattling and swerving of her brains. Something is wrong and he knows it and she knows he knows and he knows she knows he knows but they haven't said anything about it. She's worked furiously before, she's worked all day and all night for days and nights on end, but that was the crazy energy of joy, and this is wild and reckless and helpless, as if her knife is a weapon, not a key to finding something inside the wood that wants to be born, something that never was and never would be but for her brilliant fingers.

Thanks, lads, says Owen.

If she reduces this one to dust she's on her own, says Worried Man.

Has she ever thought of working in miniatures? says Declan.

There are a lot of wood chips here, says Nicholas politely.

Back to work, fellas, says Cedar, who heads back to his office, and off go the other four men to the four holy directions: Owen west to his shop, Nicholas east to his father, Declan south to no father, Worried Man north for his evening walk.

32.

Owen back in his shop hears a knock on the window and he stops working and opens the door and there's Grace O Donnell smiling.

Hey Grace.

Sorry to interrupt your work.

No no. Come in, come in.

Thought I'd stop by.

Always a pleasure.

You're sure?

Sure now. Coffee?

Sure. Thanks.

No fishing today, eh?

No.

I'm very sorry about your dad.

Thanks.

Funeral tomorrow?

Yeh. You'll be there?

Sure I will. We will. Well, not Dan. Me and Nora. Well, maybe Nora.

Actually that's why I'm here. Partly.

For Nora?

Ah, no. Can you say a prayer in Irish? At the funeral?

Ah sure. Which prayer?

Any one you like. My dad was very proud of his heritage and it seems right to have the old tongue in the air over him at the end. Peadar and Niall suggested it and Declan and I think it'd be grand.

I'll do that. You want it brief?

Well … yes.

Okay then. I'll prepare something.

Thanks so much. We're very grateful.

Does anyone in your family speak Irish?

No. Not a word. So we'd be very thankful.

Ta failte romhat. You're welcome.

Is this my Gaelic lesson now?

Ah, jeez, I was going to teach you a bit, wasn't I? I'm sorry. I've been hornswoggled lately. Don't know up from down.

This isn't a good time, is it? I'll go.

No no. Fine time. Let's do a bit. Always good to slip the old tongue in a new ear.

Grace grins and Owen flushes to the roots of his hair as black as the inside of a dog.

Ah, the old language, I mean, the old Gaelic, it's so near dead, the poor thing, any new speaker of it at all is new life in the old horse. You never know where a language will go when it finds new soil.

Okay then.

Ah. Well. Ah. This coffee, let's say. It's te.

Tea?

Te—hot.

Te.

Fuar is cold.

Fuar.

Seomra te, this room is hot.

This room is very hot, Owen. Do you always work like this?

Sa, yes. I don't know why. Nora, now, she likes a cold work room.

O?

She does. God knows why. Says she can think better when the air is crisp. The woman's mad as a mink. God knows how she stands it. Her fingers are like ice when she comes home. She slips them under my shirt sometimes and it's shocking cold.

I love heat, says Grace. I guess I spend so much time outside in the cold that I can't get enough heat.

Me too. I love heat. Hot rooms, hot weather. Maybe it's all those centuries of cold mud in our blood. My favorite month's August when the sun bears down like a burning stone. I love it. That's the one time I work outside. I set up a table out there in the heat.

Te.

That's good, Grace. You have the right touch there. Well, hey, listen, I'd best get back to work. I'm awful behind. Sorry.

No, no. Thanks for the lesson.

Sure.

And thanks for tomorrow.

Sure. I'll do my best.

Hope Daniel heals quick.

Thanks. I'll tell him you were thinking after him.

Could, can I get another lesson sometime? If it's not too much trouble. I know you're busy. Just say no if it's too much trouble.

No, no. Anytime. Just pop by.

Thanks. Well—goodbye.

Slan, that's goodbye.

Slan, Owen.

Slan, Grace.

Off she goes and back goes Owen to his bench and he tries to bring his mind down on his work like a burning stone but his mind rattles and swerves from his wife to Grace to his son to Grace to his wife to Grace to old Hugh O Donnell ah jeez the old bastard what am I going to say over that cruel old bird with never a good word for anyone and his hand as hard as his head and me saying a prayer there's a laugh I haven't said a prayer in earnest for a thousand years I bet since I was a boy younger than Danno and kneeling on that hill praying desperate that the old man and the mother would find some shred of joy between them and not crack apart into two islands cold as the tits of the queen of the sea leaving me alone between 'em alone floating alone.

33.

Owen could fiddle a bit and sometimes for no reason he'd pull the fiddle down from the shelf and fool around with it. He knew a few reels and jigs and hornpipes and airs but none so well that he could ever play them twice the same way. They were just drifting loose there in the fiddle when he asked for them with his awkward bow. There were seven of them and each had a flavor he named in Gaelic. There was a lean elegant bright reel that he called *seilistrom*, the tall yellow iris that grew near fresh water, and there was a twisting turning confusing jig he called *dris*, the blackberry bush, and there was an air that sailed up so sweetly at the end that he called it *fuiseog stairiceach*, the skylark; and whenever he played that one he would find his mind in the rocky muddy mossy lanes of his boyhood, startled as larks leapt whirring into the sulking sky.

The fourth one was Daniel's favorite, a sinuous cheerful playful reel they called the otter, *dobhran*, and the fifth was a clever elusive jig he called *madra rua*, the red fox, which always reminded him of his mother, and sixth was a mischievous riff that No Horses called the thief's theme, or *snag breac*, the magpie; and finally the seventh song was an elegant mad tune that came up every time he touched bow to string. He called it *riasc*, the heron, and he thought of it privately as Billy's waltz, in honor of his father-in-law. It was a sort of measured dance tune, a duet almost, two mirrored motifs braided and pulled apart and braided again in ever-new forms, and something in it spoke to Owen of a father's layered and confused love for his daughter, of the way a man might cherish his new babe and swaddle her in his hands and cup her to his chest as she mewled and moaned, and then teach her to speak and sing, and savor the headlong mystery of her girl years, and then war with her as a woman, and be confused and affronted, and delighted and amazed, and exhausted and angry, and patient and impatient, and watch her win a man, and birth her own child, and walk away from her father down her own road, for good or ill; and so there was in the tune both woe and wonder, and Owen never tired of playing it. More than the other six songs it was a changeful thing, each rendition different from the last, in ways he did not understand, and did not try to; but simply sat, his eyes closed, his legs asprawl, letting the bow wander gently into the song, thinking of the lanky clarity and grace of herons, thinking of Billy, smiling.

34.

No Horses finds herself up in the hills by her mom and dad's house and almost against her will she looks through the kitchen window and there's Maple Head making bread and No Horses leans on the windowsill.

Mom.

Come in, love.

I'm mid-walk. Just saying hi.

Take a loaf with you.

I'll bring it over to Daniel.

How is my little boy?

He's awake a lot more now, though he gets awful tired awful fast.

His body is still in shock, I think.

He's so … peaceful.

Pause.

He'll be fine, Nora, says Maple Head gently.

O mom, to see his legs all locked in plaster like that. …

It's alright, love. It's alright. Come sit for a minute. Here now. Sit right here. It's alright. Here you go. Here you are. When you were little we sat like this. I bet we spent a thousand hours like this rocking and rocking. We haven't sat like this for a long time, have we? It's alright. Here now. He'll be fine. Your love will heal him. You and Owen. You're exhausted, Nora. It's alright. Here's a shawl. Here now. Okay. You work so hard, love. You carry so much. There's only so much you can bear. Here now. I'll tell you a story. We used to sit like this for hours telling stories. Remember when you were little and you had those nightmares and we would tell stories to fend them off? And then you told me stories whenever I was sick. I'll tell you about Asin. Did I ever tell you about Asin? She is the wild woman of the woods. It's an old story of the People. My mom used to tell me about Asin. Asin couldn't bear being married or having children or having friends. She always wanted to run wild. She ran wild through the woods. If you saw her running you had to run to water as fast as you could and drink or her restlessness would come into you like a thirst that could never be quenched. She was happy and unhappy. She had wild long hair and she was very tall and she ran like the wind. When you saw dunegrass rippling in a line she was running through it. When the wind changed direction suddenly that was Asin. She was never satisfied or content and so she ran and ran and ran. She would grab men who were fishing alone and make love to them and then throw them down on the ground and run away weeping. She would grab children who wandered too far alone in the woods but she would return them to the same spot after three days and run away again. She would listen to women talking by the fire or working in the village or gathering berries but if they invited her to join them she ran away. You could hear her crying sometimes when the sun went down. She wanted something but she never knew what it was so she had nothing. She was as free as anyone ever could be and so she was trapped. When I was young I wanted to be Asin. Many times I wanted to be Asin and just run free. Run away. Sometimes I still want to be Asin. So do you, Nora. I know. It's okay. It's alright. My sweet love. Poor Asin. Sometimes I think that to be Asin would be the saddest thing in the world. Poor thing. Poor Nora. It's alright. I'm here. Alright.

35.

Cedar in his office is in despair over money. He has his budget books sprawled all over his desk and his head in his hands. The Department of Public Works has no money. He has no money. Worried Man has no money. No one has any money. Who has any money? He takes his pencil and makes notes on people and money.

Maple Head is a teacher and so makes a small salary and she and Worried Man get a little money from the government, but Maple Head must by law retire at the end of the school year, which looms in two weeks and after that she might or might not be rehired on a part-time one-year contract renewable only by the whim of the county school board, such decisions traditionally made about three days before the start of the new school year in September, which means a long worried summer for that astounding woman with the brown and silver hair and brown and green eyes flashing.

Cedar and Worried Man officially are employees of the county and so draw small salaries but the salaries are tied to the county budget, which is tied to the state budget, which is slashed annually by the contentious legislature, and the salaries, which are tiny to begin with, are also reduced by an arrangement with the county by which both men chose full medical benefits over full salaries, which decision is mandatory for all county employees over the age of fifty-five.

No Horses, for all the glowing reviews of her work in the city newspapers and gallery shows and glossy photographs of her sculptures in art magazines and interviews with her on alternative and progressive radio stations and the public television documentaries of her work and college students who come to worship at her feet and talk about the poetry of the grain and the soul of the tree emerging as if from a chrysalis, has sold three works in two years for cold cash and has exchanged statues recently for an eye examination, four cords of seasoned firewood, and a case of pinot noir from a vineyard on the dry side of the Coast Range.

Owen gets by with the shop but he too does far more work in exchange for services and goods than he does for cash so between he and Nora they have barely enough money to cover the bills and as he says seemingly lightly but actually not very lightly at all, which worries his wife, *we'll never be sick a day in our lives my love simply because we can't afford to be.* The first bill from the hospital in the city where Daniel had his knees bolted and sewn and stapled and screwed and stitched back together arrived yesterday and Owen was so horrified that he hid it from Nora not that she's been home to find it anyway.

The doctor who you would think would be the wealthiest man in town gets by mostly on payments, always late, from large and recalcitrant insurance carriers, and by spending one day a week in the city as a consulting general practice man. He has many times thought and dreamed and yearned for an administrative assistant in his office to deal with claim forms and phone messages and equipment purchases and warranties and prescription forms and referrals and appointments and malpractice insurance and deductions and professional memberships and patient records and a wall for photographs of all the children he has ever worked with, on, or over, but he can't afford to hire anyone at the moment.

Michael the cop makes a decent salary from the county, which would never dare to muck with the budget for public safety but he cannot bear the thought of working four more years as a beat cop to get to his twenty years for a pension, the brokenness has become too much for him altogether, and he lies awake at night pondering what he might do for money to support Sara and the girls and the baby coming.

Sara who has been a fish counter at a dam and a waitress is thinking about finding work as a waitress again, maybe at the pub with Stella the bartender, but who will hire a pregnant woman to be a waitress, bars and restaurants want lithe young girls as waitresses to add to the décor and elevate the dining experience, not women of a certain age with spectacles and a swelling belly.

The man now with sixteen days to live sold boxes and containers of all sorts, or air with boundaries, as he used to joke, but he is no longer working.

The priest is paid a small salary by his order of priests and brothers although the superior of the order, a small intense grinning man whose father was a police captain in New York City and used to let his son ride police horses through Central Park, is worried that health care costs and lack of new blood will sooner than later doom the order and maroon the men working in areas with small populations of the faithful.

George Christie who used to be a logger and then ran the Department of Public Works for thirty years has a small pension from the state as an employee of the county but the state pension fund has been plundered of late by the contentious legislature to plug the current budget crisis so the whole idea of pensions for former employees of the state or county is up in the air and the subject of much dark speculation from one end of the state to the other. His wife Anna does not work but spends her time crooning and rocking by the river. Their twin daughters Cyra and Serena are headed for public college, which will be paid for by scholarships and grants and work-study programs and some small loans which George isn't quite sure where he is going to get so he has lately quietly felled a tree here and there and cut it up as firewood for sale.

The man who beats his son works at the fish co-op, which is shockingly making a decent profit these days because the catch is so good, which worries everyone in the industry fishermen and processors and distributors and wholesalers and regulatory personnel alike because each and every one of them male and female conservative and liberal responsible and rapacious secretly in his or her heart of hearts fears this is the boom before the bust.

Nicholas, the son of the man who beats his son, just signed up to spend the summer fishing with Grace and Declan on Declan's boat, their agreement being a small salary plus ten percent of profit. Declan and Grace will split the rest of the profit. Red Hugh O Donnell's estate at his death turned out to be nothing but the old farmhouse and the land on which it muddily squats, neither worth much in the way of cash money. He also owed more than ten thousand dollars on fecking dairy equipment, which was fecking outmoded the day it was fecking hatched as Declan says darkly.

Rachel and Timmy work at the shingle factory near the old sawmill, which is the very last of the timber and logging concerns that once dominated the local economy and now are reduced and shriveled to Shingles For You, which employs seven people on a full-time basis but in the last two years has slightly expanded sales mostly to housing developments in the southwestern United States where many of the people building new houses yearn almost unconsciously for the smell of fresh-cut cedar, which reminds them of grandparents and holidays and childhood and snow; but even so Rachel who lives with her parents and saves every possible penny calculates that she can get her own place in about seven years, which thought always makes her small house seem as small and dark and cold as a prison cell in which she is sentenced to fritter away her youth.

Cedar drops his pencil and again drops his head in his hands. He has no money. No one has any money. How can he do public works without any money? How can he do what he must do? How do people get by? He can't figure it out. We're all a step from the abyss, he thinks. One slip and it's all over. We're all a car wreck or a disease or a wrenched back or a black funk or a badly hurt child or a bitter divorce away from disaster. How do we get by? He can't figure it out. Maybe cash money is the problem, he thinks. Maybe we should go to a complete barter economy. Maybe we should be hunters and gatherers like the old days. Maybe I should get my raggedy ass out of this chair and quit moaning. Maybe I should go see my boy Daniel of the three-colored hair red brown black. Maybe doing and not thinking is what I should be doing.

36.

Owen gets up at the funeral of Red Hugh O Donnell, held on the beach, and says, I will deliver a brief prayer in Irish at the request of the O Donnell family.

He is about to say, And knowing that the congregation gathered here this morning does not speak the ancient tongue of the clans I will also translate my remarks into English afterwards, but he has a sudden impulse not to translate into English at all, but just to let fly in Gaelic and be done with it, to just say what is on his mind, free from the possibility of insulting anyone, most especially the four O Donnell children in the front row, who certainly hated the old man with bitter burning hate but this isn't the time to say so publicly.

All this runs through his head in a second and he decides in the blink of an eye to just say his piece in the old tongue and let the words float mysteriously out to sea. From long bilingual habit he translates silently in his mind sentence by sentence as he goes.

So, he says aloud. A Dhia, glac chugat anois anam brúite Aoidh Rua Ó Dómhnaill, fear ceannláidir crua, taoiseach a chlainne.

God, take to you now the bruised soul of Red Hugh O Donnell, hard of head and hand, chief of his clan.

Má tá go leor trócaire Agatsa turcántachtaí an tseanbhastair a mhaitheamh, ar aghaidh leat.

If You have enough mercy to forgive the old bastard his cruelties, go to it.

Shíl mise gurb fhirín súarach a dhíolfadh a dheirfiúr féin ar phraghas gamhain mhartraithe ab ea é, agus gurb é an bhail a chuir sé ar a chuid pháistí chomh náireach sin go bhfuil cruthú ann nach dtuilleann a leithéah clan ar bith.

Personally I thought he was a mean little man who would sell his own sister for the price of a crippled calf, and the way he treated his children was a shame sufficient to prove that some men ought not be granted children at all.

Ach bronntar páistí ar chréatúir fuara cosúil le hAodh Rua, agus is cruthú dearfa é sin domsa go bhfuil Tusa i d'sheanfhear crúalach nimhneach chomh dall 's chomh crua le cloch.

The fact that some cold creatures like Red Hugh are blessed with children is to me incontrovertible proof that You are a cruel and spiteful old man as blind and bitter as a stone.

Mar sin féin, duine ab ea Aodh Rua, agus dá bhrí sin d'fhulaing sé pian cosúil le cách agus é ag troid go fíochmhar chun an grá a fháil 's a choimeád d'ainneoin na bearta gan cruth atá agatsa; agus mar sin déanaimid comhbhrón leis, mar nach é a fuair a chéasadh le himeacht a mhná chéile, agus an naimhdeas a thug a pháistí dó de bharr cruais a chroí; ach rinne Tusa é, mhúnlaigh Tusa é, 's mar sin, is féidir Leatsa é a thógáil ar ais chugat.

However Red Hugh was a human being, and so he suffered, as we all do, battling ferociously to find and harbor love against Your misshapen plans, and so we join in empathy for his suffering, which there is no question was considerable, what with his wife leaving him and all, and the enmity of his children, which he earned by the hardness of his heart, but You made him, and You formed him, and so You can have him back.

Cuimhneoimid ar a dheagníomhartha, agus céiliúrfaimid iad– mar ní hiad ach a cheathrar clainne atá ina suí sa chéad rang ansin; dá bhrí sin i ndáríre tá an ghuí seo ar a sonsa, ar son a síochána, 's ar son na lúcháire nua a bhfaighidh said b'fhéidir i saol a bhfuil fearg fhuar spairneach a n-athar imithe as.

We will remember what he did well, and celebrate that, which is pretty much the four children sitting in the front row, so really this prayer is for them, for their peace, and for the new joy they might find in a world without the cold blizzard of their father's temper.

Amen.

37.

In the pub after the funeral Grace comes up to Owen and says, Thank you for the prayer. We really appreciate it. Could you tell me roughly what you said?

Owen clears his throat and says quietly, God, take to you now the blessed soul of Red Hugh O Donnell, hard-working chief of his clan. Let your mercy pour upon the man like a sea, and bless the children You granted him, and let the waters of Your relentless love pour upon the bitter stones of their grief and wear it away utterly. In your capacious heart harbor this one poor man, and bless his suffering, and turn it all to prayers for his unquenchable soul. You made him, and You formed him, and unto You he is now returned as if a babe to the sea of his mother. We will remember what he did well, and celebrate that, which is foremost his four children sitting in the front row, so really this prayer is for them, for their peace, and for the new joy they might find in a world without the mysterious blessing who was, on this wild green earth, their one and only father. Amen.

Thank you, says Grace.

A pleasure, says Owen.

Declan is sitting in the corner with Cedar talking about fish. The halibut is almost always right-eyed, did you know that? says Declan. Not right-eyed like right-handed but actually both eyes are on one side of the creature. The top side. The eyes start out one on each side of the head and then one eye moves to join the other. Wild, huh? An eye moving from one place to another. Imagine if we could send our eyes roaming around. I'd send 'em down to my toes to feel for dabs in the tide. Flounder. We used to do that with the old man when we were little. Grace was the best. She wasn't afraid of crabs. She wasn't afraid of anything. Or I'd send my eyes behind my head so I can see trouble coming. Or send 'em down to my pecker. That'd be hilarious. I'd be a legend among the ladies. Instead of being a nothing with the ladies. It's because I stink. I smell like fish no matter how hard I wash. I wash like crazy every night. I work like crazy every day. All for nothing. All work no money, that's me. You know what the O is for in O Donnell, don't you? We O everybody. That's what the old man left us: O. Work your ass off and die in a second like the old man. Chief of the clan. Hard of head and hand. That's the O Donnell way. On O Donnell Day.

Another pint for Declan, please, Stella, says Cedar.

And one for the Department here. You do fine work, Cedar. Took balls to talk to Grace. I worry about Grace. I can't talk to Grace. She doesn't listen. She does what she wants. She's not a slut. Acts that way. Not a slut. She's a bullhead. I've caught bullhead, you know. Brown bullhead. Ugly as sin. And hagfish. Uglier. Ugliest. And dogfish and rockfish and squawfish and skilfish. I've caught 'em all. Splitnose rockfish and sharpchin rockfish and shortbelly rockfish. Greenstripe and redstripe rockfish. I know my fish. Shark and swordfish and sandfish and saury. Box crab king crab hair crab tanner crab. They'll pinch your fingers off in a second. Can't blame 'em. Hauled out of their homes. Poor bastards. Sometimes I throw a fish back. I don't know why. Some of them have the faces of people. It's bizarre. I saw a soupfin shark once with your face and a blue shark with Worried Man's face. Long thin fish too like him. Long and blue. With a white head. I threw that one back. Kept you though. We ate you. Things were tight then. When my mom left. We ate a lot of fish. A lot of mussels and clams. She used to read messages on shells. Really. I still do it. Grace won't do it. Says she doesn't remember. Liar. It's like a code. Don't laugh.

Another pint for Declan, please, Stella, says Cedar.

Cockle clams butter clams gaper clams softshells littlenecks, says Declan. Sometimes they spell words. Even urchins and mussels can be read. Like books. Grace thinks I'm nuts but there's a lot we don't know about the sea. There are a lot of worlds down there. I should know. I've hauled up skate bigger than the boat. I've seen sharks and whales bigger than the boat. I've seen whales with sucker marks from squid that must be ten times bigger than any squid anybody ever saw. I've seen sea lions that look just like beautiful women. I've seen lights in the water I can't explain. You want another pint? We just caught the two biggest halibut I ever saw off a ledge where there were never any fish of that size before. Hippoglossus is the halibut, you know. Every one a different color. Green or brown or black. Not one the same. No one knows anything about the sea. It gives and it takes. It is what it is. It's a woman. You can't understand it. I don't understand it. I don't understand anything. I don't understand my sister. I don't understand why my mom left her children. I could see her leaving Dad, he was a hagfish, but not us, we were anchovies and herring. We were little fish. How could she do that? Where did she go? I think she went to sea. I think she is an albacore, fast and silvery and long gone before you can get a good look at it. Another pint please, Stella? And one for my friend

Cedar who never says anything but just sits there smiling. Doesn't he look like a fish, Stella? Doesn't he?

38.

Worried Man and Maple Head walk home from the funeral arm in arm quietly. They have walked arm in arm for more than forty years. The first time they walked together, on the afternoon they met by the river, as Maple Head was drying the river of her hair, his arm swam gently toward hers and her hand slipped into the crook of his elbow and linked stitched woven touching skin to skin they walked and walked and walked. Their entire courtship was conducted on foot. Up hills and through forests and along the shore and through the town. Often not talking. Just walking. Thinking. Sometimes singing. One would sing and then the other. All sorts of songs. One day they came upon a cottage on a hill. Tucked in the elbow of the hill. Where the eyebrow of the hill would be if the hill was a face. It was for rent. Fifty dollars a month then. Long ago. Not long ago. The cottage smiled at them. They rented it with Maple Head's first paycheck from the school. Worried Man and Cedar built a porch and shored it up here and there though neither knew what he was doing carpentrywise really but their repairs and renovations have generally held up though the back room, which was No Horses' bedroom as a child and is now used as a guest room most often by Cedar, does slant a bit to the south just enough to notice and very slightly disorient a guest, which as Cedar says grinning is probably good for the guest. He says this sitting by the fireplace. There's always a fire going in the fireplace. Owen says his in-laws must really be Irish because there's always a fire in the hearth and two or three chairs huddled by the fire and two or three people poured into the chairs as comfortable as cats. Maple Head likes to curl in her chair as close to the fire as she can get without actually being in it so that all of her is equally and thoroughly warmed and Cedar likes to have just his feet by the fire and Worried Man doesn't like to be in his chair at all but prefers standing right in front of the fire and expounding and fulminating and lecturing and pondering and wondering and singing and laughing and hogging the fire altogether according to Maple Head who has over the years developed the habit of reaching up one lovely leg and placing her left foot on her husband's right thigh and pushing him gently over to the other side of the hearth which he doesn't even notice anymore, he just steps unconsciously to the side when he feels her touch.

She does this now and he steps to the side but he doesn't miss a beat because he has both hands on an idea now and wriggle as it will it won't get away, he's got it firmly to rights and he holds it out before him and examines it from every angle. As he speaks she watches his long face, his shock and tangle of long white hair with a black streak in it like a heron, the long excited quiver of his long lean body, his hands as big as nets whirling and swirling in the air as he juggles ideas. Sometimes when he gets to talking excitedly like this she likes him so much she wants to pull him down to the floor and cause a ruckus, which once in a while she does, just to keep him on his toes.

Now, May, he says. Consider this. We are aware of the quicksilver nature of time. Fast and slow and every speed in between. Sometimes it seems to stop. Sometimes it rushes by so fast we lose track of a day or two. I could muster a thousand examples but you know what I mean. So then time is not static energy. It is capable of changes in speed. Therefore it has a control mechanism either in the perceiver or in the delivery system. Something effects changes in speed either as perceived or as actually delivered. We will evade the question of system design and designer and focus on medium. The machinery of time, as it were. It is interesting to note that in most cases the speed of the time in question is simultaneously perceived. For example when we are exploring each other passionately we both experience timelessness. Time seems to stop. But then in moments of despair or crisis time rushes by at a terrific pace. When Daniel was hurt for example. Now if the speed of time is a matter solely of physical perception, of sensory analysis, as the doctor thinks, then understanding time is a physiological enterprise, something beyond my ken and life span, something for one of your bright young students to pursue over the course of a lifetime in the lab.

But if it is not solely a sensory matter, as Cedar and I believe, then analysis of the machinery is possible. Analysis of the delivery system. Understanding the nature of the machine. Such understanding of course leading to repair and renovation of the machine. For cleaner and more efficient operation. If you could, for example, choose moments to isolate, and slow them down, allowing for new action at the proper time, imagine the good you could do. On the local level you could rewind and repair unfortunate accidents as Daniel's. On the regional level you could for example arrest the spread of smallpox, which essentially ended the culture of our People a century ago, leaving us stranded in our time with nothing but shards and shreds of words and stories that once wove people into this place like threads in a blanket. On the national and international level adjustments could be made in situations that lead for example to endemic famine. Talk about Public Works, May. It'd be the greatest Public Work of all time. You could repair the pain and despair of millions of people. Billions. But it can't happen unless we find the machine. The locus of the delivery system. The black box.

And May: I know where it is.

And May: I have to go there.

39.

Moses floats home after the funeral and sits on the cupola of the tall house where he lives with Owen and Daniel and No Horses. He looks down through the kitchen window and sees No Horses standing there with her head bowed and her knuckles white against the white sink. He can't see her face. She doesn't look up. A shiver of fear goes through him. She doesn't look up. He stares. She doesn't look up.

When nervous or worried Moses hums, usually psalms taught him by the old nun, so he starts to hum, not knowing quite what he is humming, but after a minute he recognizes it, Psalm 34, the psalm of the broken heart, and he hums it louder and louder, and then sings his version of it in his cracked hoarse stutter of a voice like a plate breaking as Owen says like someone falling downstairs as Daniel says like an old truck wheezing its last as No Horses says:

the poor one cried
and the lord heard that cry
and saved that one from trouble
o the lord is near to them with broken hearts

and heals them with bruised spirits
and keeps them from afflictions
and keepeth all their bones unbroken
and no one will be desolate
no one no one
no one
no one

But she still doesn't look up and after watching her a long while during which time she does not move a muscle but continues to stand there clutching the sink with all her strength he floats up and away and arrows south toward Owen's shop, south where all the trouble comes from, he thinks, that's what Worried Man says, old South Wind with his fingers stirring up trouble and pain.

40.

Rain in and on and over and through the town, gentle and persistent, gray and gentle, green and insistent, thorough and quiet, respectful and watchful. On Worried Man and Cedar in the Department of Public Works where they hunch over a table strewn and scattered with maps. On Declan staggering along the beach to the hulk of his boat. On Michael the cop as he drives gently through town humming Puccini and thinking of what to make for dinner for his wife Sara and their girls. On Sara as she spades their garden with the two little girls who are digging as fast and furiously as possible looking for worms because their daddy says if they find fifty worms he will take them fishing tomorrow morning rain or shine. On No Horses walking in the hills, up the old quarry road and through the forest and back along the old quarry road once twice three times. On the young female bear two miles upriver from the village where she found a dead elk calf. On Maple Head picking salmonberries in the dark mossy places near the creek near Owen's shop. On Owen's shop where he is hammering and cursing and Moses sits silently on the old football helmet. On the oldest house in town, a cabin built by two silent brothers long ago, which slumps to the wet welcoming earth with the faintest of sighs. On Rachel taking off her shirt with both hands in the deft graceful crosshanded way that women pull their shirts over their heads and on Timmy sitting crosslegged before her watching. On George Christie the former logger oiling the teeth of his chain saw a mile from the bear. On his wife Anna who sits by the river listening to the river's excitement after three days of rain. On Grace on her knees in the mud by her father's grave in the southeast corner of the field where he thought he would die but didn't. On Nicholas relentlessly lifting weights up down more weight up down more weight up down updown updownupdownup. On his father cleaning rockfish at the co-op: you make an incision in the vent of the belly and cut up through the rib cage remove viscera remove the head remove the tail cut filet cut other filet bones and skin tossed left and filets tossed right, next fish. On the man with thirteen days to live washing Daniel's long hair in the sink of the doctor's house. On Daniel with his eyes closed and his mind filled with the ocean and his plaster-prisoned legs throbbing. On the doctor smoking his third cigarette of the day, the one called James the son of Zebedee. On the priest in the confessional in the church as he listens to Rachel's mother pour out her fears for her daughter that she too will conceive and bear a child while she is yet a child.

III

1.

Choose a morning in the Department of Public Works, any morning.
Let's say this morning. Tuesday, very early in June. Cedar in his office.
His office is a warren and a welter and a jungle and a jumble but ah,
he knows where everything is, every sheet of paper, every map, every
survey, every report, every work order, every purchase order, every
call record, every complaint sheet, every carbon copy of every letter
sent by or received by the Department in the years he has directed the
Department.

Every inch of every wall in Cedar's office is covered with maps and
charts. Even the ceiling is a vast map of the town and environs so
that when Cedar leans back in his chair and stares at the ceiling he
is immersed still in the town he has sworn with vows immense and
binding to protect and advance and celebrate and defend.

He sips his coffee and goes over his list of today's projects. He begins
his day by thinking about each one—squeezing them, as it were,
pondering them from different angles, listening to their shrill voices
clamoring for his attention, eyeing them in different lights, pondering
their substance (if any) and considering time, resources, energy, effect,
precedent, implication, and anticipated public response. Today's
projects: analyze and issue draft ruling on proposal to lease berry bushes
in town according not to property lines but traditional harvest rights.
Note to self: check laws appertaining. Check on and update as necessary
beach safety station; anonymous report of theft of surfboard(s). Note to
self: see Peadar O Donnell. Normal post-Memorial Day maintenance
work on cemetery. Note to self: request Mass for soul of nun. Issue
final budget request to county. Note to self: laugh hilariously at very
idea of county ever issuing seven cents more than what they think we
need for sewer system. Issue heated complaint to state fish and wildlife
department as to lack of assistance during massive smelt run in March.
Letter of personal thanks to sixth-graders at Neawanaka School for their
assistance in harvesting and milling several million dead smelt into fish
pellets for the hatchery. Letter to hatchery denying reimbursement for
purchase of fish pellets during month of May. Phone call to director
of hatchery with courteous request for director to get a grip and stop

blowing smoke on Public Works. Work order: destruction of beaver dam and/or construction of steel cage covering culvert draining Panther Creek through Trailer Town. Note to self: remember Michael's request to keep eye peeled for any unusual item or detail in and around creek near Trailer Town. Work order: street sweeping, southwest quadrant of downtown. Letter to Stella at pub noting gently that this is fourth street sweep of southwest quadrant in four weeks and Public Works is (a) not budgeted for weekly sweeps of area and (b) of the opinion that debris in that quadrant is traceable not to church, union hall, library, grocery, or kite shop, but to chaos and hubbub after hours in vicinity of your premises. Work order: dispose of dead owls on church property. Note to self: dead owls? See WM. Work order: construction of temporary wheelchair ramp to back entrance of library. Note to self: salmonberries to Daniel.

2.

WM his own self is in his office at the other end of the building. He is typing: *Notes, Research Results Vol. XXVI, Time Project.* There is no question at this juncture that time as we know it is not at all the ephemeral energy we commonly assume it to be. It assumes various forms at various periods. Measurement is the key. Clearly perception is the language with which we attempt to grapple with the idea, the concept, the phenomenon. List any ten speeds for time: summer morning, winter dusk, boring lecture, first time making love with woman you actually really love, drunkenness, moment of death, car crash, heart attack, any and all meetings of more than seven people, childhood, and not one happens at the same speed as the others, some are blindingly fast and over instantly and others drone and moan on until you contemplate removing your spleen with a pepper shaker just for entertainment's sake. Conclusion: time is a substance. Codicil: time unrolls, time is narrative, time is consecutive; we do know that it has not as yet reversed, rewound, been subject to miscellaneous revisits, despite popular culture adventures to the contrary. *Why cultural imagination so absorbed with time travel?* Because cultural intelligence knows full well that it is not possible. *Maybe it isn't possible* yet. Maybe so. *Are you a nut case?* My research over many years shows time to be a malleable substance, and anything that is malleable, which is to say affectable by energy of some kind, has only to have its specific affective energy to be identified. This is why we have brains. *Do you really think that you, an amateur engineer and shaman, will be able to discover the secret of time, when all the geniuses of history to date have not been able to uncover any such secret?* Perhaps the secret to discovering the secret is to *not* be a genius, in which case I am an excellent candidate.

3.

You know, says the doctor to the man with thirteen days to live, you might as well have a cigarette now, all things considered. It is late afternoon and they are sitting on the deck of the doctor's house while the doctor smokes. Tobacco is not all bad, continues the doctor. There is a certain ruminative ritual to its consumption that I enjoy. For example here is my eighth cigarette of the day, Matthew the publican. He is different from his companions. Matthew is relaxed. He is the late afternoon. He is the end of the working day. He is a publican, after all. He has seen it all. He has seen every type and stripe of man and woman. He likes people but is no fool. He works hard but there is a thoughtful social aspect to his work. With him the day draws to a close. There is a warm feeling in the air. We have worked and we are satisfied. We have done what we ought to have done and for the most part we have done it well with a few minor slippages here and there but those are things to worry about later. Right now we sprawl a little. Lean back. Ponder. Consider the sparrows of the air. The hairs on their heads. Dinner will come soon but not right now. Matthew is that moment late in the afternoon when you don't have to be anywhere in particular. Soon will come James the son of Alphaeus, before dinner, and then Labbaeus who was surnamed Thaddaeus, after dinner, and then Simon the Canaanite, and then, closing up the day, the last line of the story, the last man, Matthias, who was chosen to succeed Judas. There was a time, a long time ago, when things were different for me, that I smoked all day long, many dozens of cigarettes, more than I could count, more than I want to admit to really, and they had so many names I can hardly recall them all now. It was a hard time. Wartime. Let me think: there was Cleopas and Joses, Cephas and Nicodemus, Mnason and Manaël, Rufus and Lucius and Eurion the splay-footed, Zabdon and Zakron. And many more. I was smoking cigarettes all day long, and all night long, except when coughing or kissing, because the tenor of my life in that place was unbearable, and I could find no rest, I could not sleep, I still can't sleep. The first morning I was there I was sent to pick up pieces of men. All the wounded men and all the dead men had been carried away and there were only pieces of men left. Someone had to try to match the pieces together. That was me. Does this arm go with that arm? This leg with that leg? And worse. I was twenty years old. I began to smoke. I smoked all day long and all night long. Tobacco is not so bad. The ritual is soothing. The brief flare of flame. The sweet pull of that first drag. It makes you forget for a moment. But I remember them. Their names on their shirts. The scraps and tatters of shirts. Their names on their metal necklaces. The necklaces glittering in the mud. Let me think: there was Johnny and Joey, and Peter and Phil, and Eddy and Teddy, and Bob and Bill, and Michael and Matthew. Matthew the publican. I found some of him late in the afternoon. He was a child. The bones of a bird. A boy in a uniform asleep in a field, his head resting gently on a bed of ferns.

4.

Cedar and Worried Man stare at the maps on the long table in the cavernous central well of the Department of Public Works building. The maps sprawl and splay. In the center is a topographical map of a mountain.

That's where it is, says Worried Man.

They stare at the mountain.

No way, says Cedar.

Yes way, says Worried Man. Consider all factors. If, as we have discussed, time is capable of different speeds, let us say ten speeds for ease of discussion though there are certainly more, then it is akin to film or video and can be sped up and slowed down. There is a master mechanism for its control. We do not know the master mechanism, nor the master mechanic, nor if there *is* a master mechanic. Such questions are not our purview. However the actual material at hand, the stuff of time, *is* our purview. Such material must be tactile. It cannot be ephemeral. Time does move, it does pass, it consists, it exists, it is not a dream, it is a thing. If as we have agreed we are talking not just perception but reality, actual phenomena perceived by more than one person at one time and not attributable to mob psychosis or misperception, then we are talking about tactile material. For ease of operation such material would be stored near the site where it is to be processed. For ease of storage after use it would be stored near the site where it *was* processed. A sensible arrangement would be to divide the processing areas into regions. Suitable storage places in regions would require isolation, difficulty if not impossibility of discovery, and, I believe, inasmuch as they are probably filmic, temperatures at or below freezing. In this region only two sites present themselves as serious candidates, and of the two sites one, Lavelatla, the fire mountain, is dangerously active seismically. The other, however, is essentially stable, is sufficiently remote and isolated in its nether parts, bears ice every day of the year. And I would argue further that it is agreeable as a storage site because of its very proximity to a large urban area. One would never think something so valuable would be stored in plain sight, as it were. If there is a master mechanic we can assume he is as devious as all other mechanics, exhibit A being you. Therefore.

Both men stare at the map some more.

No way, says Cedar.

Yes, says Worried Man.

You make a good case.

We have to go there.

Do we?

We do.

Billy, we are neither of us young anymore.

Yet we have to go.

Do we?

We do.

What about May?

I'll talk to May.

What if we don't come back?

We'll come back.

What if we don't? What if we freeze or fall off a cliff or get buried in ice?

We won't. What's the matter with you?

She'd be alone. We'd be leaving her alone.

Cedar. We've waited all our lives for this. This is our chance. This is it. I know it is. It's there. If we wait we will just get older. If we wait we will lose the chance. If we wait we will always be waiting. We'll regret not going the rest of our lives. And if we find it we could change everything. We could fix everything. We could save millions of children. Billions. We could feed the world. We could stop wars. We could change everything. We are the Public Works. This is the greatest work of all time. Brains against pains. We have to go. It's what we are here for. It's our calling. You know and I know that you get a set of tools and talents and experiences and you have to meld them into your work. What you are here for. This is what we are here for. You know it and I know it. We have to go.

Do we?

We do.

5.

The river thinks too, you know. Did you think that rivers did not think? The Mink is thinking. Salmon and steelhead and cutthroat trout, it thinks. Fir needles. Salmonberries dropping suddenly and being snapped up by trout who think them orange insects. Alder and spruce roots drinking me always their eager thin little rude roots poking at me. Rocks and pebbles and grains of stone and splinters of stone and huge stones and slabs and beaver and mink and crawdads and feces from the effluent treatment plant upriver. Rain and mist and fog and gale and drizzle and howl and owl. Asters and arrow-grass. Finger creeks feeder creeks streams ditches seeps and springs. Rowboats and rafts. Canoes and chicory. Men and women and children. Dead and alive. Willows and beer bottles and blackberry and ducklings and wood sorrel and rubber boots and foxglove and buttercup and rushes and slugs and snails and velvetgrass and wild cucumber and orbweaver spiders and that woman singing with her feet in me singing. Baneberry and beargrass. Thrush and hemlock and coffee grounds. Thimbleberry and heron. Smelt and moss and water ouzels and bears and bear scat. Bramble and bracken. Elk drinking me cougar drinking me. Ground-cedar and ground-ivy and ground-pine and groundsel. Sometimes a lost loon. Cinquefoil and eelgrass. Vultures and voles. Water striders mosquitos mosquitohawks. Dock and dewberry. Moths and mergansers. Huckleberry and snowberry. Hawks and osprey. Water wheels and beaver dams. Deer and lupine. Red currant. Trees and logs and trunks and branches and bark and duff. I eat everything. Elderberry and evening primrose. Bulrush and burdock. I know them all. They yearn for me. Caddis fly and coralroot. I do not begin nor do I cease. Foamflower fleeceflower fireweed. I always am always will be. Lily and lotus. Swell and surge and ripple and roar and roil and boil. I go to the Mother. Madrone and mistmaiden. The Mother takes me in. Nettle and ninebark. Pelt and peppergrass. She waits for me. Pine-sap and poppy. I bring her all small waters. Raspberry and rockcress. I draw them I lure them I accept them. Salal and satin-flower. She is all waters. Tansy and trillium. She drinks me. Velvetgrass and vernalgrass. I begin as a sheen on leaves high in the hills, a wet idea, a motion, a dream, a rune, and then I am a ripple, and I gather the small waters to me, the little wet children, the rills of the hills, and we are me and run to Her muscling through wood and stone cutting through everything singing and shouting roiling and rippling and there She is waiting and whispering her salty arms always opening always open always o.

6.

Today is June ninth, the feast of Saint Columba, says the priest as he steps down into a beam of buttery light from the shadowed altar and begins his homily at the noon Mass. There are four old women in the front row and three old men in the rows behind them and one youngish man he doesn't know who must be from out of town a trucker perhaps and to his surprise there in the back nestled together hand in hand are Rachel and Timmy and as the priest's eyes adjust to the light he also sees amazingly Grace O Donnell deep in one corner and deep in the other shifting restlessly from foot to foot Owen Cooney who has never ever not once in eight years set either of those restless feet in this church. The priest resists the urge to say something to Owen and indeed being an experienced campaigner he knows to not even look in his direction although he cannot resist looking at Grace again to be sure that it's really Grace sitting primly half in and half out of the fat golden light. Well, he says, Columba is celebrated as a great saint of the Scots but he was not Scottish, nor was his name Columba, and for much of his life he was hardly a saintly man, which makes him an apt figure for us to ponder this morning. He was born in County Donegal of the O Neill clan of the north, his father being Fedhlimidh, great-grandson of Niall of the Nine Hostages, and his mother Eithne, granddaughter of the King of Leinster. He was christened Colm and he grew in learning and stature so wonderfully that by the time he was twenty-five years of age he was renowned throughout the North for his skills as a poet and his physical strength and his voice so loud and melodious it could be heard a mile off. He loved books and traveling and he went everywhere in his country preaching and teaching. However he also had a violent temper and after a friend of his was slain over a sporting accident Colm instigated a vendetta that left thousands dead at Cuil Dremne. This horrified Colm so much that he fled the country, taking twelve of his cousins with him to sea in a small boat built of wood and leather. They landed on the island of I, also known as Iona, and there he spent the rest of his life as abbot of the island community, receiving visitors of all sorts and stripes from every walk of life, most of them in some sort of physical or emotional or spiritual pain and seeking his counsel, which he gave most generously and continually in payment of the deaths his temper had caused, though he offered counsel in an austere and brusque fashion, it being said of Colm that of all his qualities gentleness was precisely the one in which he failed the most. Yet gentleness was the trait he sought above all others, seeking the limitless joy to be found in good work that leads to a peaceful nature, not in strife either in himself or with his companions and enemies, and many enemies he had, though as Colm said his greatest enemy was finally himself, for each of us, man and woman alike, is a seething sea of desires and shadows, of illusions and dreams, of courage and cowardice, and we arrive in peaceful harbors only by sailing ourselves true, by finding and wielding our talents as tools to help others. In a real sense we arrive home only by leaving the island of I. This is the message that comes down to us through the years and across great waters from the man called Colm; and it is the thought I leave with you this morning. Amen.

7.

Ite missa es, the Mass is ended, go in peace, says the priest at the end of the Mass, and he gathers up his chalice and paten and white hand-towel, the tools of his trade as he likes to say, the minutiae of the miracle, the stuff of the sacrament, and he walks briskly into the tiny sacristy, the locker room for the performance, as he likes to say, and as he disrobes he ponders the five people he saw this afternoon whom he never saw before in his church: Rachel and Timmy and Grace and Owen and the youngish man who might be a trucker or something passing through town.

Rachel and Timmy leave the church and hand in hand walk downhill past the school and as they cut through the schoolyard they stop in the dark lee of the building where the gym overlaps the auditorium, there is a little half-alley there where the older schoolchildren smoke cigarettes and make out sometimes carefully not knowing quite yet whether or not to take your glasses off when you kiss intensely or where to put your hands exactly or whether to keep your eyes closed all the time or not and there in that little half-alley russet-shadowed in the bright blinking young afternoon Rachel leans back against the brick wall and lifts her skirt and stares at Timmy and Timmy slides into her gently and they rock gently against the wall for a while staring at each other their eyes locked their loins locked her fingers locked in his hair.

Grace leaves the church hurriedly by the side door and puts her head down so no one can see her face and starts to walk as fast as she can but she walks bang! right into the shoulder-bone of the youngish man who might be a trucker or such who has paused outside the church to light a cigarette.

Hey now, he says, smiling.

Sorry, sorry, says Grace, walking on.

No need to be sorry, he says, falling into stride with her. What's your name?

None of your business.

People call me Denny.

Do they?

But you can call me Dennis.

Okay, Dennis: piss off.

I need coffee. Been driving all night. There a shop near here?

I don't know.

Bet you do.

Grace stops walking and rounds on him and says angrily, Leave me alone! Walk somewhere else! There's a coffee shop down the hill!

You're a wild one, he says calmly. Can I buy you a cup of coffee?

What do you want? says Grace angrily. You want me? You don't want coffee. You want me naked. Someone told you I was easy. Isn't that so? Someone told you that. Didn't he? Didn't he?

Well, he says, staring at her.

Not today, pal. Kitchen's closed.

Whatever, he says, and he walks away, turning to look at her when he gets far enough away that he thinks she doesn't see him but she does.

Owen leaves the church and starts to walk home but on a hunch he tacks south toward the Department of Public Works and indeed as he walks toward the shaggy green building he hears music from Nora's studio. On impulse he swings himself up and over the porch railing and knocks gently on the porch window shaped like a woman. She's so intent on gouging the wooden man on the table that she doesn't hear his knock and for a second he stands there fist poised to knock again but he lets the second drag a little so he can savor her at work, her hair half wild and half hurriedly caught up in a red rubber band, her blue work shirt sprawling over a chair, her tight black jersey with a soak of sweat between her breasts, her brown bare shoulders flexing as she leans both arms and all her weight into the gouge. He knocks again and this time she hears him and turns and he smiles and she half smiles and opens the door.

Hey now, he says.

Hey, she says, wiping her brow.

Just came by to say hey, he says. And to see if there's any wood left.

I think I finally got it, Owen, she says.

That's great, love.

I think so anyway.

I trust your eye, Nora.

I don't. I've been so off lately. All that wood.

Yeh. The guys were getting sore.

Sorry.

It's okay.

Let's go see Daniel.

Sure? If the work's going well ...

This is a good place to stop. I was just working on his ...

I see what you were working on, you lusty thing.

She grins.

His is ... I feel so inadequate, he says, smiling.

Don't, she says, smiling.

And to think of you alone in here all day with him.

He can't touch me though, she says smiling. No hands yet.

Ah, now, *I* can do that, he says smiling. I've been told by a woman I trust that I have good hands.

So touch me, she says.

Hey now, hey, he says.

Lock the door, she says.

8.

Michael the cop and his wife Sara and their two girls, three if you count the girl inside Sara, are driving to the beach in the police car, it being a beautiful day, one of those days washed clean by yesterday's thorough rain. It's lunchtime and on a lark Michael swung by the house in the cruiser and laughing carried Sara in his arms into the car the girls giggling behind them and the girls are in the back seat now eating french fries and slurping milkshakes and being Extra Careful not to spill in daddy's car although in about four minutes the younger girl will indeed do so.

This is fun, says Sara.

Just seemed like the thing to do, *mia sirena*.

Sirena?

My beauty, my love. From *Tosca*.

Loud slurping and giggling from the back seat.

Michael.

Sara.

Why … why do you like Puccini so much?

Are you serious? he says.

Yes, she says, annoyed.

Well. First for his music.

But there's other great music and you don't listen to that.

That's true.

So why Puccini?

Well, his music means the most to me, I guess. I'd like to be much more open to other music but it just doesn't get to me in the same way. I mean, I like all music, you know, but when I choose which music I want to really lift me it's always *Tosca*. I know it seems crazy but there it is.

I didn't say it was crazy.

I know you didn't, Sara. It must seem crazy, though. One opera over and over.

You can listen to whatever you want.

And there's something about Puccini the guy that appeals to me too.

What?

He's a genius and an idiot.

That appeals to you?

I find it fascinating. That a man could be so stupid and greedy sometimes but make such wonderful music, that's really interesting. I don't understand it.

So why listen?

Sara, what's the matter?

Nothing's the matter. I didn't say anything was the matter.

You seem …

The younger daughter, leaning over the front seat to ask her mother if she could have the rest of the french fries, spills all of the rest of her milkshake on Sara's shoulder, the cold shock of which makes Sara shout, which frightens the girl, who leaps back into her seat but bangs her sister's shoulder, which makes the sister punch her angrily in the shoulder too, and the younger daughter bursts into tears, and Michael yells at the older daughter, who yells back quick as lightning quick as a snake's tongue *You can't yell at me! You're not my father!*

They drive along in steaming silence.

Well, says Michael, trying to get things calm again, I listen to Puccini because somehow the music always gets to me. Of all the music I have ever heard, *Tosca* means the most to me. I've thought a lot about it. Maybe I am obsessive or something. But I figure you are attracted to some things and not to others. Some things matter to you and not others. Something about Puccini's opera just gets to me and I'd rather go really deeply into one thing than enjoy a lot of things lightly. It's like being married to you. I'd rather go deeply into you than anyone else.

Anyone else like who? says Sara.

Well, other women.

You think about other women?

No, Sara, I don't think about other women.

They drive along in tense silence again. The girls hold their breaths.

Michael, why do you love me? says Sara.

Sara, the girls, he says.

But why? Tell me.

He turns and looks at her.

Because I do, he says. I just do. There's something about you that attracts me very much. And the more I know you the more attractive you are.

You married me because of the baby, she says quietly enough for the girls not to hear.

No I didn't, he says just as quietly.

You had to marry me.

No, Sara, I didn't have to. I wanted to. I asked you, remember?

You were just trying to do what an honorable guy would do.

Another tense silence.

You want me not to love you at all? he says, trying to make her smile.

Do whatever you want.

Michael pulls the cruiser into the beach parking lot and they all get out and the girls, sun-struck, surf-addled, float like gulls to the water. Michael and Sara mop up the milkshake silently with the girls' beach towels.

Sara, says Michael.

I'm sorry, says Sara.

What's the matter? he says gently.

We can't afford this baby, she says.

Sure we can.

I don't have any money.

We have enough money for another baby, Sara.

You have money.

No, Sara, *we* have money.

I don't think I should have this baby.

Sara, what are you saying?

I'm saying I shouldn't have this baby.

It's *our* child. *Our* baby.

You want me to be like Tosca.

What?

But I'm not Tosca. I'm not a princess.

What?

I'm just me. And I can't afford another baby. What if you leave? Then what?

Sara, he says, shocked and finally beginning to be angry.

I don't believe you! I don't! she says and she runs to the beach.

He stands there gaping for a minute and then picks up the milkshake-sodden towels and wrings them out, the thick cold milk dripping on the hot asphalt, and rolls them tightly, and tucks them under his arm, and carries them to be rinsed in the sea.

9.

The man who beats his son is beating his son. His fist makes a hollow sound on Nicholas's back. Why don't you listen to me? he shouts at Nicholas. Why don't you do what I say? Who do you think you are? Nicholas has his arms folded over his head. I am your father, shouts his father, raining punches on Nicholas. I am not some kid in the street. When I tell you to do something you do it. Nicholas jumps up suddenly and runs to the dining room and gets the table between him and his father. I pay for everything here, shouts his father. You pay for nothing. I bought the food. I pay the rent. I clean the clothes. I cook the food. All you do is eat. All you do is give me lip. Always lip. All day and night I get lip. I won't take it. I don't care how strong you are. I don't care how much you lift weights. You'll never be stronger than me. I am your father. I made you. Say something! Nicholas says nothing but gauges the distance between the table and the back door and feints to his right which draws a left hook from his father but as his father's arm is fully extended Nicholas shoves the table at him and sprints for the door so just as the table's edge hits his father sharply in the groin the screen door bangs and Nicholas is gone. His father furiously hammers his right fist on the table until his knuckles bleed and then he stops, shaking, and gets his cigarettes and sits shaking on the back steps. He tries to light a cigarette but his hands are shaking too much. I hate this, he thinks. I hate this. I love him. I hate me. I love us. I hate this. This has to stop. I'll hurt him. He'll hurt me. He has shoulders like an ox. He's no boy. What's the matter with me? Why does this happen? Where is he? What am I going to do? He tries to light the cigarette again but his hand shakes so badly that he burns his lower lip.

10.

Worried Man and Cedar roll up the maps of the mountain and put them in tubes and rack the tubes and then walk outside into the crisp noon sunlight and sit at the rickety alder table in front of the Department and split a beer and slowly eat salmonberries.

We have to go, says Worried Man.

I know, says Cedar.

May would want us to go, says Worried Man.

Would she?

She would. She knows us. She knows me. She desires my joy. I desire her joy. That's the point of being married. To want the other to be joyfully at peace.

She won't like this. We're too old.

But she'll want us to go.

I don't think so. Not this time.

Then we'll go ask her, says Worried Man, but just as he says this he freezes, his glass halfway to his lips, and then he sets his glass down so hurriedly that he spills his beer, and he stands up, craning his head this way and that, and then he climbs right up on the rickety table and balances there turning this way and that, eyes closed.

What? Where? says Cedar.

This is bad, says Worried Man. This is raw green fear. This is bad.

Who is it?

I don't know. A girl. A child. You have to go right now, Cedar. Run. I can't go fast enough for this one. This one is real bad.

Cedar jumps up, his heart suddenly cold. He's only seen this look on his friend's face a few times in all their years together and each time it boded evil.

Bring a stick or something, says Worried Man, his face pale.

Where?

South. Quarter mile maybe. A narrow room? White shingles? I see a girl, I feel the girl. A sink. White siding ... a trailer! It's a trailer! The trailer park! I'll take the truck. Run! Run! Last trailer! Green door! Run!

And Cedar runs, he's the fastest sixtysomething man you ever saw, lean and wiry and relentless and angry and frightened, his heart cold his heart hammering with fear and the pace of his sprinting through the woods down the hill from the Department through a fringe of woods; he sees the trailer park below him bucolic the white rectangles of the trailers like cottages their friendly windowboxes abloom with daffodils their little knee-high fences and plastic mailboxes shining in the sun and he races down among them his heart racing and he sees a blue door a red door a brown door a white door where is the green door? where is the green door? there it is! green! green! he hammers on it with all his strength and inside a high screaming stops suddenly and his rage rises in his throat and he can hardly see he is so angry and frightened and he grabs a rake leaning against the side of the trailer and smashes in the window and at the sound of the glass smashing two faces turn to look at him one a man in a big brown coat and the other a girl maybe twelve years old the man has her pinned against the sink and Cedar opens the door and runs in and the man shoves the girl aside and swings at Cedar but Cedar smashes the rake handle against the man's face just as the truck fishtails to a halt by the door and Worried Man jumps out yelling Cedar! Cedar! and Cedar smashes the man again and again and again with the rake handle as Worried Man runs in yelling Cedar! stop! enough! and the girl at the sink watches horrified her face as white and ancient and remote as the moon.

11.

Rachel, walking home from work at the old shingle factory near the old sawmill, worries about missing her period. Sara the wife of Michael the cop feels a flutter in her belly when she kneels to plant the pole beans. Rachel tries to stay calm and count the days before during and after. Sara throws up behind the little row of white cedar saplings. Rachel walks faster and faster. Sara gets a shovel and buries her vomit and scatters leaves and sticks over it for good measure. Rachel walks in her house and says *Mom? Mom?* and hearing no reply goes straight to her mom's bedroom and gets her mom's desk calendar the one with all the holy days marked in blue and counts the days since. Sara kneels again and plants the beans in five long rows. Rachel hears her mother coming up from the basement and hurriedly puts the calendar back and goes to the closet and pretends to be rooting around for shoes. Sara thinks a row for each of us if I keep this child. Rachel grabs two shoes and runs down the stairs and runs into the bathroom and throws up in the sink. Sara feels the flutter again but it feels like bubbles this time. Rachel flushes the toilet to cover the sound of her gagging. Sara's daughters pat down the soil over the beans with their fingers small and gentle and active and dirty and lively as earthworms. Rachel's mother passes the

bathroom door on her way upstairs with an armful of laundry up to her
eyeballs and she hears the plumbing humming and she says, Rachel?
Sara's daughters throw dirt clods at each other. Out in a minute Mum,
says Rachel rinsing out the towel with which she cleaned the sink. Sara's
daughters wander off behind the house and Sara on her hands and
knees in the dirt watches them go. Rachel washes her face and pinches
her cheeks to get her color back. Sara presses her hand against her belly.
Rachel slips out the back door and runs down the street and just as Sara
stands up in her garden she sees Rachel flash past as leggy and free as a
young deer and Rachel sees Sara as strong and wise as the sea. Rachel's
mother comes back down the stairs and says, Rachel? and then notices
two mismatched shoes under the sink in the bathroom and a moist
towel folded on the edge of the tub.

12.

After Michael the cop comes for the man in the big brown coat and
Worried Man and Cedar drive the girl who is indeed twelve years old
to the doctor's for an examination and a night's sleep in the doctor's
custody it is dusk and they are famished and drained and they head
home to Maple Head who is stirring a stunning stew and there are two
loaves of fresh bread on the windowsill and she says grinning to Cedar,
where are my fresh salmonberries old man?

But when the two men sit exhausted at the table and explain their
afternoon she stops grinning and the meal is quiet.

Near the end of the meal Worried Man begins to say something and
completely loses track of his thought and he sits there startled and blank.
Maple Head leads him over to the couch and says, you are exhausted
love, you lie down for a few minutes, just close your eyes, there you go,
just let go, we'll knock off the dishes, just rest a minute, there you go,
and he drifts off in seconds, her hands cupping his face.

When she turns back to the kitchen table she sees Cedar with his
head in his hands.

That bad? she says quietly.

This one got me, May, says Cedar, looking up. That girl's face.

You did the right thing.

I couldn't stop hitting the guy, May. I really hurt him.

She sits down and cups his hands in her hands.

I'm worried, May. I'm getting too angry. I can't let go of things. If I feel they are wrong I can't let go of them. Billy was right about that time we went to talk to Grace. I embarrassed her. I said things I should never have said. I'm not her father or brother or lover. I am no one to her. I'm no one. I have no right. You have to love someone before you can say something searing. Isn't that right? You have to love people to hurt them. Isn't that right? I'm getting too angry. I'm doing too much work. We're starting to do more things maybe than we should. Billy tried to talk to me about it but I wouldn't listen. I don't know when to stop.

She says nothing but holds his hands and stares in his eyes.

I'm no cop, he says. I'm no judge. I'm the public works guy. Sewers and water mains. Highway maintenance and storm drains. That's what we are supposed to do, not fix people's lives. Billy's right. I got some kind of god complex or something.

Cedar, says Maple Head.

What am I doing, May?

Cedar. You did the right thing. You saved that girl.

Billy saved that girl, May. He smelled her pain from half a mile away. He knew. All I did was run. All I did was break the guy's face with a rake. That wasn't hard. That was easy. That was too easy. It's easy to hurt someone. I'm good at that. I was real good at that once, remember?

Who was the man? she says, changing the subject.

Her *father*. The guy is her *father*, May. Michael told us the story. The kid is always calling in sick to school. She goes to school two towns over. No one knows them here. The mother left and the girl stayed with the father. There's no other family. There's no neighbors down there in Trailer Town. That kid was skinny, too, May. Too skinny. She looks like a ghost. She's just a kid.

How long will she be at the doctor's?

Michael didn't know. Could be a while. The father's at the county jail and he's not coming back for a while. Could be a long while. If ever.

I'll go visit her. I was going to tuck Daniel in anyway. Want to come?

I'm beat, May. I'll bump off the dishes and keep an eye on your man there.

She stands up to go.

You're doing the right thing, Cedar, she says quietly.

I always thought I was, May. I really did. All I wanted was to take care of things. To make them right. To make them okay. To protect people. To be there when it counted. To *be* there. Billy and me. We were a team. He smelled trouble and I solved trouble. But even Billy looks at me funny now. He thinks I'm trying too hard. But I can't let go. I can't stop. But I'm getting too angry. But who will take care of things if I don't do it?

People are stronger than you think, Cedar. People can take care of themselves more than you think.

Could that kid take care of her trouble, May?

Maple Head gets her coat.

What am I going to do, May?

You're going to help Billy to bed when he wakes up.

Who will take care of kids like that, May?

You can't take care of everyone, she says, pausing at the door.

Then who will, May?

13.

The girl twelve years old is sitting with the doctor. Her name is Kristi. He has examined her thoroughly and she is mortified. He is silent. She gets dressed. He fills out pages and pages of forms and reports and assessments. She sits primly. His pen scritches and scratches. She ties her sneakers again and again.

Are you hungry, Kristi? he asks.

I could eat.

Would you like a pear?

I could eat.

He cuts two pears into cubes and they eat.

What is going to happen to me? she says.

Well, you get to live here for a while.

With you?

I live downstairs. You'll be in a room on this floor. Your own room. With a lock on the door.

You lock me in?

No, no. You can lock it yourself. For safety. For peace of mind.

Peace of mind.

There are two other patients on this floor also.

Okay.

One is a boy your age and the other is a man who is very ill. Both are gentlemen. You'll like them. I'll introduce you now if you like.

Okay.

The man with twelve days to live is asleep in the reclining chair in the corner by the maps of the sea but Daniel is awake and curious in his bed.

Dan, this is Kristi. She'll be living here for a while in my care.

Hi, Kristi.

Hi.

I'll go now, says the doctor. I'll leave you two to get acquainted. I'll be downstairs in my study when you are ready to get to bed, Kristi.

They watch him go silently.

Want to sit down? says Daniel.

No thanks. What happened to your legs?

Crashed my bike. Went off the path in the woods by the sea lion cove.

Hurt a lot?

I don't remember much, to be honest.

Who's the man in the corner?

He's real sick.

How sick?

He says he has twelve days left before he dies. He's real clear about it. He's a nice guy. Quiet. He's a real good listener. You find yourself thinking aloud when you talk to him. Nice guy. Are you sick?

No.

Why are you here?

Some things happened.

Oh.

Family things.

Okay.

I should find my room.

Okay.

Nice to meet you.

Nice to meet you.

Kristi goes to find the doctor who is downstairs in his study reading the Book of Job. Wearisome nights are appointed to me, he reads. Kristi walks down the stairs. When shall I arise and the night be gone? She walks through the kitchen. I am full of tossings to and fro until the dawning of the day. She sees a dark hallway and thinks, his study must be down there but I am not going down there. My days are swifter than a weaver's shuttle and are spent without hope. Doctor? she says. Doctor? O remember that my life is wind, he reads, and hears her voice, and he closes his book, and stands up, and closing his eyes, he folds his hands together in the ancient gesture of supplication and helplessness, and says aloud, in a clear voice that carries down the hallway to the kitchen, here I am, Kristi. Here I am.

14.

Maple Head walks over to the doctor's house, cutting along the beach in the moonlight, the tide is low, thinking about her husband, about all the hours and days and weeks and months and years they have spent together, about all the arguments they have had, all the laughter, all the exhausted moments with the baby, and then raising a girl and then a young woman, and trying to have more children but not having any more children, that was hard for the longest time, that was a deep wound between us, he wanted more children and so did I but I stopped wanting more children before he did, and maybe we spoiled Nora a little because of that, but what can you do, you do the best you know how at the time, and we never really had any money, and I made more money than he did for the longest time, and that was hard for him, that was a small wound between us, and he had all these wild projects, and I love that, because he is his dreams, and without his dreams he'd be empty and tired, but those dreams were crazy sometimes, all the projects, all the stuff in the house, all the machines, and all the thousands of hours he could have been doing something for money, but he is who he is, a dreamer, impractical and practical, I know that, and I love him for who he is, I know that, and I am not perfect either, a dreamer too, I always wanted to open my own school and never did, never never never had the money, but it wasn't the money I sometimes think, it was the leap, I never took the leap, but how could I?

At the doctor's house she knocks and he opens the door and a smile spreads across his face as he sees her and he adjusts his spectacles cheerfully and says May, it is always the highlight of my day when I see you standing before me. Come right in. He's still awake. I was just getting a new patient squared away.

Billy and Cedar told me about her. Can I help?

You might just look in on her, May. She'd be happy to see a friendly woman's face, I think. She's in the back bedroom upstairs.

Maple Head sits on the edge of Daniel's bed and tucks the blanket around his shoulders as tight as a tick as he says and she kisses him on the forehead and he tells her about his sea lion dreams.

You know what your grandfather would say about these dreams, Dan.

What?

That they are visions of your guiding spirit.

Really?

Really.

What will I be, then?

Well, I don't know, Dan. Clearly something to do with the ocean. We can ask Worried Man tomorrow.

He'll know.

He knows a lot, love.

He knows everything.

Well, she says smiling, he *thinks* he knows everything. Go to sleep. I'll come by tomorrow with your grandfather.

Okay.

Night.

Love you, Gram.

I love you too, Daniel. Deep dreams to you.

Maple Head knocks on Kristi's door and Kristi opens it a crack and says, yes?

168

My name is May, says Maple Head. I'm visiting my grandson Dan and thought I'd say hello.

Hello, says Kristi, not opening the door any wider.

Settling in? asks Maple Head.

Yes.

Can I help at all?

No.

Well, I'll be here every day to see Dan. Tell me if I can help at all. Maybe tutoring or something. I'm a teacher. Sixth grade. Most of my students are about your age. You'll need to keep up with your schoolwork, I guess.

Thanks.

Okay. Well. I'll be going.

Is Dan asleep?

I think so.

Did … did you tuck him in?

Yes, I did.

My name's Kristi.

Well, Kristi, I did tuck Daniel in. Tight as a tick.

Could you … tuck me in too?

Yes, Kristi, I could, she says, her heart twisting, and she does, her hands wrapping the sheet and blanket around the girl's shoulders narrow as bird bones, her face pale against the pale sheets. All the way home Maple Head sees the girl's white face in the white moon trailing its white cloak over the restless sea.

15.

In the morning Owen wheels Daniel out to the little deck over the sea and they watch the gulls and cormorants and pelicans wheeling. Sea lions power through the surf heading south in little pods of three or four. Daniel sees a seal. Owen sees a whale's spout. Three terns flash past and skim fish from the sea. The ocean hums. Owen makes breakfast and brings it out to the deck. The man with eleven days to live goes for a walk along the beach. The doctor takes Kristi off to some appointments of a legal nature. Owen and Daniel bask in the late spring sun.

Tell me about your mom and dad, Dad, says Daniel.

Is maith an scealai an aimsir, says Owen dreamily.

What's that?

Time is a great storyteller.

Does that mean you won't tell me the stories?

No, no, says Owen, shaking himself awake. You've a right to know. What is it you want to know?

Your mom lives on a hill?

Yeh.

Where?

Kilfinnane, in Limerick county. Near Clare and Kerry.

She won't come down anymore?

No.

Why?

She's afraid.

Of what?

I don't really know, Dan. I haven't spoken to her for years and years.

Why?

Just haven't.

And your dad?

He's buried along a road nearby.

I knew he was dead but not how he died.

No.

I always wanted to know.

I'm sorry, Dan. It's been hard for me to talk about it.

I'm sorry.

Yeh.

How did he die?

He worked himself to death on the road. He kept working until his heart gave out. Some people think he did it on purpose.

Was he young?

Sixty.

I'm sorry, Dad.

Thank you.

What was he like?

Quiet. He never said much. I don't think he was ever very happy. He never found the work he really wanted to do. He had a hard life. I understand him more now that he's gone than I did when he was alive. He confused me when I was your age.

Did you fight with him?

No. He was very quiet.

And your mom?

She's very quiet too. They married late. He was much older than she was. He lived up on the hill and she passed him in the road every day at dawn and dusk. They'd stop to talk. She found him more interesting than the boys in the town and he thought she was the most beautiful girl he'd ever seen. He was very lonely. She thought he was fascinating and handsome. She began to bring food to his house sometimes, berries and milk and such, and one thing led to another, and that led to me. There were only seven people in the church when they got married, my mother says. Her father refused to come. She never forgot that. Her sisters keened at the wedding.

Keened?

Keening is wailing for the dead. They were saying she was dead to them. My mother and father never forgot that either. They went to live in my dad's house on the hill and that's where I was raised, on the hill, until my dad died, and I left for America.

Why?

I had to leave.

Why?

Lots of reasons, I guess, says Owen, rubbing his eyes with the heels of his hands. I didn't like myself then, I didn't like my home, I wanted to be new, I wanted a fresh start. I felt stuck there. Trapped. I had to get out. I wanted a new country. A new self. A new start. I wanted to be born again, in a sense. I wanted my own life without everyone else's stories in it. I wanted to write my own story.

Do you miss your mom?

Yes.

Did you ever go back?

No.

Do you write?

No.

Does she write to you?

Yes.

Do … do you read her letters?

Yes. You can read them. They're in the shop.

Do you want to see her again?

O yes, Daniel, sure I do. But I can't. We haven't a penny, it's all long ago and far away now, and I feel I've hurt her so with my silence that I can never make it up. You can't heal everything, Dan. You just can't. It's better left alone now. Time is the great healer, eh?

I'd like to meet her.

Maybe someday.

Maybe soon.

Maybe.

We'll figure out the money, Dad.

Yeh.

Really.

Sure we will, son.

Tus maith, leath na hoibre, says Daniel, and Owen's mouth falls open just like in the movies or in the cartoons, it opens like the hinges to his jaw suddenly surrendered, he is open-mouthed and gaping, and then grinning in the broad morning light.

And what does that mean, o young scholar of Gaelic?

A good start is half the work.

That's well said, son.

Yeh.

All right, then.

All right.

16.

At noon Cedar and Worried Man are drinking beer and eating salmonberries. Between them is one empty beer bottle.

It has had many names, says Worried Man. Captains Meriwether Lewis and William Clark called it Falls Mountain and Timm Mountain, *timm* being a word of the local people meaning the falls in the river nearby. The French voyageurs who may have climbed it in their pursuit of furs called it Montagne de Neige, the mountain of snow. Some say it was called Waucoma, also the name of the little river flowing north from it to Nchiawana, the grandfather of rivers. Captain John Fremont, the Pathfinder, who was a dog and a coward, saw it "glowing in the sunlight," as he wrote, from his camp in the Blue Mountains, hundreds of miles away. The Scottish botanist David Douglas may have climbed it in the summer of 1826, after he lost all his papers and tools and seeds in the Fraser River that spring. He was a fine and good man and my greatgrandfather walked with him and told stories of him. A very gentle man, said my grandfather, the sort of man who sat down so as not to be taller than the child telling him the story. Remind me to tell you a story about my greatgrandfather and David Douglas.

You were telling me about the mountain, says Cedar patiently.

I walked to it once when I was young, says Worried Man. That was one long walk! I walked as far as I could go, past all the trees, past juniper and ravens, into the dust and snow, where all things are silent, even *asayahal*, the south wind, and there I found my colors, blue and white, and my work, which is seeing clearly, and my spirit, which is the heron. And now I have to go back. We have to go back. That's where the time is, Cedar. I know it. I am absolutely sure.

Did you talk to May about this trip?

Not quite yet. Tonight.

At dinner?

Yes.

What's for dinner?

You know, my friend, I think I will eat with May alone tonight. This is a talk we must have heart to heart, eye to eye, wife to husband, lover to lover.

Sensible.

Don't be hurt.

I'm not hurt.

You're hurt.

I'll miss May too, you know.

I know.

I love her very much.

I know.

She's an extraordinary creature.

I know.

She's my closest friend.

Now *I'm* hurt.

They grin and stand up simultaneously to get back to work.

The holy mountain Wyeast, says Worried Man, staring.

The icy mountain Hood, says Cedar, staring.

It will save us all, says Worried Man, his eyes closed.

It will try to kill us, says Cedar grimly, his eyes open.

Wyeast was a great chief, says Worried Man, opening his eyes, and he was in love with Loowit, the most beautiful woman in the West. So the mountain named for Wyeast is powerful for love. I hold onto that. Names matter, you know.

If names matter then I worry, says Cedar, for Hood is what people call it now, and the name is an inappropriate accident. A young British Navy lieutenant wanders by one day and names the mountain for a famous man of his place and time, Alexander Hood, and because the young guy, William Broughton, makes a map, the name sticks, but it's the wrong name, it doesn't matter here, it's an accident of history, it's awkward, it's ungainly, it's wrong. So I worry about accidents.

Then I'll call you Worried Man.

I'm serious.

Cedar. All will be well.

17.

When dawn comes Owen reaches for No Horses but she's not there. Uncommon but not unusual. He figures she's at the doctor's with Daniel. He showers and shaves and makes coffee. He ambles down their front path to the mailbox to get the paper and on his way back detours past the back garden to see if the beans are up yet and he finds his wife sitting crosslegged in the wet soil. Robins are whinnying and crows barking.

Nora?

She stares at him silently.

Nora, he says, squatting down to look her in the eye.

I can't get out, Owen, she says.

Out of the garden?

The room. The black room.

Owen's heart goes cold.

I'm really afraid, Owen.

Lean on me, Nora. Here now. Take my arm.

I haven't told you. I haven't told anyone. I've been crying all the time. I can't stop crying. I can't sleep anymore either. I'm really afraid.

He drops the newspaper on the tiny eager bean curls and hoists her up out of the moist garden. All her lithe lift and verve is gone, she weighs a thousand pounds, his heart quails.

I'm so tired, Owen, she says.

Nora, how long have you been out here?

I couldn't sleep. I woke up at three o'clock. I wake up every night now. I lie there praying. I think about everything. I can't get out from under this anymore. I'm so afraid. I can't command my mind. I can't command my body. I try to walk and I can hardly move. I try to sing and I can hardly speak. I feel so heavy, Owen. I'm so tired. What am I going to do? I don't feel like myself. I feel trapped and useless. What am I going to do?

He walks her into the house and sits her at the kitchen table but her eyes are so hollow and her face so gaunt and pale and her unshakable sense of herself so shaken that he doesn't ask her if she wants a cup of coffee, he doesn't tease and josh her, he doesn't ask questions on other matters to lure her out of her thicket, but he picks her up in his arms and carries her down the hallway and takes her clothes off gently and curls her into bed and all the time that he is taking her wet muddy clothes off she sobs quietly and it is ten minutes later or maybe twenty or thirty until her shoulders stop shaking and she falls asleep and he sits by the side of the bed terrified.

18.

Nora was the fastest girl in Neawanaka at age ten, the fastest girl or boy in Neawanaka by age twelve, the fastest girl in the county by age fourteen, the fastest girl or boy in the county by age sixteen, and the fastest girl in the state of Oregon by age seventeen. That year, as a junior in high school, she won state titles in all three sprint events. The next year, when she was eighteen, she won state titles in all three sprint events, and the half-mile, and the mile. There was a lot of talk about her future in track, college scholarships, Olympic teams, national titles, meets in Berlin and Oslo. Reporters from all sorts of newspapers and magazines came to the Department of Public Works to interview her colorful father, who said that his daughter had inherited her natural speed from her mother, who was so fast she could catch birds on the wing. Maple Head, smiling, refused all requests for interviews and Nora never had much to say. I like to run fast, she would say. I just run. I just run and other people measure how fast I run. I just run. She was a striking sight at age eighteen, her long hair flowing out behind her as she flew through the shouts and cheers of the crowd, her legs long and lean as a deer, and photographers jostled for position at the side of the track when she ran. Sometimes, when she ran in city meets or ran against local favorites, there would be jeers from the crowd, but she said she never heard anything or saw anything, not even the other runners. I just run, she would say. One magazine published a story about the mysticism of her running, and another collected all the quotes attributed to her by reporters and rearranged them into a sort of zen poem that was widely reprinted in running magazines. Her choice of a college was briefly a heated matter in sports sections but then she chose a small art college on the coast and after several columnists opined that such a bizarre decision was only to be expected in today's mangled and twisted moral environment the attention died away. She kept running. The art college had no sports teams but she kept running. She ran on the beach at low tide. She ran faster and faster but no one timed her anymore. After a while people all over that little town where the college was marked their tide charts for low tide and made a place in their day to go to the beach and watch her run. People of all ages would do this. She would start at one end of the beach and run lightly up and back the strand to get loose and then she would start flying. On the days when she had the wind behind her you never saw anyone run so fast in your life. One time an old man who used to be a track coach brought a stopwatch to the beach and timed her and did some calculations and then threw his stopwatch into the sea. That really happened.

19.

Rachel is also up at dawn and she dresses for work at the shingle factory but skips breakfast altogether and slips out of the house an hour earlier than usual and walks to the doctor's and taps gently at his window. He is up and dressed and sipping coffee and he opens the door so quickly that she is startled and wonders if he was waiting for her.

But that's not possible, she thinks. He didn't know I was coming. He doesn't even know me. Does he?

May I help you? says the doctor.

I think I'm pregnant, says Rachel.

Well, says the doctor. Let's see about that.

In his office he asks her name and address but she politely declines to identify herself and they look at each other.

It would be best if you were honest with me, he says. I will keep all information confidential if you can assure me you are eighteen years old or older. Also a formal record of your visit protects both you and me against possible malpractice.

I am twenty years old and I would rather not share personal information right now, she says politely. I hope you'll understand. Also I would like to trust you.

They look at each other again for a moment and then the doctor says okay.

He examines her carefully and conducts tests and after she is dressed again he comes back into the room and sits down and looks her in the eye and says, yes, you are pregnant.

I am, says Rachel.

You are.

I thought I was.

Is this good news?

No.

They sit quietly for a minute, looking at each other.

Thank you, says Rachel.

Will you be carrying this child to term? asks the doctor gently.

I don't know.

Will you tell your ... partner?

I don't know.

You may notice an increase in breast size during the next few weeks, says the doctor, taking refuge in information. Your breasts will also probably become very sensitive and tender. And you may feel nauseous a good deal of time.

Rachel stares.

People call it morning sickness but really it can come at any time. That's why it's very important to eat well in these weeks. For yourself and your son or daughter.

My son or daughter.

Chances are the child will be male or female.

Thank you. I'd better go. What do I owe you?

You can pay me later if you'd like me to be your attending physician.

I'd rather pay now. Thank you.

Do you have insurance through an employer?

Yes.

Then I can bill the insurance company.

Through my employer?

Yes.

Then my company will know I've been here.

Yes.

No. I'll pay myself. What do I owe?

Tell you what, says the doctor. Why don't you come back in two weeks for a check-up, and we can square away the bill at that time. By then your child will be developing his or her major organs. That's a critical time.

No, thank you, says Rachel politely. Do I owe you fifty dollars? A hundred?

Thirty dollars is the fee for a standard examination, says the doctor, looking at her closely.

Rachel takes three ten-dollar bills from her purse and puts them on the table between them and stands to go.

If I can be of any assistance at all … says the doctor.

Thank you.

Remember to eat well, says the doctor.

Thank you.

Please be careful.

Thank you.

He holds the door open for her and watches her walk away and notices that when she turns the corner she breaks into a run.

20.

When school ends at three o'clock Maple Head's students file out of her classroom politely but as soon as they are loose in the sunshine they sprint and sprawl and fling bags and shuck jackets and huddle laughing and drift home in gaggles and flocks and knots and trios and pairs. Four walk alone shuffling home in the four holy directions. Moses drifts over the school dreamily surfing the intricate afternoon winds from the ocean. A hawk floats overhead like a burnished russet tent and Moses dogs it on principle but his heart isn't in it, the afternoon is too crisp and lovely and bracing for war, and he wheels back over the school, watching the groups of children below disperse and dissolve, some on bicycles, which reminds him of Daniel, which sends him to the doctor's house, where he lands *plop* on the porch railing, startling the man with ten days to live but delighting Daniel, who cradles the big bird in his lap like a glossy croaking child.

Maple Head stacks mathematics papers to the left of her desk and literary essays to the right, glances at her lesson plans for tomorrow (morning theme: statistics and demographics; afternoon theme, theater and debate) and stands to go but finds herself looking into the grinning eyes of her husband.

May I walk you home, young lady?

If you carry my book bag.

It's an honor.

Let's walk along the beach, says Worried Man. Such a clear day.

Low tide, the tidal flat gleaming and threaded with rivulets and ripples. Here and there a crab shell flipped and emptied in minutes by the merciless gulls. Along the high tide line a wavering green path of kelp fronds, sea-lettuce leaves, tiny crab legs, mole crab shells, sand hoppers, gull feathers, net floats, driftwood, fish bones, occasionally a shoe, occasionally a beam of a boat, occasionally an entire dead creature: murre, cormorant, infant seal.

Maple Head kneels by the seal pup and examines it closely.

Such an intricate miracle, she says.

Such a brief one, says her husband.

They walk on silently arm in arm.

May, there's something I'd like to talk about. I was going to save it for dinner but this is a good time. As good as any.

What is it?

I am planning a trip.

Mm?

With Cedar.

You and me and Cedar?

Just Cedar and me.

Where are you going?

To the holy mountain.

Wyeast?

Wyeast.

Why?

I think time is there. I think it's stored there. On the north side.

So you and Cedar are going to find it?

That's the idea.

Just you two?

Yes.

How?

Well, our plan is to climb the mountain carefully, and explore. If my calculations are correct, the north-northeast side of the mountain, where caves have occasionally been reported when the ice is in retreat, is a serious possibility for ...

You are going to climb the mountain.

Yes.

You just had a serious heart attack. So serious you told me you thought it was the end. So serious you couldn't breathe.

Well.

Now you're going to climb a mountain eleven thousand feet high. At your age. With your heart.

We won't be going all the way to the summit. There's no need for that.

She withdraws her arm from his arm and stops walking and turns to look him in the eye.

Are you asking me or telling me about this trip? she says.

I'm ... asking for your blessing, I suppose, he says.

No.

No?

No. Why are you doing this? You are in no condition to do this. It's dangerous. It would be dangerous for anyone at any time but for you now it's deliberate danger and I don't understand it. I don't see any reason for this. You could send someone else.

May ...

I know what you are after and I understand it and I have always thought it creative and quite possible and possibly world shaking but this—this is crazy, Billy. Crazy. And you know it. This is self destructive.

May, it's something I have to do. You know that. There are just things you have to do. Things for yourself. Things to *be* yourself. Believe me I have thought it over. Believe me I know how I am not the best candidate for such a trip. But I feel that I *have* to do it. I feel that all my work is pointless unless I prove it to be true. And I know in my bones it's true. I am convinced. Dead sure.

What if something happens?

Cedar will be there.

You're risking all the people you love. You're risking losing Nora and Daniel and Owen and Cedar and me. And your work. And all the people you might save with that nose of yours. Your talent. All the people who love you.

May …

She spins on her heel and walks off down the beach again and he hurries to catch up to her.

May, please.

She takes her book bag from him.

Do whatever you want, she says.

May, please.

I love you, Billy. I love you dearly. But I don't love this. This is wrong. This is *wrong*. This is putting yourself in danger deliberately. This is selfish. That's why I am upset. You're never selfish. But this is selfish. Do whatever you want. But don't ask me to like it. Don't ask me to smile and say it's fine. It isn't fine. Go ahead and go. It's your decision. It's your life. Do whatever you want.

21.

Worried Man tucks Daniel into his bed at the doctor's house and sits on the edge and cups the boy's face in his enormous hands.

Tell me a story of the old days, Gramp.

Ah, I am filling your head with stories, boy.

I like to hear them. I feel lucky when you tell me stories that no one knows anymore.

Mm.

Tell me a funny story.

Well, I don't know. I am a little rattled tonight. My memory isn't what it was. I am getting old, Dan. No way around it.

Just one story.

I'll tell you a story if you promise to go right to sleep afterwards.

Deal.

Well, hmm. I'll tell you about when the People first started to celebrate the Fourth of July. It wasn't *our* holiday, you know—we were always an independent people, England was never our mother—but my grandfather remembered when we celebrated it for the first time. It was maybe 1877 or so, a few years before the Ghost Dance War east of us, when most of the tribes and clans rose up one last time against the loss of their lands and language and stories. That's a sad story. They wore white leather shirts, Daniel, because they were convinced bullets couldn't pierce white leather shirts. But they were wrong. That's a long sad story. That was the end of all the People east of us. And we were ending too but we didn't know it then. We didn't know it for the longest time. My father was the one who saw it clear finally. He was the one who spoke it and the People never forgave him for it. He was a brave man, my father.

What was his name?

Sisaxai, which means *healer with two hands*. He was a body healer and a spirit healer too. Very few people could do both healings. He had a healing sign carved on his bed. My mother carved it for him. My mother was one of those crazy Cheamhills! She lived in a place called Wamka, the Valley of the Gophers. Her name was Wocas, which is the bright yellow lily in ponds and lakes. My father met her when he was berrying there one summer. They were in thickets by a creek. He didn't know she was one of the crazy Cheamhills. He saw her through a thicket. He said hello and she ran away down the creek quick as a deer. He used to tease her about that all the time. *When you saw me you ran away!* he would say to her to make her laugh. *I must be as ugly as a cod!* he would say. He was always trying to make her laugh. She liked to laugh. They were always laughing. He was a brave man, my father. He walked into that Cheamhill village one morning shirtless with his hands empty and his hair unbraided. I have no war for you today, he said to the Cheamhills. Their warriors surrounded him. They were furious at his cheek. *Tunaqayu*, o warriors, I saw a woman of your people in the thickets and there's nothing I can do to control my heart now, he said to them. The *tunaqayu* men did not want to listen but their old women made them listen. I am here with no weapons, said my father. I am here with my hair undone. I am here without armor. I am here without brothers. I am here without friends. I am here without the heart I used to have. I lost it there in the thickets. I wish only to speak to the woman I saw. I wish only to see her again. Her face is now my food. If she tells me to leave I will leave. If she tells me she does not like me I will leave. I have no war for you today. That's what he said. He was a brave man. My mother liked to tell that story.

What happened? says Daniel.

Well, they called my mother out to look at the crazy man from Neawanaka.

And?

They understood each other.

What does that mean?

They liked each other.

Did they get married?

O, not for a long time. But eventually yes.

Why so long?

There were many negotiations, not least between them. They were from different people, and different countries, and they lived in different ways, and even ate different foods. My mother never did like fish and fish is about all my father ever ate. But they understood each other. It's like your mom and dad, Dan. They understand each other. Now there's another story. They met by the ocean. And your grandmother and I met by the river. And your great-grandparents met by that creek in the Valley of the Gophers. So we all met by water. Be careful, boy. Your woman will be waiting by water. That's just the way it is. She's probably waiting there for you right now. Time for bed.

You never told me about the first Fourth of July here.

Ah, you're right. Tomorrow.

Goodnight, Gramp.

Goodnight, boy.

I love this, Gramp. When you tell me stories.

Me too.

I love you, Gramp. I love you very much.

Me too, Dan. Me too.

22.

No Horses goes up the coast alone for a couple of days.

On a clear day the Oregon coast is the most beautiful place on earth—clear and crisp and clean, a rich green in the land and a bright blue in the sky, the air fat and salty and bracing, the ocean spreading like a grin. Brown pelicans rise and fall in their chorus lines in the wells of the waves, cormorants arrow, an eagle kingly queenly floats south high above the water line.

She lies in the hot sand half-asleep, thinking.

Am I insane?

Owen tries to lose himself in his shop but work doesn't matter and he isn't hungry anymore and he can't sleep, so he goes to the Department of Public Works and kneels down in the grass and stays there for an hour in that position, his face pressed into the grass, the hot dying smell of it filling his nose and mouth and eyes, his sobs muffled by the embracing grass, his tears sucked down by the thirsty grass, his body grateful for the gentle grass, and then exhausted he sprawls full length in the endless grass and stares at the sun and tries to burn his eyes out of his head, my eyes are holy and burning like Billy says, he thinks, but soon his eyes can't endure the pain anymore and they close protectively and by that time Owen's mind is driftless and exhausted and he falls asleep.

Cedar sees all this from the window.

23.

The man with eight days to live is thinner and thinner. The bones of his face are sharper and sharper. He spends more and more time in the chair by the window under the maps of the sea. Daniel reads to him. The doctor sits with him morning noon and night. Moses floats up every afternoon to sit with him also. The man and Moses have become friends. When Moses floats up and lands *plop* on the railing the man rises slowly from his chair and helps Daniel into his wheelchair and wheels the boy out on the porch in the fat salty sun. Today man and boy and crow are talking about water and daughters. I love both my daughters the same but in different ways, says the man. One is a challenge and the other is a comfort. One is a battle and the other is a refuge. One is brass and the other is velvet. One is a knife and the other is a spoon. Daniel tells the man about his grandfathers and grandmothers. One grandfather is alive and the other is dead, he says. One grandmother walks like the wind and the other never walks anywhere. One grandfather fights against time and the other one fought against hunger. I guess everyone fights against something. I fight hawks, says Moses cheerfully, and they all laugh. A fourth voice laughs: Kristi, who has been listening from the porch door. Come out, come out, Kristi, it's sunny, says Daniel. I am afraid of the eagle, says Kristi. I am no eagle, says Moses, startled. The bird talks! says Kristi, startled. That bird is my friend Moses, says Daniel. Moses, Kristi, Kristi, Moses. Moses bows and says the honor is mine, Kristi. The bird talks! says Kristi. Indeed he does, and with a great deal of sense, says the man with eight days to live. Not to mention a terrific grasp of the Psalms. Moses is fully as astute on the Psalms as our host the doctor is on the Acts of the Apostles in particular and the Good Book in general. He rises slowly and offers Kristi his chair but she declines politely, still staring at Moses. Did you teach him to talk? she asks Daniel. No no, says Daniel, Moses works with my dad. Actually I was instructed in your language by a wonderful woman now deceased, says Moses quietly. Tell us about her, says the man. O, says Moses, she was a wonder in every way, a remarkable creature. Never lost her temper. Never did her hands rest for an instant except when she was asleep. Sang all day long. An excellent cook. She was a nun. She died recently. I think of her every hour. Her soul shone like the face of the sun. Moses stops speaking, unable to go on. I'm so sorry, whispers Kristi, and she reaches out tentatively and strokes Moses' gleaming back and for the first and last time in his long life he begins to cry, long ragged aching sobs, the sound of lost, the sound of empty, the sound of alone. Daniel stares at his lap and the man stares out to sea but Kristi stands up and gathers the weeping crow into her chest and belly and bends over him and croons, the sound of healing, the sound of warm, the sound of yes.

24.

I am of the clan of crow, Moses explains to Kristi. They are still sitting on the porch, Kristi stroking his back and Moses humming with pleasure. Daniel and the man with eight days to live have wheeled inside for naps. I am no eagle, says Moses. God forbid such a thing. The clan of raptor is a mean clan. Their minds are small. Their horizons are meat. They take pride in their violence. They tear and shred each other with no regret or compunction. Their hearts are limited. They have no sense of time. They have no perspective. They have no past and no future. They are never sad, having no past to mourn and no future to fear, but they are never happy. They glower and snarl. They live for blood. What kind of life is that? They glory in power. What kind of life is that? They have no humor and their affection for their children is measured out in meat. What kind of life is that? Whereas my tribe is motley and chaotic. My tribe is dense and tumultuous. We argue and tease and wrangle and goof and fly upside-down. We are brilliant and stupid. We are lonely and livid. We lie, we laugh. We are greedy and foolish. Sometimes we all sing together. We tease dogs. We can be cruel but never for very long. We just can't sustain it. If we could sustain and organize our cruelty we'd rule the world. But what kind of life is that? We all fly home together at the end of the day. We have no kings. We have no outlaws. We have no ranking. We have no priests. We have no status. Age confers nothing in our clan. Size confers nothing. We have no warriors. We have no beauties. That's just how it is. We all look the same. Our stories go on all day long. We remember everything. Our life can be maddening. It gets loud. We never agree on anything. We bicker. We play jokes. We take chances. I have often taken refuge with your tribe just to escape the hubbub of my tribe. Your tribe is better able to be alone. Lots of you are alone. Lots are lonely too. The old nun who raised me, who saved me from death in the mud, my dearest friend, she was alone and sometimes lonely, but she fought loneliness with calm ferocity. She was a most remarkable woman. You look like her. She was a most remarkable creature. You have the same eyes. It is remarkable. Is her soul now in your body? I do not fully understand the ways of human beings. They are a curious and remarkable tribe altogether. They are capable of anything. I know that much. They are a constant surprise to me. They are a constant surprise to themselves also. They appear to live in a state of constant amazement. This makes them refreshing and infuriating. But there is a greatness about them sometimes. More perhaps than they know. Or a capacity for greatness. More than they know. It's confusing but I know this to be true. I have learned that much in all these years.

25.

The man who beats his son goes to the priest to see if there is some way
he can stop beating his son. I don't want to hit the boy, he says. I hate
myself when it happens. I love that boy. He's not really a boy anymore.
He's a young man. I love him dearly. He's never had a mother. I've tried
to do everything. I am all balled up inside. I have a dark place inside.
I don't know what to do. Can you help me? I can't go on like this. He
can't go on like this. What can I do? I am afraid. I am afraid of myself.
I am afraid of losing control. I have nothing but Nicholas. If I lose
Nicholas I don't know what I would do. Maybe I am so hard on him
because I am afraid of losing him. He's going to leave the house soon, I
know it. That's okay. That's natural. That's normal. I know that. That's
good for him. He's a young man now. He's very strong. He's a bright
boy. He's a gentle boy. I think of all the blows I have rained on him and
I am ashamed. I am mortified. I lose my temper. There are days I can't
look at myself in the mirror. There are days I hate myself. He's all I have.
He's all I'll ever have. I clean fish for a living. I smell like fish. I have to
let him go. I know that. I just want him to be okay. I have to learn to
trust him. I have to let him live his life. I have to let him leave. It's okay
to be alone. I don't mind. I like being alone. It's okay to be alone. It'll be
good to hear from him sometimes. Whatever he does. Maybe he'll go
to college. Maybe he'll get a job. Maybe he'll stay nearby. Why would
he though? Probably he hates me. Certainly he hates me. How could
he not? Sometimes my mind is unclear. Sometimes I have to sit down.
I love that boy. I want everything to be okay. I want him to be all right.
I love that boy. Can you help me?

The priest wants to say something wise, wants to say something
piercing, wants to reach across the table where they are sitting in his
kitchen and hold the man's face in his hands, the man's heavy face, the
faint smell of fish and ice, the man's salt and pepper hair, the faint smell
of fear and love, the man's heavy bowed shoulders like the shoulders of
a bear, the faint smell of his loneliness and pain, the sleeves of his red
sweater poking out from the sleeves of his blue coat, which he would
not remove, but the priest can bring no words to his lips, nothing easy
or facile comes to mind or mouth, yet he knows his moment is at hand,

a heart is gaping open in front of him, his work is staring him in the face, so he reaches out wordlessly and cups the man's hands in his hands, and brings up one word from deep in his throat, up it comes flashing and struggling like a silver fish from the murky green sea: Yes.

26.

On Saturday Sara and Michael and the girls, three of them if you count the one in Sara's womb, have breakfast together, waffles and jam and peanut butter, and peanut butter gets all over the table, but just as Michael is about to growl at the younger girl who made the mess she bursts out laughing with such a peal of hilarious clear clean unadulterated unmodulated unselfconscious artless merriment that he has to grin, and then he takes the two girls to the beach for the morning, it's low tide and they can piddle and putter and puddle in the tide flats, digging for mole crabs, screaming at the occasional scuttling scuttering Dungeness crab, trying to catch the infinite number of half-inch transparent mottled fish of no determinate gender or species, and Sara cleans up the peanut butter and then she goes for a long walk, along the river and then through the woods on the path where Daniel flew off, and then suddenly, without forethought, as she passes the Christies' house, the one with the mammoth statue of a logger in front, cut and carved by George Christie as a monument to his former profession, a dying way of life, as he says, an American subculture worthy of preservation but ignored by everyone, he says, a crucial art and craft and labor of this region but no one cares, he says, we had our own language and manner of dressing and sense of humor and it's all gone now he says, and as Sara prepares to knock on the door he yanks it open and he actually is saying these things into the telephone, some newspaper guy is interviewing me, he says to Sara, hang on a second here he says to the phone, what can I do for ya? he says to Sara.

Is, is Anna home?

Out back by the river, follow the path, he says to Sara, no, not you, he says into the phone.

Sara follows the path through fern and Oregon grape and salal and elderberry, alders leaning over the path protectively, and when she gets to the river she looks for Anna but doesn't see anyone, and the path just stops, so she steps closer to the river, looking both ways, and then what appeared to be a rock moves, it's actually Anna wearing a hooded brown shawl, and the two women look at each other silently.

My name is Sara, says Sara.

Anna says nothing. The river sings.

You don't know me, says Sara, but I heard you sing years ago and I never forgot it. You were amazing.

Anna says nothing. The river mutters.

I know you sang with orchestras and operas and things.

The river hums.

I have sort of a favor to ask.

Deep basso notes from the river as it rolls rocks.

I'd like to learn to sing. Like you do. Well, not that well, but the way you do. Beautifully. Real singing. I want to surprise my husband. He loves opera, and I …

Which operas? says Anna, her voice rough from disuse.

Tosca.

What else?

Just *Tosca*, really. That's his favorite opera. He only has that one tape in his car. He listens to it all the time.

Anna says nothing.

I'd like to take lessons is what I mean, says Sara. Voice lessons. I don't have much money but I thought I could trade work for the lessons. I could clean your house. Or work your garden. I have two daughters and they could work with me.

Anna says nothing. The river sighs.

It's a lot to ask but it would mean an awful lot to me.

Is this for you or for him? says Anna.

Well, says Sara, startled. It would be a gift for him, I guess. I'd like to surprise him. But I—I've always wanted to sing. Sometimes when I am alone I sing. I would never sing in front of anyone else, but I sing alone.

Sing, says Anna.

Now?

Yes.

What … should I sing?

Sing the river.

The river?

There's a high voice and a low voice in the river, says Anna. Those are the easiest to hear. There are a lot of voices in the water but those are the easiest to pick out. Sing the high voice. Find that note and just sing that note. Follow that note with your voice. Listen.

Part of Sara wants to bolt back up the path but she takes a deep breath and listens to the river and after a minute yes indeed she hears the high tone in the water, maybe it's the edge of the river where it spins along the patient shore, that's where the high pitch comes from, and the low tone is in the middle, over the thrumming rocks, who knows, no one knows, there seem to be a lot of tones once you really listen, and then Sara opens her mouth and starts to sing, and she sings in and around the high tone, playing with it, and Anna rocks back and forth and the river sings and Sara sings and sings, and afterwards, when she is walking home along the river, she is rattled and elevated and not quite sure what just happened, she thinks maybe she heard *three* voices singing, and as she gets close to the house she *does* hear three voices singing, it's the love duet by Cavaradossi and Tosca in the opening act of *Tosca*; Michael is singing Cavaradossi's part and the little girls are singing Tosca's part together.

27.

And there is a moment there, as Sara stands by the fence humming, when everyone in town is singing: Sara is humming Tosca's part with her daughters, and Michael is singing Cavaradossi, and No Horses, back from the beach, is humming in her studio and Owen in his shop, and Declan and Nicholas are trying to remember the fight song from their high school, of which no one can remember more than the first two lines, and Worried Man is humming a war song his grandfather taught him from the time the People went to war with those crazy Cheamhills, and Maple Head is teaching her class a song in the key of C as they study harmony and melody, and Daniel and Kristi and the doctor and the man with seven days to live are singing a song about the sea that the doctor learned from the old Navy sailor who had been twice lost at sea, and Moses is croaking along with them, and the priest is humming William Blake's poem "Jerusalem," and Stella the bartender is humming as she swabs and swipes the bar, and Grace is singing cheerfully as she goes back to work slicing apart the car in the field with her blowtorch, and Timmy is humming into the back of Rachel's neck, and Rachel eyes closed is humming with pleasure, and Anna is standing knee-deep in the river and singing with the baritone groaning of the river rumbling rocks, and George Christie is singing a lewd logging song into the telephone, and the man who beats his son is walking along the beach humming the song he used to sing to Nicholas when Nicholas was a toddler and could not sleep for fear of the dark. Even the young female bear is singing, or humming, or making a music deep inside her, a long contented basso throbbing thrumming that fills the tiny cave where she has curled around her two new cubs; and they are singing too, two high sweet new notes never heard before in all the long bubbling troubled endless bruised pure violent innocent bloody perfect singing of the burly broken mewling world.

28.

No Horses stops humming suddenly and sits down on the floor of her studio amid the wood chips and bows her head into her lap and puts her arms over her head to fend off the black snow she feels falling faintly and faintly falling. She begins to weep, but she's dry as a bone, not a tear left in her head, and after a minute she stops sobbing and kneels on the floor her forehead pressed into the wood and her hair filled with alder chips and sawdust. Her mind spins and careens. Too much snow. It's in my hair. What's happening to me? I can't get out of this place. I am so sad. Snow should be white. Alder is red. *Fearnog* is the Gaelic word for alder, Owen says. Owen will help me. *Alnus rubra* is the Latin name for alder. Owen can't help me. The birds associated with alder are crows and gulls. I have to help myself. Alder resists water. Why am I so sad? What's happening to me? Alder is white when first cut but from it comes a sap that runs like blood. I've lost the me of me. Alder is usually found near running water and will not thrive on dry ground. I am so dry. Alder heals doubt. I need water. I feel withered. Alder blooms at the equinox. My seasons are turning. The catkins are female. I have been daughter and wife and mother. Alder is rebirth. The wood when young is easily worked. Alder is resurrection. Alder is healing. The bark when decocted cures swelling and inflammation and sore throats and ague and rheumatism. The wood when older is veined. The catkins are female and the sap is as red as blood. Alder is steadfast. It endures under water for many years. Alder is true. Alder is healing. Alder is rebirth. Sap as red as blood.

She stands up suddenly and shakes back the river of her hair and the alder chips float to the white floor like red snow.

29.

Owen takes Worried Man for a dry run to the holy mountain. From Neawanaka they head east along the river through endless marching lines of enormous cedar and spruce, past Panther Creek, past Rose Lodge. They stop to pee and collect hatfuls of salmonberries for the ride.

Past Boyer, past Fort Hill. Talk of forts leads to talk of soldiers, which leads to Owen singing a song Union Irish soldiers sang to Confederate Irish soldiers and vice versa at night as campfires flickered through beech trees during the Civil War and then in the morning they slaughtered each other without mercy or remorse.

Past Gold Creek, past Willamina. They emerge from the forest into open country where every tenth fencepost has a glaring hawk. It's sunny on this side of the Coast Range hills and they stop for a minute to stretch. This is the Cheamhills' place, says Worried Man. All the way from the forest back there to the big river ahead. Those crazy Cheamhills. They're all gone. They liked this country because it was open. Lots of berries grew here. The berries are still here and the people are all gone. That's what happens.

Past Sheridan. Named for another Civil War soldier, says Owen, Phil Sheridan. The Cheamhills hated Phil Sheridan, you know, says Worried Man. You could always get a rise out of them by saying something admiring about Phil Sheridan. Touchy people, the Cheamhills. Your boy's great-grandmother was a Cheamhill woman, you know. Wocas, the bright lily. Bright woman. Touchy.

Past Dundee.

Do you think about your mom much? says Owen.

More at certain times than others, says Worried Man. When the first forsythia comes out, when the salmonberries flower, when the pond lilies open. Then again when the leaves fall. Beginning and ending times, that's when I think of my mother. I don't know why. She died in the autumn, maybe that's why.

Past Six Corners and Frog Pond and Pulp and into the city of Portland, past the old train station. That's where Cedar got on the train that took him to the world war, says Worried Man.

Cedar was in the war?

Yes.

I didn't know that.

He didn't like it.

I'll be darned. I didn't know that.

Past Boring and Kelso and Sandy and now both men feel the mountain rising beneath the road, feel the air crisper, feel a stony intelligence somewhere ahead behind the rows of screening trees.

Past Shorty's Corner, Cherryville, Marmot. Both men are silent, savoring the cold air, the sugaring of snow amid the trees, the unbroken ocean of fir sweeping away east as they round a turn.

Past Alder Creek.

I think your daughter has finally settled into that alder log we hauled in there, says Owen.

Alder was always her wood as a child, says Worried Man. Her crib was alder, her bed, her first little canoe. Even her hair was red when she was small.

Past Salmon and Welches and Wildwood and Brightwood and Rhododendron and just there as they passed over the Salmon River bridge Worried Man saw the bright white mountain and a shiver went through him from the top of his imperious white head to the tip of his toes.

Past Zigzag, past Government Camp. Also named for soldiers, says Owen. Funny how many places remember warriors.

They turn off the main road after Government Camp and take the spur road to Timberline Lodge and walk up past the old stone and fir building, past gaggles and straggles of teenagers and tourists, and sit for a moment in the juniper scrub behind the lodge so Worried Man can catch his breath, and then they walk up the mountain as high as they can, their boots caking with dust. Owen quietly falls behind his father-in-law just in case.

Worried Man stops to point out places. That's Palmer Glacier, which opened in 1924 and swallowed a horse. Those teeth there are the Hawkins Cliffs, and there's Crater Rock, right in the center of the ancient mouth of the mountain. Zigzag Glacier starts right there. Joel Palmer walked on that glacier barefoot because his moccasins gave out.

Where's the summit?

Just there to the right, above that sheer cliff face.

That'd be quite a climb.

It's more than eleven thousand feet above sea level, Owen. People get dizzy on the peak. Hard to breathe. Sometimes people bleed from the eyes and ears. But we are not going to the summit.

Where are you going?

To the northwest side, above the Sandy Glacier. There's a huge area there that is remote and isolated, so much so that there are no records of any climbers or exploration or survey parties in that area. That's where we have to go.

That'll be dangerous.

I suppose so.

Even for experienced climbers.

Yes.

Certainly for amateurs.

Owen, says Worried Man, we might as well be straight with each other. I have always liked you very much. You love my daughter with grace and patience and I love her more than I could ever explain to you or anyone or even myself. You work hard, your humor is a pleasure, your heart is large, you gave me my grandson. You are a good man, a real man, not a boy in a man's body. And I too am a man and not a boy. My body is old. I am not stupid. I see the danger. I know what might happen. But this is crucial to me. This is the end of a dream. I have worked for years to be here, and I know deep in my heart I am right. To not go would be to surrender to age, to frailty, to time, and if there is one thing I will not do on this green earth it is surrender to time. So we will go, Cedar and me. Do you see? It would help me if you understood. It would matter very much to me. I love you like a son and I want matters to be clear between us. Sometimes you have to make journeys that are hard. There are all kinds of hard journeys. This one isn't as hard as most. Your greatgrandfather walked through a vast hunger. My grandfather watched his people vanish before his eyes. Your son will have a hard journey. My daughter is on a hard journey. But we make our journeys. We have no choice. We can't hide from who we are. That's no life at all. You know that.

I do, says Owen.

They stand silently for a minute looking at the mountain and then Worried Man says, we'd better get home and they turn and start back down and Owen speeds up a little without seeming to so he can walk in front and after a couple of minutes when they hit a particularly steep patch Owen feels Worried Man's hand on his shoulder for support but he doesn't say anything and neither does Worried Man and all the way home in the car they talk about journeys and voyages and voyages and journeys.

30.

These things matter to me, Daniel, says the man with six days to live. They are sitting on the porch in the last light. These things matter to me, son. The way hawks huddle their shoulders angrily against hissing snow. Wrens whirring in the bare bones of bushes in winter. The way swallows and swifts veer and whirl and swim and slice and carve and curve and swerve. The way that frozen dew outlines *every* blade of grass. Salmonberries thimbleberries cloudberries snowberries elderberries salalberries gooseberries. My children learning to read. My wife's voice velvet in my ear at night in the dark under the covers. Her hair in my nose as we slept curled like spoons. The sinuous pace of rivers and minks and cats. Rubber bands. Fresh bread with too much butter. My children's hands when they cup my face in their hands. Toys. Exuberance. Mowing the lawn. Tiny wrenches and screwdrivers. Tears of sorrow, which are the salt sea of the heart. Sleep in every form from doze to bone-weary. Pay stubs. Trains. The shivering ache of a saxophone and the yearning of a soprano. Folding laundry hot from the dryer. A spotless kitchen floor. The sound of bagpipes. The way horses smell in spring. Red wines. Furnaces. Stone walls. Sweat. Postcards on which the sender has written so much that he or she can barely squeeze in a signature. Opera on the radio. Bathrobes, backrubs. Potatoes. Mink oil on boots. The bands at wedding receptions. Box-elder bugs. The postman's grin. Linen table napkins. Tent flaps. The green sifting powdery snow of cedar pollen on my porch every year. Raccoons. The way a heron labors through the sky with such vast elderly dignity. The cheerful ears of dogs. Smoked fish and the smokehouses where fish are smoked. The way barbers sweep up circles of hair after a haircut. Handkerchiefs. Poems read aloud by poets. Cigar-scissors. Book marginalia written with the lightest possible pencil as if the reader is whispering to the writer. People who keep dead languages alive. Fresh-mown lawns. First-basemen's mitts. Dish-racks. My wife's breasts. Lumber. Newspapers folded under arms. Hats. The way my children smelled after their baths when they were little. Sneakers. The way my father's face shone right after he shaved. Pants that fit. Soap half gone. Weeds forcing their way through sidewalks. Worms. The sound of ice shaken in drinks. Nutcrackers. Boxing matches. Diapers. Rain in every form from mist to sluice. The sound of my daughters typing their papers for school. My wife's eyes, as blue and green and gray as the sea. The sea, as blue and green and gray as her eyes. Her eyes. Her.

31.

After Michael the policeman brought Kristi's father to the police station, Kristi's father was photographed and fingerprinted, interviewed at length by two detectives in an attempt to elicit inculpatory statements, and finally released, still wearing his big brown coat. He denied all wrongdoing adamantly and threatened legal action against both detectives as well as the arresting officer. The detectives issued a no-contact order, informed him clearly that he would be arrested again if he made contact or sought to make contact with his daughter, and sent the case on to the district attorney's office. Both detectives reported to their chief that although they had both developed a dislike and distrust of the suspect almost immediately, they could not in their professional opinions find enough evidence to keep him in jail pending review of the case by the office of the district attorney.

Two days later the district attorney's office reviewed the case and, finding sufficient cause for further review, sent it on to a grand jury. One day later the grand jury, composed of nine citizens of the county impaneled for thirty days, did find probable cause of crime, and instructed the district attorney's office to issue a felony indictment. Warrant for the arrest of Kristi's father was issued the next evening by teletype and by direct phone call to all police stations in the county. Michael's shift supervisor presented him with a warrant sheet in the morning at roll call, which is why Michael is now cruising Trailer Town looking for a man in a big brown coat.

Three days, thinks Michael. Three days have passed and he could be in Mexico or Canada by now. He could be anywhere. I had him in the car. I had him in cuffs. I had him. Now he could be anywhere. He didn't seem like a runner to me though. He seemed like a badger, not a deer. He'd hole up. He wouldn't run. He'd hole up. He'd want revenge. He'd hole up.

But where?

So he cruises the town: Trailer Town, the beach road, the old quarry road, the back of the railyard, the fringes of the woods, the empty summer rentals, the alley behind the old hotel, the sheds and shacks at the sawmill, the alley behind the shingle factory. The veins and arteries of his town, through which his black and white car moves unhurriedly, sharp-eyed, worried.

32.

Cedar hears No Horses scream in her studio and he comes running. For once the door between her studio and the cavernous central work area is unlocked. She is still shaking the alder chips from her hair onto the floor.

Nora!

Cedar.

Are you okay?

No.

What's …

I can't bear it anymore. The black snow.

Nora?

Everything's sad. Everything's empty.

He reaches to take her in his arms, as a grandfather would embrace a granddaughter, but her face is so gray and gaunt that he is startled and his arms stop on their way toward her shoulders.

Nora, are you ill?

Uncle, I feel nothing. I can't feel anymore. I can't think. I can't work. I can't see straight. I'm so afraid. I don't feel anything. I poke myself with the chisel sometimes to make sure I am here. There's a snow. I can't sing. I am so afraid. I'm lost. I'm lost at sea. Will you help me? I'm so afraid. I don't know what to do. I don't have any more hope. I ate the hope. I used it up. No more hope. Where is the hope? Will you help me? Will you hope me?

I have seen this face, thinks Cedar. I have seen that face. That boy in the war. That woman on the beach one day. The man on the train.

Nora, he says quietly, come walk with me. We'll take a walk.

A walk, she says dully.

Take my elbow, he says. Here we go. Lovely day. We'll take a break.

A break.

One time, he says—wanting to keep words in the air between them, words to lead her out of the chip-strewn room, down the hallway smelling of oil and paint, through the cavernous central work area smelling of dirt and wood and burst fuses and turpentine, and out into the newborn air—one time when I was in the war there was a guy who lost his way.

You were in the war?

I don't like to talk about it.

I'm sorry.

It's time to talk, I guess. This young man was named Harry or Barry or Larry. He had been on an island in the Pacific. I disremember the name of the island. This guy was young. He was just a kid really. He'd been under fire for weeks and weeks. We went to get him and his friends off that island. Most of his friends were dead. He lost something on that island. Something in his head. The thing that makes you *you*. He couldn't speak. He didn't say anything for days after we got him off. He just stared. The thing that got him talking finally was a cigarette. We were on the next island over from the one where we got him. I asked him if he wanted coffee and he said no. I asked him if he wanted food and he said no. I asked him if he wanted fresh fruit and he said no. But when I asked him did he want a smoke, well, you should have seen his face light up, Nora. I had to light it for him and put it in his lips. His arms didn't work very well. I lifted up his helmet and tucked the butt between his lips and he took a drag like it was the most nutritious and necessary air. After that he started to come back a little. It took an awful long time but he came back, Nora.

He came back?

He came back. Funny the things that bring you back to yourself. Somehow that cigarette got him started back on the road. I knew another guy that a song brought him back from darkness.

I'm afraid. I'm so tired, Uncle.

That young guy on the island, Nora, he told me he ran out of bullets and hope on that island. He wanted to die. But he got himself back, Nora. He started again clean. He was born a second time. He used to say that his old self died on one island and his new self was born one island over. I disremember the name of the second island but he used to call it Resurrection Island. He used to wonder if there were lots of resurrection islands. I think maybe there are. I think maybe they are all over the place. I think maybe we don't even see the half of them. They are invisible maybe. They are tiny maybe. They're all over the place. That's what I think.

You think so?

I do, sweetheart. I do.

33.

Today was packing day at the shingle factory and Rachel has glue in her hair, splinters in both hands, sawdust in her eyes, and the smell of cedar in and on and through her from tip to toe. Generally she loves the smell of cedar, such a sharp friendly smell, but on packing day at the factory she *hates* the smell of cedar and she wants it *off* her, and it's such a crisp warm day, and the river looks so clean and inviting that she walks briskly up past the school to where a bend in the river makes the Cool Pool, a haven in the dog days of summer, and there she shucks her clothes in about an eighth of a second and slips in easily, she loves water and the river and swimming, the feeling of moving water against her skin. The water is a *lot* colder than she expected, but rivetingly clear, and she lazes and luxuriates and ruminates and meditates, her whole body submerged except for her nose and eyes. A thrush pipes.

A *baby*, she thinks.

A robin whinnies.

Timmy's baby.

The salmonberry bushes ringing the pool quiver in the nervous breeze.

My. Son.

In the distance log trucks shiver the highway.

My. Daughter.

She dives to the bottom of the pool.

Our son or daughter.

She holds on to the patient rocks at the bottom of the pool and faces upstream into the current.

My poor mama.

She surges up to the surface for air.

But I don't have to have the baby.

She dives down to the bottom again.

I could make an appointment somewhere.

A trout whirls past her face.

I wouldn't have to tell mama.

A crawdad pokes his head out from under the rock she's holding.

Poor mama.

She drifts up to the surface again for air.

So quiet down there.

Sinks back down to the bottom and closes her eyes and for a long minute she is completely at peace, held gently by the river, cupped by the river, saved and salved by the river, at home at peace at rest in the gentle green light, the furry rocks, the smiling pebbles, the curious crawdad, the murmuring current, the flitting trout fingerlings like tiny silver birds, and then she has a cramp so sharp and sudden that she gasps and thrashes choking to the surface and then another like a horse kicking her in the belly and then another twice as bad as the others she is doubled over her face in the water her hair trailing like kelp she stumbles to the edge of the pool and *another* and kneels *another* and something inside her twists savagely *another* and her salty blood pours into the river *another* and she sobs terrified *another* mama mama! *another* and between her legs her son the size of a finger is born into the river and he spins away end over end a tiny silver bird flying toward the sea.

34.

Past a blue heron who snaps at him thinking him a fish, and past Anna Christie rocking and singing with Sara also singing, and past Timmy whistling as he saunters along the river fingering the engagement ring for Rachel in his pocket, and past a merganser duck with eight ducklings soon to be seven courtesy of the female mink watching them, and past Cedar and No Horses who are sitting on Cedar's hand-hewn salmon-watching bench on the riverbank watching the young osprey in their enormous nest in a fir snag, and past the two mule deer fawns hidden in the cattail thicket behind Trailer Town, and past the man in the big brown coat also hidden in the cattail thicket pondering his options and courses of action and snarling belly, and past Maple Head approaching the thicket her hair silver and black flowing behind her in the breeze her feet light as feathers on the path, past alders mourning into the river and cottonwoods, past salmonberry and blackberry, past Michael the cop in the parking lot behind the fish co-op thinking hard about where Kristi's father could be hiding, past Owen taking half an hour off to cast for steelhead on general principles and on the off chance that if he catches one the look on Nora's face at dinner will be a pleasure and a wonder absolutely, under the porch of the doctor's house where Daniel and Kristi and the man with five days to live are laughing, past Worried Man and the doctor taking a lunchtime stroll along the riverbank, past an ouzel underwater, past trout, past a sturgeon the size of a leg near the effluent plant, under water striders, over beaver kits, under coot, over crawdads, past Grace and Declan and Nicholas patching and hammering the boat as it sprawls like an exhausted walrus on the beach where the river meets the sea, over rocks and sticks and cans and bones, past the pair of hungry sea lions at the mouth of the river waiting for salmon and steelhead, on and on he tumbles and whirls, Inch does, his heart hammering, his arms and legs milling wildly, his eyes open, his mouth open, breathing the moan and whir and rumble of the river, the hiss and roar and ripple of it, but as he nears the sea he fails, he fades, he ebbs, his span is spun, his heart slows, his brain cools, and just as he is startled by salt for the first and last time in the eleven minutes of his life he closes his eyes, puts his thumb in his mouth, and enters the ancient endless patient ocean, where all stories end, where all stories are born.

35.

Sometimes sadness swept over the town like a tide or a mist, fingering first one and then another until all of Neawanaka was quiet and still and chilled to the bone. At such times the library was empty and the church emptier, the strand stranded and the streets filled only with salt and wind. The pub was the last outpost of the defiant, with a handful of huddled patrons; but even Stella, not usually prone to prevailing sentiment, sat in the yellow kitchen behind the bar and stared out to sea and wondered at the wander of her life. As a girl she had hoped for only as much as anyone else: someone to love and be loved by, work that mattered, a child or three to be amazed and exhausted by, a home in the wild world where she would feel rooted and safe, warmed and webbed; but the story of her life was fits and starts, roads that led nowhere, lovers who lied, jobs taken out of desperation, insurance lapsing unawares, cars born four presidents ago. Too proud to lean on anyone, she soon trusted no one, and watched wary when man or woman tried to peer through the bars of her gates. By the time she was out of her twenties she was leery of love; by the time she was out of her thirties she was so lonely she would not mouth the word even to herself. When her mother died and she had inherited what there was of her parents' estate she bought the pub, almost on first impulse, dreaming inchoately of communal verve and laughter, softball and bowling teams, dart contests, impromptu speeches, all you can eats, barbecues, business partners, church suppers, bus trips, surfing competitions, fiddles and guitars, hilarious wakes and solemn wedding receptions, smoking in the back and singing in the front, children and sawdust underfoot, plaques and trophies, framed photographs, decks of cards, regulars, chaos and hubbub, motley energy, a tribe of friends, an almost family; but as the years passed she increasingly found herself alone in the kitchen, staring at the bills, staring at the griddle, staring out to sea.

36.

Worried Man spends the afternoon in the Department of Public Works laying in supplies for climbing Wyeast. He is a cautious man, for all his exuberance, and he creates two piles, one for him and one for Cedar. First I'll make sure each of us has everything we could possibly need and then we can pare the piles. Clothing: boots, gloves, socks, wool underwear, sweaters, hats, sunglasses. Better bring lots of socks because if he doesn't change his socks it will be a very short journey indeed. Housing: tent, tent stakes, sleeping bags, blankets. Better bring an extra blanket we can share. Tools: ice axes, crampons, rope, more rope, carabiners, skis, ice screws, ice saw, pickets, belay loops, snowshoes, shovel, knives, iodine tablets, matches, more matches. Better bring *way* more matches. Walking sticks. *Two are better than one; for if they fall, the one will lift up his fellow; but woe to him that is alone when he falleth, and hath not another to lift him up.* Ecclesiastes. Waterproof match cases. Maps. Batteries. Compasses. Flashlights. Headlamps. First-aid kit. Wristwatches. Ham radio. Toothbrushes. Toothpaste. Because his breath in the morning smells like an old elk. Bandannas. Because my nose runs at high elevations. *That which is far off, and exceeding deep, who can find it out? I applied mine heart to know, and to search, and to seek out wisdom, and the reason of things.* Ecclesiastes. Toilet paper. Better bring a couple extra rolls of paper. Notepads. Camera. Film for camera. Dried berries. Dried elk jerky. Dried salmon sticks. Walnuts, almonds, pine nuts, peanuts. Water. Beer? No beer. Aspirin. More aspirin. We are neither of us young. *Be not thou foolish: why shouldest thou die before thy time?* Ecclesiastes. One whistle each in case we get lost. He perches the bright steel whistles on the apexes of the teetering piles of stuff and grins to think that they look like nipples on breasts which makes him think of Maple Head's breasts which makes him sit down on the floor with his head in his hands and think What am I doing? What poor fool walks away from such a woman? His mind spins through a thousand moments with her: her combing her wet hair by the river, her eyes flashing green and brown and rebellious and alive, their daughter sliding out mewling and wet, their bitter arguments, their wild hot lovemaking, her helpless laughter, the smell of fresh hot bread, the avalanche of her tears, the hopeful sound of her steps on the path outside, light and quick as the eddying air. But still inside his head like a grain of salt is Wyeast, the castle of ice. *Great things are done when men and mountains meet.* Blake.

37.

Cedar walks No Horses over to the doctor's house but the doctor is not there, and Kristi has wheeled Daniel over to the river for the afternoon, and the man with five days to live is asleep in his wheelchair on the porch, so Cedar and No Horses keep walking along the beach.

Uncle?

Girl of my heart.

Do you ever ... have you ever ... been dark?

O Nora, yes. Yes absolutely, as your father says.

What did you do about it?

Do? Well, when I was young I was always trying to find reasons for it. So I could assign blame. And there were some good reasons. There was lots to blame. I nearly drowned, and I don't remember my childhood at all, and I was in a war when I was young. But blaming those things didn't seem to help any.

What did help?

Work. Friends. Your mother and father have been an immense help to me. Also, how would I explain it … a certain ferocious attention to things.

How do you mean?

An intense attention, so to speak, says Cedar. It clarifies your mind. It could be anything. For me it's nearly everything. See that black bird low in the water there? In front of the last breaker?

Cormorant?

Red-throated loon. *Stellata,* the starred one, because of the shape of the red mark on its throat. And there's a red-necked grebe, which *loves* to eat newts. There's a story in everything and the more stories I hear the less sad I am. See now, those little black ducks in the waves are scoters, which fly underwater like ouzels do in creeks. Ouzels are your spirit birds, Nora, you remember. With their extraordinary songs and relentless spirits. That's you, Nora, extraordinary and relentless.

I don't feel that way, Uncle.

You will, Nora. I am sure of it. You'll sing. Not all birds can sing, you know. Grebes yelp, and wigeons say *whew*, and swans say *wow*, and oystercatchers yell *wheee*, and knots murmur *want want*, and dowitchers mutter *tu tu tu*, and auklets moo, and … what are you smiling at?

You are the most unusual man in the world, Uncle.

No, no, child. That would be your father. Not to mention your husband. And I have high hopes for your son as the eventual world champion most unusual man in the world. He's got the hair for it, too.

Tu tu tu, says Nora, and they howl with laughter, howl so loud that the loon at sea turns to look at what it takes to be two new loons on land.

38.

Maple Head is trying to write a history of Neawanaka. She has been writing the history for more than twenty years. She is up to volume fourteen in a series of slim black notebooks. She carries one of these notebooks with her wherever she goes. Sometimes she writes in the notebook during study halls or lunch periods at school. Sometimes she writes in the halves of hours while soups simmer. Sometimes she writes when she is on the telephone. Sometimes she writes by the fire at night. She has written at the bedsides of the sick and the dying. She has written during wedding receptions. She has written during meetings at school. She has written during Department of Public Works picnics. She has written early in the morning when the light is pale as the pearl lining of a shell. She has written on the beach as the pages of her notebook fluttered. She has written in playgrounds and parks and on the edges of pools with her legs refracted in the glimmering water. She has written in the library. She has written on her ironing board. She has written on Worried Man's naked back as they sprawled in bed. She has written in the bathroom. She has written on the porch. She has written in her daughter's studio and in the cavernous central work area of the Department of Public Works. She has written in every seat of various cars. She has written on buses and trains. She has written in church when there is a visiting pastor during the summer. She has tried to account her town, the poetry and pain and poverty and plainness of it, the bravery and belly laughs, the stunning volume of rain, the sadness of winter, the petty crime, the smell of manure, the squelch of mud, the smell of skunk cabbage, the burble and babble and bubble of the children in her classroom, the endless fleeing of children to the city as soon as possible, the sticky smell of cottonwood buds opening, the prevalence of mold and mildew, the gargling snarl of chain saws, the violet green sheen of a swallow, the hollow eyes of retarded children, the stunning sunlight after rain, the prevalence of car parts in yards, the mustiness of basements, the prevalence of divorce, the slam of screen doors, the paucity of voters, the night oratorio of tree frogs, the smell of fish like a wall near the co-op, the smell of beer like an aura around the pub night and day, the thrill of thrushes, the smell of a crate of new school books, the riotous vegetation, the patient heartless brooding watchful sea.

39.

Cast thy bread upon the waters: for thou shalt find it after many days, that's from Ecclesiastes, says the doctor, and smashes the bottle of champagne against Declan's newly repaired boat, which accepts the blow wooden-faced.

I wish the crew of this boat fine fishing, safety, peace, joy, and halibut the size of doors, he says, and everyone cheers. Champagne droplets scatter like sweet rain across the heads and shoulders of those in attendance.

A suitable baptism, says the priest, smiling.

Fecking waste of wine, says Grace, smiling.

Cast thy champagne upon the waters, for it shalt sweeten all that salt, says Nicholas, smiling.

Thank you, each and every one of you, for coming this evening, says Declan, earnestly. And special thanks to Stella for all the beer. Speaking of which the first round is on me.

Sometimes in a town a small event grows into a big event. No one plans it, no one directs it. It just happens. It happens with wedding receptions and funerals and sporting events. Spontaneous parades after the high school team shockingly wins the league title. Hilarious evenings in the pub when a boat comes in loaded to the gunwales. Poignant evenings in church when a child thought drowned is found wandering dazed in the woods. Testimonial dinners. The Fourth of July. Car-wash afternoons that get wetter and funnier as the day wears on. Farmers' markets that turn into block parties. Block parties that morph into neighborhood parties that last deep into the night and in the morning when you go to get the newspaper you see the street littered with beer bottles, lawn chairs, several bicycles, two folding card tables, torn bunting, scraps of cookies, tiny volcanoes of charcoal ash from grills and hibachis, hamburgers burnt to the color and consistency of charcoal, uncooked hot dogs, wine bottles, paper cups, plastic cups, two broken frisbees, a bra on a bush, and someone's mangled eyeglasses.

In such a way did the rechristening of the *Plover* after its repair and renovation become an Event, morphing from three crew members and two dozen friends and family gathered at the main dock to what Michael the cop estimated at nearly a hundred people crammed laughing brawling kissing shouting weeping yelling wrestling grinning into the pub long past its official closing hour of two in the morning. Not even Michael, usually a stickler for rules and regulations as the fair bounds of human concourse, had the heart to close down the pub; and when Declan, with a half-drunk's lurching majesty and rubbery grace, hopped up on the bar, Stella rapping at his legs with a mop handle to get him off, and grandly bought the last round of the night, Michael accepted the pint that Stella poured for him, and sipped it long, and toasted the *Plover*'s return to the sea. Then he did, without fanfare, with professional skill and calm, shut down the pub, table by table, group by group, couple by couple, with a quiet word; but he also without fanfare drove the incapacitated to their homes. Stella counted three round trips and seven passengers total for Michael before she too, after mopping the floor, went upstairs to bed.

40.

As he drove through the moist salty night with his singing or sleeping passengers Michael hummed Puccini but the rear of his mind was preoccupied with a big brown coat. If the guy was smart he'd ditch that coat right off, he thought. The coat's a marker. The kid mentioned it, Cedar and Worried Man mentioned it, the guy was photographed in the coat at the station. He's smart enough to know we'll be looking for the coat. But he needs a coat. The nights are cold. He needs food. He needs a bed. He won't go back to Trailer Town. He'd know we are watching it. He's long gone. The guys at the station say so. But I don't think so. I think he's here. He's angry. He wants revenge. He's humiliated. He'll want to get even with Cedar. He knows Cedar. He knows where they work. Did he see Worried Man? Does he know Maple Head? And he wants Kristi. He doesn't know where she is. He'll hang around the school looking for her. He'll hang around Public Works looking for Cedar. Cedar can take care of himself. Maple Head is a slip of a thing, though. I'll swing by their house with my lights off. Just in case. You never know.

41.

Maple Head has read every account of the birth of Neawanaka, which is to say that she has read both of them: *Some Annals of Neawanaka*, a booklet published privately in a limited edition of fifty copies by a Presbyterian minister named Youatt in 1901, and the mimeographed transcript of an interview with her father-in-law Sisaxai, recorded just before his death in 1933. The interview had been part of a high school oral history project, and the transcript, which ran for more than fifty pages, was wholly unedited, and so it faithfully recorded Sisaxai's riverine speaking style, which veered off without warning into disquisitions on plants, animals, women, songs, myth, lore, medicine, spirituality, politics, timber, oceanic current patterns by season, music, bone density, skin grafting, geology, ethnobotany, evolution, literature, tribal relations in Oregon pre- and post-contact, Captain Robert Gray, sexual practices, dreams, *more* sexual practices, Captains Meriwether Lewis and William Clark, sculpture, his wife Wocas, food, one last note on sexual practices, and the peculiar character of their young son Billy.

However Sisaxai did also mention three times in the course of his lengthy interview (which so addled the high school girl who interviewed him that she went on to later earn a doctorate in journalism) that Neawanaka had begun at the source of the Mink River. He gave three wildly different accounts of the town and the river, Maple Head noted with a smile, but in all three stories the place of nativity was clear: the town was conceived at the place where a spring emerges from the side of a hill that looks like a woman's breast.

In one story Asayahal, the south wind, emerged from his cave on that hillside, and fell in love with Xilgo, the wild woman of the winter surf, whom he could see from his hill, tossing her long white hair, and he cracked the hill with his fist and made the river come out to carry him to her.

In the second story—told with the same complete assurance as the first—Asayahal, the south wind, grew so angry with the People that he blew ceaselessly for a month, drying up the creeks and streams and rivers, withering the trees and plants, choking the animals and birds with dust, until finally little Mink, brave beyond her size, bit into the very rock itself and brought forth the river named for her.

In the third story—told with such confidence that you would swear the teller had never even considered, let alone just *told*, any other possible story of the river's birth—a woman named Queku became very sad and went off alone into the hills looking for hope. She wandered for one year, never resting in the same place more than one night. At the end of one year she was still without hope and she sat down on a rock to make an end of herself. She was a magic woman, a spirit doctor, a *sisasun*, and she thought she would try to suck out the hopelessness in her blood, so she cut her arm and sucked out some blood and spit it on the rock, and out of the rock came living water, clear and clean, a bright wriggling hopeful singing river, and she stretched out and let the river flow under and over and in and through her and hope came back into her and she was healed.

So say I, Sisaxai, and what I say is true, and I tell it so that you who hear it may be healed too.

42.

Declan takes the day off and Grace and Nicholas take the *Plover* out for halibut. They check gear before they go.

Bait? says Grace.

Salmon heads, says Nicholas, and mackerel guts, octopus, herring, crab, cod guts, and squid.

Jigs?

Lead heads, darts, zingers, stingers, spinnows.

Line?

Kevlar 80 and 120.

Beer?

No beer at work.

Huh. Lifejackets.

Two.

Float suits.

Two.

Beer.

No beer at work.

Brains.

One—mine.

Piss off, says Grace cheerfully, and guns the throttle and they roar out.

Neither says anything for the longest time as the boat hums and slices west into open water. The morning is clear and calm. They see a pod of sea lions heading south. They share coffee. Grace drives and Nicholas dozes in the stern. The water gets bluer. They see a solitary humpback whale big as a bus.

A few minutes later they stop over what Grace says is a valley on the sea floor and they set out their long lines. They have another sip of coffee.

Wonder if Declan is out of bed yet, says Nicholas.

Better be. He's supposed to sell the fecking cows today.

Really? The whole herd?

The cows were my dad's thing. We kids hated them. All that mud and shit and work. We hated it. It was some kind of Irish thing for my dad. Connection to the land. Connection to shit and snot machines, if you ask me. I'd be happy to never see another cow ever. My kid brothers have to take care of them now and they hate it more than me and Declan did.

What will you do for money?

Fish, I guess.

What about Peadar and Niall?

They still have years of high school.

You like fishing?

It's better than mucking with cows.

They pull in lines and up come three small halibut, a vermilion rockfish that is the reddest thing Nicholas has ever seen, and a ling cod with a gaping mouth the size of China. They clean and ice the fish. Gulls wheel and dive at the offal flung into the water.

See? No snot, no shit, and birds clean up after you, says Grace.

Can I ask you a question? says Nicholas.

No.

Do you miss your dad?

No.

Is your mom dead?

No.

Should we bait up again?

Yes.

Am I bugging you?

Yes.

I'll stop talking.

No.

43.

Declan rattles into town in his truck for his appointment at the bank. He is to meet an estate appraiser named McCann at ten in the morning. They were friends as boys. McCann has been out to the farm twice, has walked the boundary, has been in contact with state and county agricultural organizations as to the present value of cattle and land, and has a sheaf of reports as thick as his hand to show Declan.

Cut to the chase, Dennis, says Declan. What's it all worth?

Less than you want, says McCann.

How could that be?

No one wants the cows and the land isn't zoned residential.

Meaning what?

No one wants the land either. If you can't build houses on it facing the sea then it isn't worth much.

It's decent farmland now, after a century of fertilizer.

It's mud if there's no buyer.

This is a joke, Dennis. A fecking joke. My father spent his whole life on that land. It's cleared, well-watered, decent soil, a hillside view of the ocean. It can't flood and there's acres and acres of it. And most of it is forested.

You could log it.

Then it wouldn't be forested, would it, Dennis?

Don't get mad at me, Dec. I'm just telling you the facts. Property is only worth what a buyer thinks it is. If you have lots of buyers then it's worth a lot. If no one wants it then it's worthless.

Worthless.

Essentially.

Even the cows?

Especially the cows. The dairy market is very poor right now. I couldn't even find a taker for a donation. I called all over the county. Not even the ag schools or high-school ag clubs will take them. They cost too much to maintain if you aren't set up for them. Only a big co-op could take them and they're selling surplus now too. It's just a market thing, Dec. Don't take it personal.

Feck.

Sorry.

This isn't what I need right now, Dennis. I need the money. I'm fishing for a living, for Chrissake.

Hard work.

Fecking right it's hard. And I have to take care of my sister and brothers. It's not like the old bastard left us any money when the log punched him out.

Hard times, Dec.

Fecking right.

Sorry.

You want to buy six cows?

No, Dec.

The bank doesn't want 'em? Your own herd, Dennis. You'd be the only bank in the country with your own herd. Think of the marketing possibilities. Cash cows. We herd your money right. Photo op. That kind of thing.

I have another appointment, Dec.

I'll give you all the stuff that goes with 'em, Dennis. Milk cans, syringes, pasteurizers, all of it. Hell, I'll give you the barn.

Dec ...

We'll take the barn down *and* cut it up for you, Dennis. Free wood. That's good spruce, last you three winters I bet. Good firewood.

Dec.

Come on, Dennis. I need some help here.

Dec. I did my best. It's worthless. They're worthless.

Worthless.

Essentially, says Dennis with finality, and he stands up and extends his hand but Declan ignores him and Dennis leaves.

Declan drives home slowly, taking the long way home. It has begun to rain. He drives along the beach road, thinking of Grace and Nicholas at sea. The rain is a gray sheet. He drives along the river, thinking of his father. It has rained since fecking November, he thinks. He drives past the school, thinking of his brothers Niall and Peadar. Maybe it will rain until next fecking November. He drives up the long serpentine driveway to the house, thinking of his mother bumping down the driveway with her suitcase. Just as he steps onto the porch he sees a long low gray creature slipping fast and low along the far fence-line and he spins and grabs his rifle from inside the doorway and sprints to the corner of the pasture to get a shot at the fecking coyote but the rabbit-eared thing is amazing wily and slides away among the legs of the cows and vanishes into the trees. The cows startle and lurch. Declan is so angry that his eyes ache. He fires the gun into the rotting fence post, splintering it to bits, and then without thinking he swings the gun up and shoots the nearest cow in the ear, and then the next and the next and the next and the next and the last, the gun booming like a cannon, the dying cows moaning, the birds that had been sitting on the fence chaffing each other now flying away as fast as their wings can whip.

44.

Daniel Cooney has a long talk with the pain in his legs. He and his legs are in the bed by the window under the maps of the sea. The pain has a flushed face and hair the color of sand. The pain is restless and keeps changing shapes: now a thin man with thin hands, now a jay, now a fish of indeterminate species. Daniel tries to keep the pain clear in his sights but he can't seem to catch the moment of morph. He asks the pain to keep one shape but the pain says politely that it cannot. Daniel drifts and dreams. He dreams that he is swimming with sea lions through caves at the bottom of the sea. He dreams that his mother wraps him in her hair and lifts him from the bed and carries him to the sea. He dreams his legs have no flesh but are only bones blinding white. He dreams his father comes with all his tools jingling and singing and hammers him a new pair of legs made from the brightest steel. He dreams that all the shatters and splinters of bones in his legs are tiny fish quick and silver in the shallows of the sea. He dreams that he is in a country where all the people and animals and trees are made of salt. He hears the bugling of elk and the hoarse roaring of sea lions. He hears all the fish in the sea singing their songs. He hears a sighing and roaring and sighing and roaring and a high voice like a bird in his left ear and a low voice like a bear in his right ear and he opens his eyes to find his mother on his left and his father on his right their arms around him thick and soft as kelp his legs bathing in the swirl of the surf and the moon hanging over the shimmer of the sea.

45.

Declan walks back to the house and puts his rifle back in its rack by the front door and makes a cup of tea and calls the Department of Public Works. He explains what happened to the herd he used to have. Worried Man listens quietly. He discusses the matter with Cedar who points out sensibly enough that there is now enough meat in the meadow to feed the whole town. Worried Man calls Maple Head for advice. She notes that it would be a useful public work to feed the whole town, and she notes further that the employees of the fish cooperative are expert editors of meat, and she notes further that alerting the entire population of Neawanaka to a free picnic the next afternoon wouldn't be especially hard if some husbands and doctors she knew used their evening circumference stroll to inform rather than to ruminate, and also that Michael the cop's patrol cruiser had a loudspeaker attachment, and that Daniel's bicycle brigade friends had a really startling range with those speedy little bicycles, and that Michael's wife Sara was a member of a telephone tree for expectant mothers, and that the priest was hosting a meeting tonight of his parish council, and that No Horses was the fastest runner on the planet and that such a stellar sprinter armed with suitable posters might very well paper every wall in town in a day, and that such posters could easily be produced on the printing press in the basement of the Department of Public Works if someone she knew would stop fooling around with pipe fittings and get his ass in gear on the printing press, and that Nicholas and his weightlifting cronies at the high school could very easily assemble hundreds of picnic tables under the astute direction of the engineering and carpentry professional Owen Cooney of Auto & Other Repair, and that George Christie the former logger could very easily assemble sufficient seasoned wood for a massive roasting and grilling project, and that all six grades of the Neawanaka School could very easily be assigned a natural history project to collect ripe salmonberries and thimbleberries from miles around in the morning, and that Stella at the pub would certainly not be averse to contributing a barrel or two of beer considering the public relations value of such a gift to the community, and that the O Donnell brothers Niall and Peadar were reputedly now past masters of the arcane arts of grilling and roasting beef, and that Rachel and Timmy and the other employees of the shingle factory could perhaps fairly easily be persuaded to assist in the distribution of food, and that various other people she could think of, if given a moment, could fairly easily be persuaded to cover dish duty, and that despite the pissing and moaning of some men she knows about lack of time to prepare such a public event, and lack of money, and how it would be easier to just bury the cows, that in her considered opinion a *real* Department of Public Works would *leap* at such a unique chance to strengthen the communal fabric, and make a silk purse out of the sow's ear, or cow's ear, of Declan's, ah, accident, and perhaps she was wrong to think so highly of certain Departments of Public Works that she knew, but maybe not, and it was her assumption that the men she knows would rise to their best selves in this matter, that she would be very disappointed if they didn't get hopping on this matter pronto and instantaneously, which is how an enormous and immense picnic was scheduled for the next afternoon at three o'clock, on the sprawling football field of the school, to commence as school let out early for it, all invited, bring your friends, bring your appetite, all the meat you can eat, courtesy of the O Donnell family, in celebration of the unique character, history, and communal good will of Neawanaka, long may it wave.

46.

I'm going way out, says Declan. I am taking the fecking boat and going way way out. Tomorrow morning after the picnic. Way out is where the big fish are and I am going there. Enough of this day trip crap. Enough of what every other fecking fishing boat on the coast does. Enough of this fecking farm and the fecking mud. Let's shoot the moon. Let's go hundreds of miles out. Let's get us some deep blue water. Far away from here. Weeks at sea. Let's go for it. Let's do something big. A real voyage. We can fit out the boat for a trip like that without much trouble or much money. Are you with me or not?

Grace and Nicholas exchange glances. They are all three sitting on the rickety wooden steps of the farmhouse. Midmorning, just as the last tendrils of sea fog melt off the meadow and are caught in the fingers of the firs.

How far out? asks Nicholas.

Way the feck out, says Declan.

Ah … why? asks Nicholas.

To work the canyons.

What canyons? asks Grace.

There's a whole line of deep canyons off the edge of the continental shelf, says Declan. From Rogue Canyon, sixty miles off the mouth of the Rogue River, to Astoria Canyon, a hundred miles off the mouth of the Columbia. That's the shelf line and that's where the lunkers are and we are going to get them and get us some serious money. Bluefin tuna, marlin, swordfish, and halibut bigger than the boat. I need big fish. I need big money. I'm tired of this chickenshit. Tired of banks and loans and payments. I'm going for it. I'm shooting the moon. You with me or not?

For how long? asks Grace.

Long as it takes, says Declan. We can clean and ice the catch on the boat and stay out for a week. Then back in to sell and then out again. Long trips. Big fish. We'll be rich by the end of summer. We can sell this place for the nothing it's worth and do whatever we want, Grace. Live in town. Move to California. Hell, move to Japan or Africa or Mars. We don't have to stay here. The boys can finish school anywhere. What are we here for, anyway? You should be in college. We're only here because we're here. Mom left and the old man is gone and the cows are gone. So what say? You with me?

Lemme think about it, says Grace.

Nicholas?

Ah, I don't know, Dec. Working days is one thing but weeks away is another. I'll have to ask my dad.

You have to check with the guy who punches you out every day?

Back off, Dec, says Grace.

Ever hit him back, Nicholas? says Declan. Because I would.

Back *off*, Dec, says Grace.

I'd punch his fecking face in, says Declan, standing up slowly. I punched my fecking old man and I'd punch yours. Feckers.

I don't think I'll be on the boat tomorrow, says Nicholas, also standing up.

I don't think you have any fecking balls at all, says Declan.

Jesus, Dec, shut *up*, says Grace, jumping up.

See you at the picnic, Grace, says Nicholas grimly, turning away.

Yeh, see you there, Nicholas, she says. Three o'clock at the school. I'll be there early to help you with the tables. I have to run a couple errands first. See you there. Okay. See you there. *Ass*hole, she snarls at Declan, who stands smiling calmly though his face is webbed with jagged red lines of rage. What's the *matter* with you? Why pick on him? What's he done to you? You're a bully. You're just like Dad. You want everyone to be as mean as you. What's the *matter* with you? Take your fecking trip by yourself. Do the work yourself. He's not going and neither am I. *Ass*hole.

Fine, growls Declan, turning toward the house.

Fine, snaps Grace, turning toward the road.

47.

The manager of the shingle factory gives everyone the day off for the picnic, what the hell, sometimes you just do things for the hell of it, what the hell, but he comes into the office alone early to wrestle with numbers. Rachel and Timmy take a picnic lunch and go up to her friend's cabin on the Mink to make love all morning. The manager makes coffee and spreads reports and ledger books on a long table. Timmy makes coffee and Rachel spreads fresh sheets on the bed. The manager slowly eats an apple as he stares at the numbers. Timmy and Rachel slowly eat grapes as they stare at each other. The manager takes off his sweater. Timmy takes off Rachel's blouse. The manager unbuttons the top button of his shirt. Rachel unzips Timmy's jeans. The manager removes his eyeglasses and knuckles his eyes. Timmy removes Rachel's underwear as she kisses his eyes. The manager studies income. Timmy slides into Rachel. The manager studies expense. Timmy comes immediately. The manager curses at the numbers. Timmy curses in embarrassment. The manager rubs his jaw as fervently as if his chin was a magic lantern and a spirit might appear to make everything all right. Rachel strokes the soft hairs on Timmy's chin and tells him it's all right. The manager leans back in his chair and moans in despair. Rachel leans back in the bed and moans in delight. The manager leaps up and paces around the room. Timmy leaps up and paces around the room. The manager reaches into his briefcase. Timmy reaches into his backpack. The manager brings forth a small battered leather wallet from which he extracts a handwritten note from his father that has been folded and unfolded so many times the quadrants of paper are held together by the merest faintest latticework of fibers. Timmy brings forth a small square black box with a filigreed silver hinge and a thick velvet lining like the fur of a mole. The manager reads the note written to him by his father fifty years ago when he was a boy and his father had just borrowed four thousand dollars to start the shingle factory. Timmy kneels naked by the side of the bed and opens the box in which there is a ring. The manager kneels by the side of his desk in his office.

I have to shut down the factory, whispers the manager.

Will you marry me? says Timmy.

No! says the manager. No!

No, whispers Rachel. No.

IV

1.

Dawn. A pregnant green moist silence everywhere; and then the robins start, and the starlings, and the jays, and the juncos, and the barred owl closing up shop for the night, and a hound howling in the hills, which starts a couple other dogs going, which sets a guy to shouting at the dogs to shut *up* for chrissake, and someone tries to get a recalcitrant truck going, and the truck just can't *get* going, it gasps and gasps and gasps, which sets the owl going again, which sets the mice and shrews and squirrels nearby to chittering, which worries the jays and robins, everyone has the owl shivers, and then the truck *finally* starts but then immediately dies, which sets the driver to cursing steadily feck feck feck which sets his passenger to giggling and the passenger's giggle is so infectious that the driver can't help but laugh either, so they sit there laughing, which sets two crows laughing, which sets the hound to howling in the hills again; and then another car across town starts and a church bell booms brazenly and a house alarm shrills and three garage doors groan up at once and a gray whale moans offshore and there are a thousand thousand other sounds too small or high to hear, the eyelids of a thrush chick opening, the petals of redwood sorrel opening, morning glory flowers opening, refrigerators opening, smiles beginning, groans beginning, prayers launching, boats launching, a long green whisper of sunlight sinking down down down into the sea and touching the motionless perch who hear in their dreams the slide of tide like breathing, like a caress, like a waltz.

2.

Owen Cooney is up early and eager because today is the day he is going to carry Daniel home from the doctor's house, and today is the day No Horses says she is going back to work in the studio after some long talking walks with the doctor and her mom and her dad and her husband about what No Horses calls the black dog at her heels, and today is the day of the picnic with all the meat you can eat courtesy of Declan O Donnell, and Owen is in charge of assembly and disassembly of the tables, and also today is the last day of equipment preparation before Owen drives Worried Man and Cedar to the foot of the mountain where they are to set forth on their voyages, and Owen feels very responsible indeed for the engineering and mechanical quality of the mountaineering material in question, he swore and vowed and promised No Horses that he would fourple-check the ice axes, crampons, carabiners, skis, ice screws, ice saws, pickets, belay loops, snowshoes, shovels, knives, batteries, compasses, flashlights, headlamps, first-aid kits, watches, radios, and whistles Worried Man and Cedar would carry, and finally he wants to bring Daniel's repaired renovated and restored bike from the shop to the house so it will be waiting gleaming glittering cheerfully in Daniel's room when Owen carries him up for bed that night after the picnic, so Owen is up with the first tentative tendrils of dawn (No Horses stirs but doesn't wake) and dresses in a flash (no shirt no socks) and is out of the house (scattering a chitter of sparrows on the fence) and strolling along the river (leap of salmon, float of heron) and into the shop (soon redolent of coffee) when the sun finally peers over the eastern ridge and fills the shop with light just as Moses floats through the window and takes up his spot on the old football helmet.

Morning, bird.

Morning, man.

Busy day before us, Mo.

A most interesting day.

I'll say.

I worry about the mountain, Owen.

Well, my friend, they are set on it, so …

Still.

I know. Me too. That's why I am going through these piles of stuff.

Is Nora worried?

Yep.

Is Nora okay?

Owen stops tinkering with the carabiners and looks up at the crow.

I don't know, Moses, he says slowly. She's drained. Empty, she says. But she said last night she wanted to work today. First time she's said that in days. That's a good sign. And she wants to come to the picnic. And Daniel coming home will give her a lift. I don't know what to do. I want to help but I don't know what to do. Somehow she lost her compass. Her engine failed. Her gyroscope broke. She's … lost. She says the road she was on isn't there any more and she doesn't know where to walk now.

I'm very sorry.

Moses, do crows ever … lose their way?

O yes. I think it's a function of intelligence, Owen. The more complex the brain the more ways it can twist and turn. We are electrochemical beings. Anything can go wrong. I have seen crows go blank. I have seen crows deliberately cause their own deaths. I had a friend who dove into the sea. She was a most amazing creature. She had the most amazing capacity for languages. She could speak with any other creature. She had a most astounding mind. Something happened to her and she dove into the sea in a thunderstorm and she never came back up. I think of her every day. I think perhaps she is a fish now. She was a most remarkable creature. I think of her at dusk. When the light is blue and black and brown and everything smells like salt and sand and spruce I think of her. I think of her every day. She was a most remarkable creature.

3.

Enter into the rock, into the holes of the rocks, and into the caves of the earth, into the clefts of the rocks, and into the tops of the ragged rocks, that's from Isaiah, says the doctor, stooping to pick up a rock from the sand and skipping it out over the quiet morning ocean. Into the clefts of the ragged rocks, Billy, that's where you are going. Are you really going?

We are really going, says Worried Man.

After the picnic?

Tomorrow at dawn. Owen is driving us.

Don't forget the medicine. It will stimulate your heart in case of arrhythmia.

I won't forget.

I'll give you a second bottle.

Okay.

I'll look in on May.

I'd be grateful.

Maybe I'll ask her to marry me.

I'd be hateful.

They walk along the beach silently for a moment.

I'll miss our walks, says the doctor quietly. The evening ones especially.

Me too.

I have come to depend on them for clarity and perspective.

Me too.

And for the startling talents of my friend who can sniff out pain and trouble.

You know, says Worried Man so quietly that the doctor has to strain to hear him over the lap lap lap of the patient ocean, I am tired of pain.

I know the feeling.

I have smelled it all my life and I am tired of it.

Yet we are professionals, Billy.

Mm.

Who volunteer for other people's pain.

Mm.

To carry their pain.

Mm.

To heal their pain.

Mm.

But we don't, do we?

We ... what?

We hardly matter most of the time.

What?

We don't, Billy. We make our holy gestures, we conduct our intricate and complicated rituals, we apply salves and poultices, elixirs and potions, and people remain broken and torn. The best I can do is just witness the pain. Just stand there and watch it eat my patients. I can't help the man who sold boxes and containers. He will die before Tuesday night. Mark my words. I wave my arms and apply magic liquors but nothing really matters. I can't help Kristi. She's broken in places you can't see. I wave my arms and say magic words and they don't matter. I am like your father who used smoke and spit and magic words on his patients. Sisaxai, the healer with two hands. With the healing sign carved on his bed, carved by the woman he loved. I have no sign on my bed. I have no woman. I have no magic. I just stand there and watch. That's what I do. Pain comes to me and I wave my arms and conduct my intricate rituals, as ephemeral as the wind, as insubstantial as shadows, as elusive as smoke.

4.

Cedar at his work table at the Department of Public Works is thinking about money again. Because there is no money in town people do all sorts of things to get money. Stella the bartender for example collects ferns and thyme and cedar needles and dries them and packages them in sachet bundles. Maple Head applies relentlessly and tirelessly for grants from historical societies and cultural associations and preservation agencies and any and all other grant-issuing entities whose mission statements emphasize the preservation and promulgation of regional character and heritage. Declan O Donnell has done the odd bit of quiet fishing and hunting out of season, on the theory that seasons are really ephemeral administrative ideas and bonehead legislative dodges anyway, and he has also quietly logged here and there without what you might call a permit or permission, and he has also engaged in what he calls entrepreneurial agricultural production but Michael the cop has called illegal marijuana production. No Horses briefly executed commissions for what turned out to be a short-lived company selling authentic genuine handmade carvings of totem animals by living American Indian artists and craftspeople none of whom actually received a check for her or his work and some of whom continued to receive notices of bankruptcy proceedings long after she or he had forgotten that peculiar chapter in her or his artistic career such as it was.

George Christie the former logger tried his damnedest for the longest time to get his beloved logging museum up and running, said museum being as he said an extraordinary opportunity for the people of today to visit a place and a time fading away as fast as smoke and fog, a place and a time and a craft and a breed of men and women with their own lingo and tools and humor and horrors and style and skills and stories and pride in their work, which was of a kind never done before and never to be done again in Neawanaka and environs whereas only the once would men and women of such strength and courage come to the woods to drop the big trees with respect and awe in their hearts and a crosscut saw the size of a boat in their meaty hands, but that time has well passed and even the memory of it is fading faster than the kids of today can spit on its coffin as it trundles by pulled by draft horses of the kind that were once endemic and necessary in these very woods.

Cedar grins and winces as he remembers what George Christie did to the beautiful cedar and spruce cabin he had built with his own hands to house his beloved logging museum. He chopped it down, alone, working every day from dawn to suppertime, and then he sawed and split the logs into firewood, and so burned his dream, as he said, so at least his dreams would provide some heat for his children, at least they would be good for that. Damn it all.

5.

George Christie the former logger stands in the DPW truck and pitches logs and splits down to No Horses who carries them two by two to the serpentine ranks of grills the O Donnell brothers Peadar and Niall have arranged for the picnic. After twenty minutes George and Nora switch places and after forty minutes they take a break in the cab of the truck where they drink beer and talk wood.

Lot of alder there, George, says Nora.

Lotta everything there, kid.

I swear I smelled juniper.

You gotta real nose there, kid. You work the wood?

Sometimes.

What does that mean?

I do some carving.

I seen your statues. They're good statues.

Thanks.

Ever cut your own wood?

You mean logging? No.

You should. Learn the wood when it's alive.

Well, I'll think about that, George. I certainly will.

Me, I like the big trees.

Spruce?

Well, kid, your spruce tree is a good tree, a real good tree, but I'm a cedar man, myself. Most important tree in the woods, the cedar is. Hell, your dad's people, now, they used the cedar for everything from houses to diapers. I always cut a cedar with respect. For one thing they get amazing old, more than a thousand years. Hell of a tree. Now, I would imagine working with a wood like that would be an amazing thing. That so?

I've only worked a few pieces, really. Mostly I use oak or alder.

Oh, hell, I'll get you some big old cedar. There's something special in an old cedar. It's seen an awful lotta life. It's a smart old thing and the smart stays in the tree. Sounds crazy but it ain't. There's something in a cedar just isn't in another tree. Not even your big old redwoods, which they are a hell of a tree also. But your cedar now, that's the tree of here. You gotta know the cedar if you want to really know these hills. I'll get you some really old cedar and that'll get you going something amazing. It's a hell of a tree, kid. I'll get you some.

Thanks.

Well, kid, glad we had this talk. Let's get to work. Listen, you gotta learn to quiet down a little. I don't mean to get on your case or anything but we gotta lotta work to finish here. You gotta learn to let the other guy say something sometimes. That's only fair. You know what I mean? You take turns. That's only fair. What the hell. Here we go.

6.

Michael the cop walks the perimeter of the football field with Cedar just to make sure that there are no obvious safety problems considering the size of the crowd expected. They argue cheerfully about whether or not this event should fall under the purview of the police department, which is charged with public safety and civic order, or the public works department, which is charged with civic safety and public order. The day has opened into that fat heat that presages real summer, the sort of broad heat that has young men shirtless, babies peeled down to shirts and diapers, and old folks carefully removing their blazers and jackets and draping them primly on the rickety folding chairs. The tables are all set up and the wrestling team is finishing the chairs. Frisbees float in the distance. Dragonflies and damselflies drone by like tiny glittering airplanes. Owen and Grace rattle off in Owen's truck headed back to his shop to get ten more tables. Swallows swim and swifts slice the gleaming air. Maple Head leads a giggling gaggle of girls in unrolling and cutting butcher paper into tablecloths and taping the paper to the tables. Two ground-squirrel kits who graze the field every morning after the bell for school rings wander up over the bluff edge of the field unconcernedly and freeze with horror at the incredible welter of human activity before sprinting away in the desperate zigzag tail-high way of ground-squirrel kits who hear a hawk or feel a fox somehow somewhere staring. George Christie the former logger is cursing cheerfully at the O Donnell brothers Peadar and Niall as they try to get all George's wood burning properly to be coals properly at three o'clock when the damn picnic is scheduled to start if ever yer damn brother shows up with yer damn meat. Gulls wheel overhead clockwise and above them buzzards counter-clockwise. Declan rattles up in his truck with the meat. The priest joins No Horses and Anna Christie and Sara and Rachel and Timmy and Rachel's mother and the manager of the shingle factory in laying out knives and forks on the tables on which the butcher paper riffles and rattles in the breeze. A gleaming biplane drones by high above the shoreline like a huge dragonfly. A gray seal pops his head out of the near surf and cranes his neck to see what They are doing up there this time. You never can tell with Them, he thinks. Dangerous and riveting creatures altogether. Best to avoid Them, because They can and do and will bring you violence, and being anywhere close to Them is certain to mean pain, but They are so utterly fascinating, so unpredictable, so alluring, that you find yourself drawn to Them almost against your will, against your better judgment, against all sense and sanity, day after day after day, like the tide is drawn reluctantly and joyously to the moon.

7.

Worried Man and Cedar find a table under a spruce and sit for a minute and split a bottle of beer and handful of salmonberries that Cedar has requisitioned from one of the kids in Maple Head's sixth grade. The two men eat the berries and sip the beer very slowly. The kids collecting thimbleberries blackberries run past in pairs and trios with their buckets and bowls thumping against their legs. By now the football field is a seething laughing sea of people and smoke from the grill is pouring into the sky in a geometric gray curtain that obscures the coughing O Donnell brothers Peadar and Niall.

You know, says Worried Man, looking at his friend through the brown beer bottle, in the old days here, when the People set out adventuring, there was always a feast first. You wouldn't think of a major journey or voyage without a major meal. It was a sort of communal prayer. So the scent of grilling meat must be in the topographical memory of Neawanaka. The old trees remember it. Maybe the hills themselves.

And the sea.

And the sea. My grandfather now, says Worried Man, grinning, he used to tell stories about the great feasts he remembered. He said they always got delightfully out of hand. He said maybe that was what great feasts were for, to let things get out of hand. He said sometimes there were fights and sometimes there were trysts. Sometimes there were fights and then trysts. Sometimes there were fighting trysts and trysting fights. Sometimes the people who were supposed to leave in the morning were nowhere to be found in the morning. Feasts changed things. All that gathered energy.

And meat.

And meat. My father now, he used to say he did a lot of healings at feasts. People were more open then and sadness could be driven out. One time … Are you going to eat that last berry?

Let's split it. Be a good omen for tomorrow. Shared load.

They split the berry carefully, grinning.

How often have we done this?

Thousands of times.

Forty years?

I disremember exactly.

Let's say forty.

Times, say, three hundred lunches a year.

Or so.

Or so.

That's twelve thousand bottles of beer.

Or so.

A thousand gallons easy.

Or so.

And God knows how many berries.

God knows.

Does God know?

God knows. The doctor says so. Not a sparrow or salmonberry falls but the Father knows.

8.

The pub is filled with a rich golden buttery sunlight so dense and thorough that it seems for a minute to the doctor that maybe he is having an epiphany or a vision like Saul of Tarsus on the road to Damascus but when he, the doctor, pushes through the swinging screen door to the kitchen he finds Stella under the stove cleaning the grease trap. All he can see of her are the bottoms of her shoes. The bottoms of her shoes are filthy.

Stella?

I'm busy. Come back later.

I've come to help with the beer for the picnic, Stella.

Hang on.

She inches backwards and he watches her emerge feet first as if breeched from a dark metal womb.

Ah, doctor. Hang on a minute. I'm a mess.

He watches with a professional eye as she washes up.

Kind of you to help, she says, looking sideways at him.

Happy to help.

Place is a mess. Sorry.

I know the feeling, he says politely. My office is a mess. Books and papers everywhere. I should hire an office manager but I can't afford it.

I'd hire someone to replace me if I could afford it, she says, smiling. Funny how owning a place means you work the hardest and get paid the least.

Do you like owning the pub?

I used to, she says simply. Not any more.

Why?

I'm tired of it. The grease, the stench, the drunks. You see a lot. It's fun sometimes early in the evening, when people stop in for a beer on the way home, and there's that companionable feeling in the room. But then it gets edgier. More sour. And the work never ends. Cooking and cleaning, purchase orders, deliveries messed up, the staff drinking up all the profits, the breakage. It's a hard business. But so is your business, eh? I mean, you're in the business of fixing broken people. That must be hard.

It's hard when I can't help, which happens a lot.

Do you ... is it awful when a patient dies? I don't mean to pry. Sorry.

No, no. Well, yes, it's hard. But it happens and you have to ... adjust. You never get used to it but you have to deal with it. You do your best and accept what happens. It's hardest when it's a child, of course. That just seems cruel. That has happened to me eight times and I remember every taut pale face. Five girls and three boys. I think of them as my children somehow sometimes. Because I lost them.

Sorry to ask.

No, no. It's actually a bit of a relief to talk about it openly. I don't talk about it much. It's good to talk.

We better deliver the beer.

Yes, yes. The beer. Well. How can I help?

Thanks for talking, she says, watching the sunlight glint off his glasses.

Thank *you*, Stella, he says, making the slightest of bows.

All right then, she says.

Here we go, he says, but neither of them moves, not a muscle, not a finger, not the twitch of an eyelid, the dense yellow light filling the little kitchen, glinting off the pots and pans, the grill, the steel sink, the stack of empty steel barrels, the racks of mugs, the towers of plates and saucers, the mound of freshly washed silverware, the cracked wall tiles that had once been white, the scrawl of penciled phone numbers on the wall by the phone, the battered old yellow phone, the battered old yellow boots by the door, the battered old yellow door covered with yellowing notes.

9.

The smoke and smell of the grilling meat rises and spreads and soaks through the hills and draws the most heartfelt and genuine attention from a most remarkable variety of creatures in most every element. The bear who can smell meat from half a mile away cuffs her cubs into parade position and all three of them trundle cautiously toward the picnic along the old sand quarry road. The old bobcat who lives in the sand quarry and is gruff lord of all he surveys there smells the meat and has dark squirming visions of all the sorts of meat it might delightfully be and he too sets off evanescing through the salal and huckleberry thickets. The two adult eagles nesting in the third cove south of town, the one that you can't get to except by sea or air, the one where the sea lions haul up at low tide to preen and bake and flirt, actually float through a column of smoke over the football field on their way north to see if anything good to eat died in the river, and their awkward new daughter trailing them, still wobbly on her wings after only a few weeks aloft, veers to avoid the column of smoke, not quite sure if it's a sudden amorphous cliff or a really tall gray tree or what, and she nearly falls out of the air altogether absolutely while making a most uneaglelike sound, a sort of terrified *sqwork?* Elk and deer smell the smoke and know what it means and drift silently deeper into the woods. Cows smell the smoke and do nothing. Vultures see and smell the smoke and in the mysterious sky code of vultures they come from miles around, even from adjoining counties, riding thermals along ridges to get enough loft to turn and cruise the rising south wind toward Neawanaka, each one seeing the next one dropping toward meat and following it so there is a ripple of vulture in the air for many miles. The smoke swirls and eddies and intrigues dogs and cats, weasels and martens, butterflies and bobcats, snails and slugs, squirrels and scrub jays, crows and cougar, mice and voles, foxes and fox sparrows, gulls and geese, dragonflies and damselflies. Most of all the redolent greasy smoke rivets the lean intense raptors of the insect world, the clan of wasp and hornet, who rise humming from every dell and dingle and rill and hill, from their holes and nests and dens and secret humming caves, and turn to face the sweet smoke, and fire themselves humming toward its source as if from a thousand angry yellow rifles.

10.

Owen and Grace jounce in his truck toward Auto & Other Repair for ten more tables but along the way Grace says can we swing by my house, I hafta get my tools, so they do, driving up the ridge road and up the serpentine driveway along the pasture line where Declan shot the cows.

Ought to be a historical marker there, says Grace.

Owen grins.

They pull up by the house and Grace hops out and goes to get her toolbox from the shed. Owen turns off the engine and sits meditatively for a minute and then gets out and walks the fence line. The grassy golden meadow curves gently down into a dark ravine filled with the thick matted jungly stand of spruce and hemlock that Red Hugh never cut; a second meadow curves up from the shadowy ravine, and beyond that second gleaming coppery meadow is the endless green sea. The morning haze has burned off and Owen can see for miles and miles. Not a cloud in the sky. Goldfinches are working the thistle in the meadows and swallows are mowing the insects rising from the warming grass.

Is mo lau nad muir n-oited imma-rau, he whispers, thinking of his greatgrandfather Timmy Cooney.

What's that mean? says Grace, who is suddenly next to him.

It is many a day since I sailed on the sea of youth, says Owen. My greatgranddad used to say that when he was old.

Was he a sailor?

No no. He was a teacher, sort of. A storyteller.

Here?

Ireland.

He still alive?

Died when I was a kid. He was a great guy.

Sorry.

Yeh.

We better go.

Yeh.

They get back in the truck and as Owen turns the key Grace says, tell me about your family?

Not much to tell, says Owen. My greatgranddad survived the Hunger and had a son, his name was Cathol, who married my gram, her name was Maighread, and they had one son, my dad Martin, and he married my mum, her name is Maire, and they had me, and here I am.

How did you get here from Ireland?

Ah, there's a long story there, Grace. It'd take all day.

I have all day.

Short version is, I took a ship.

Come on. Tell me.

I ran away from home, basically, and got on a cargo boat in Galway, as a loader, and we went across the pond to Rio, and then around the Horn, and then back up the other side. The ship was supposed to dock in Seattle for repair work but by the time we came past here I had had enough. It was a scummy hole of a boat and I never got paid. So as we passed the headland there I jumped off.

Out *there?*

Yeh. I was a good swimmer, it was a calm day, I figured what the hell. I was young and strong and stupid. Nearly broke my neck. Nearly drowned too. Landed on the beach right near the doctor's house. I was *tired*, I can tell you that. I was never so tired in my life. Nora says I was born from the ocean like Cedar was born from the river. Daniel gets a kick out of that. I hear him telling his friends that his da was born at sea.

How is Dan?

Better. Doesn't get woozy like before.

How's Nora?

Good. I guess.

You guess?

She's, ah, not feeling well. Lately.

Sorry.

Yeh.

By now they are at Auto & Other Repair and they hop out to get the tables.

I had to store 'em in the auto half, says Owen, leading the way through an unimaginable welter and thicket of car parts and pieces of cars and towers of tires. You take five and I'll take five. They're not that heavy. Strong kid like you can handle 'em, maybe.

Piss off, says Grace sweetly.

The tables are stacked on an oily dark table in the oiliest dark corner of the shop and as they lean over to get a good grip on the tables their shoulders and hips and thighs align firmly for an instant, half a second maybe, not long, bone to bone, just long enough for Grace to shiver and Owen to cough. They carry the tables out to the truck, blinking when they emerge from the cool dark of the shop into the bright heat of the afternoon, and drive back to the picnic, talking about ships.

11.

The picnic gets louder and louder as the afternoon deepens. Near dusk Maple Head finally sits down to eat at a table in the end zone of the field under the uprights. Her daughter is there talking animatedly with George Christie the former logger and as Maple Head folds herself on to the bench and slices a piece of steak and sighs with pleasure at the masterful grilling job No Horses turns to her and without a word folds her arms around her and leans her head on her mother's shoulder and Maple Head is wise enough to say nothing whatsoever but to just sit and accept and savor these arms, this face, these tears.

Anna Christie the singer is sitting next to her husband rocking a little and she stares at the mother and daughter across the table and says nothing. Next to her is Michael the cop's wife Sara with one of her girls asleep in her lap and the other running around crazy with a bunch of other kids at the edge of the woods beyond the end zone. Sara is humming Puccini. Every time she gets to a passage where the tone deepens her baby kicks her in the spleen. The dusk deepens infinitesimally minute by minute, as if someone was adding grains of darkness to the bowl of brimming light on the field, and at exactly the right sifting moment for swifts to appear they appear far overhead, chittering and flittering, taking over the sky from the barn swallows, who swirl and whirl into their muddy tenements and fold themselves up tightly and cleanly as gleaming blinking blue and black and orange knives.

It gets dark enough for Owen and Nicholas and the wrestling team to ring the field with hanging lanterns, which cast gentle scalloped pools of light on the dark field. Talk and song and hubbub and laughter and shouts rise and fall. Smoke still towers from the grill and the O Donnell brothers Peadar and Niall are black-faced and grimy and grinning. Cedar finds a corner and has a long talk with Nicholas. The doctor and Declan O Donnell go to get the man with one day to live from the doctor's house and Declan carries the man in his arms from the house to the truck and from the truck to a chair by the bonfire and Daniel wheels over to chat and Kristi toasts marshmallows for the three of them. The night sifts down like charcoal mist. Bats take over from swifts. Worried Man quietly folds himself onto the bench on the other side of No Horses and takes her in his arms and she puts her head on his chest like a boat docking. Owen, passing by with Nicholas to fix the handful of burned-out lanterns, leans in and kisses his wife's turbulent hair.

Michael the cop walks the fringe of the field, no particular reason, just keeping his eyes peeled, not looking for anything in particular, not breaking up the teenage couples leaning against trees, not breaking up arguments, not even breaking up a wrestling match starting to boil over and ringed by shouting boys, just walking, just keeping an eye peeled, just keeping the legs loose, no problem, listening to the music, grinning at the teasing he gets from those who notice him, accepting a beer that Stella hands him as he passes the kegs but not drinking it, clapping the priest on the shoulder as he walks by, waving to a table of teachers, glaring at a table of boys drinking too much beer, just walking, just keeping moving is all, no problem, noticing as the old folks put their sweaters on and then their jackets and coats, noticing coats hung on chairs, noticing a coat made of gleaming silver, which turns out, when he casually walks over and looks at it closely without looking at it directly, to be the nylon lining of a coat that's been turned inside out, a brown coat, he keeps walking, no problem, keep moving, stay calm, no problem, but when he comes to the corner of the field where an old hemlock offers its ancient shaggy darkness he quietly leaves his beer on an empty table and steps under the hemlock and vanishes.

12.

That guy weighed about fifty pounds, says Declan to the doctor. I've carried fish weighed more than that guy. His wheelchair weighed twice as much as him. He can't have much more to go. The guy's all edges. His skin is like paper. Nice guy. Quiet. Was he a little guy before?

Not especially, says the doctor.

That's amazing, says Declan. You wouldn't think a guy could get that papery and all. You wouldn't think he could stay alive and all. He's hardly there. It's like all his insides got sucked out and all's left is the shell. Like gulls do with crabs that get caught up the beach.

He has what we call a voracious tumor, says the doctor.

So it's eating him from the inside?

Essentially.

Man. That's evil. Poor guy. You couldn't take it out?

No.

Man.

They both watch the man with one day to live as he sits by the bonfire. Daniel leans in grinning and says something and the man grins and Kristi kneeling by the fire grins and offers the man a marshmallow smoking on her stick which the man declines gently with a wave of his hand nearly as slender as the stick.

He loves the sea, you know, says the doctor.

I thought he was a sales guy.

That was his job, yes.

Did he fish?

No. He just loves the sea. He was born here, you know.

Yeah, well, I was born here and I hate the sea.

Really?

Well—I hate depending on it. I hate working it like it was a farm. It's alive, you know. It moves around. You can't trust it. It does what it wants. It's not like land. Nothing's ever the same twice out there. Never the same color or weather or smell or anything. Everything moves around. You find the best fishing spot ever and the next time you go there's nothing there. And there's a lotta ways to get killed. I might like the ocean if it wasn't my job. I'd like to like it from a safe distance, you know?

Are you going out tomorrow?

Yeh. Way out. Out to the shelf. I need big fish. Going alone. Grace and Nicholas bagged out on me. Chickenshit.

Why don't you take him with you?

Who—him?

He'd like that.

He's dead weight. So to speak.

Yes.

What if we get hit with weather?

What if you do?

He could drown.

Yes.

Oh.

Yes.

Well, hell, says Declan.

He told me he's never actually been on the ocean, says the doctor.

Well, hell, says Declan. I got room, I guess. Might as well. Poor bastard.

He'd like that.

What the hell, says Declan. I could use the company.

Yes.

What the hey.

Yes.

Poor bastard.

Yes.

13.

Me and a guy in a fecking wheelchair, says Declan to the doctor, staring at the guy sitting in the freckled light of the bonfire. What a crew. Never a dull moment at sea. See what I mean? Nothing ever happens the same way twice. Up is down and down is up. Whatever you think will happen will *never* happen and what you *never* dreamed of will happen for *sure*. It's the craziest thing. I stopped trying to understand it a long time ago. Now I just go out and come in. Gracie watches the birds and all but I just try to get some fish and not get killed. I'm a simple guy. I remember one time a reporter guy was at the dock when we came in, he wanted to do an article on the heroes of the salt sea and all, the decline of the fishery, the end of a way of life and all, all this literary poetical crap, and I had to laugh. I mean, really. The poor dope. None of us would do it if we could do something else, that's the funny thing about meat fishing. Guys who fish do it because that's what they do. Guys who hit the big day generally quit the life. They start fishing for tuna and swordfish and such, specialty fish for the Jap market. Or run charters for tourists. That's easier. You get paid even if there are no fish. Or like the guy in Depoe Bay who takes people out to see whales. Now there's a fecking gig—*watching* whales! You don't have to catch a thing except a sight of a whale. There's a gig for sure. He says it's the fecking future but I don't know. People need to eat. The thing is I like being my own boss and all but there's no romantic crap in it. Man, we laughed that morning at that newspaper guy. We laughed fit to choke. Fishing is heroic and romantical for about an hour. By the end of your first day you were never so sore and tired before in your whole life, and your hands are all bloody, too. Then you add up your profit and you realize you lost fecking money on the day. Right then you either quit or laugh. What else can you do? There was an old guy in Newport I remember that was the name of his boat, the *Quit 'r Laugh*. He drowned, of course. Went down laughing I bet. A huge storm got him out by Rogue Canyon. He must have laughed when he knew it was the end. What other end is there for a fisherman? What else can you do? It's quit or laugh. No truer words ever spoken. Or painted on a boat at the bottom of the sea.

14.

Maple Head, relishing the last of the salmonberries on their table as the bats flicker past like afterthoughts, quietly tells No Horses that she has decided to make a journey on foot to the source of the Mink River starting tomorrow at dawn, for two reasons.

One: to find the prime seep or spring from which the river begins its trip to the sea, such a primary spring being, in every culture on every continent, a place of healing and restoration, and it would be a very good thing for me to find such a place, for all sorts of reasons. Imagine how we could quietly bring people to the spring to be restored, Nora. The good we could do! Billy and Cedar talk about public works all the time, but what a public work *that* would be!

Two: to discover if the ocean surf can indeed be seen from the hill where the source is found, which would corroborate Sisaxai's first story of the town's birth, the one in which Asayahal, the south wind, falls in love with Xilgo, the wild woman of the winter surf, whom he could see from his hill, tossing her long white hair in a most alluring fashion. One of my theories is that you and I are related to Xilgo—all the women in our family, you know, for as far back as anyone remembers, had long rich curling hair like the surf. I mean, look at Daniel. That boy has hair most women can only dream about. Red black brown.

Plus kid, I need to stretch my legs, and get all those sweet wild voices out of my hair, and get away from the school for a while, and get out of town, and anyway your father and Cedar are off to the mountain on their own journey tomorrow, and the doctor says he'd like Daniel to stay with him for a few days more, so there's a clear stretch of days here for both of us, and the weather's fine, and it's high time for a trip. Will you come with me, Nora? I'd be very honored if you would. Just you and me and the river. We'll bring a little food. We'll pick berries. We'll tell stories. We'll rest. We'll walk and walk. Please say yes. It would be wonderful to just walk quietly in the woods by the river, you and me. We haven't done that in ages. Remember all the walking we did when you were young? In the woods and by the sea. You would hold my finger when you were little. I loved those times, Nora. Especially the woods in late spring, when everything is opening and everything has hope in it for a while. We would walk and walk, do you remember? Will you come with me?

Yes, mama, says No Horses, lifting her head from her mother's shoulder. Yes, I will. Yes.

15.

Cedar and Worried Man start clearing off tables. People are starting to drift home. The wind rattles the lanterns. Cedar organizes what remains of the wrestling team for cleanup duty. Teenagers in cars peel out of the school parking lot in squeals and screeches of rubber on asphalt. Raccoons slip onto the field and quietly snare meat and berries from sopping unattended paper plates and slip back overjoyed into the ragged fringe of the woods. All the hornets leave and the wasps think about leaving. Nicholas sits quietly at a table with his father and the priest and the two young women who teach second grade. A young screech owl wakes in an old spruce and shakes and shivers and stretches and steps out of its hole and gapes in amazement at the wild lights where usually she can cruise silently along the crewcut grass scaring mice and voles into motion and so to their sudden and piercing deaths. Owen reminds Worried Man and Cedar that he will be at the Department of Public Works building in his truck at dawn to take them to the mountain. The young owl thinks her jumbled and furious thoughts. Rachel tells Timmy that she has decided to quit the factory and go to college in the fall. A coyote approaching the field upwind suddenly smells Michael the cop standing in the shadow of the shaggy hemlock. Two yellowjacket wasps linger by the grill where shreds of meat adhere until Cedar says something quietly to them in their language and they rise quietly into the air and go home. The wind dies down to a whisper. The first stars appear and Maple Head whispers them to her daughter as she has done a thousand times over the years: Dubhe and Merak, the brother stars who point to Polaris, the north star, and red Antares to the southeast, and yellow Arcturus overhead, and blue Spica to the south; and across the table Anna Christie the singer listens in silence and then suddenly stands up on the bench and opens her mouth and fills the field with her enormous voice, singing a river song.

16.

Michael the cop is now only a shadow in the shadow of the shaggy tree. He wants a cigarette something fierce and he has to pee like a horse and his knees hurt but he doesn't move a muscle. He breathes slowly and carefully. He watches the coat. Once a boy comes by and picks it up and Michael tenses but it's not the kid's coat and he puts it back and runs on and Michael breathes again. Wait. Another time a man puts his hand on it but it turns out he's old and he's only leaning on the chair for support and he walks on and Michael breathes again. Slow. Easy. Wait.

Then the guy picks it up.

That's the guy

He doesn't put the coat on.

That's him

He looks around carefully.

Don't breathe

He walks toward Michael.

Don't breathe

Ducks beneath the shaggy arm of the hemlock.

Don't even think

Brushes past Michael by maybe two inches.

O

And walks off briskly through the woods on a trail kids use to get to the beach.

He knows the trail!

Michael counts to ten slowly and considers whether to nail him right here right now but it's too dangerous with people around he could be armed so he detaches himself from the shadow of the hemlock and eases down the trail after the guy one shadow in the vortex of another shadow their shadows moving through the shadows of the trees the ferns the bushes the whispering trees the watchful trees the murmuring trees. Below their twinned yoked moving shadows the hungry patient ocean.

17.

Grace goes to the pub after the picnic and downs a shot and then another and another and another and another and another and then picks out a guy and takes him out to his car and she tears open her shirt and he gropes her greedily but when the guy tries to kiss her she spits on him and kicks open the car door and stomps back into the bar and has another shot and then goes to pee. Some guy says something leering at her on the way to the bathroom and she tips his table over in his lap so there's wet broken glass everywhere. The backup bartender jumps out from behind the bar and grabs her by the shoulders and marches her out the back door saying c'mon now easy now c'mon now. She tries to spit on him too but instead she throws up. He dances out of the way cursing. The vomit splashes on the patio and chairs. He stalks back inside and slams the yellow door. She's on her hands and knees on the patio throwing up. Overhead owls, nighthawks, stars. She can't stop throwing up. Then someone is kneeling next to her holding her shaking shoulders. Fuck off, she says, choking. Easy now, Grace, says Nicholas. Easy now.

It takes Grace a while to quit throwing up but after a while she does and she sits down heavily with her back against the wall.

What do you want from me, Nicholas?

Nothing.

Then why are you here?

Heard you barking.

Everybody wants something, Nicholas.

I guess.

So what do you want from me?

Nothing.

Bullshit.

Why do you fight everybody, Grace?

I don't fight everybody.

Yeh you do.

Piss off.

You don't trust anybody.

Piss off twice.

You could trust me.

I don't know you from a hole in the ground.

Pause.

Why don't you try trusting me? See how it feels.

Why don't you go piss off?

I'm serious.

So am I.

Pause.

So you don't want any friends, that what you want?

Pause.

I asked you a question, Grace.

Piss off.

You got to throw up some more? I'll get out of the way.

Grace starts to say piss off again but instead she cries. Nicholas doesn't say anything. Overhead owls, nighthawks, stars. Grace stops crying after a while and she doesn't say anything and Nicholas doesn't say anything. After a while Nicholas unfolds himself from kneeling and sits down against the wall next to Grace. He doesn't say anything and she doesn't say anything and they just sit there for a while looking out to sea their legs pointing out to sea.

18.

The O Donnell brothers Peadar and Niall are sixteen and fourteen years old respectively and they are sick and tired of being the youngest brothers of a snarling older sister and a testy older brother. They disliked their dad as much as Grace and Declan did though without, as Peadar says snickering, Declan's whole oedipal battling the king thing and Gracie's rage that dad made mom leave or mom left because of dad or whatever.

Plus Red Hugh is Dead Hugh now anyway, says Niall.

Dead as a doornail, says Peadar.

They are sitting on the beach in the starlight drinking beer. They have had a lot of beer since the picnic ended.

Let's go surfing, says Peadar.

In the dark?

What the hell.

What the hell hey.

They fall down laughing.

We don't actually hey have boards, says Niall.

There's boards in the surf shack, says Peadar.

Shurf sack, says Niall and they fall down laughing.

They take two longboards from the safety shed where all that stuff is stored: ropes, life preservers, first-aid kits.

Shore stuff stored, says Peadar.

Hey hey, says Niall. It's awful dark. And cold.

Chickenshit.

And we are no good at shurfing.

What the hey hey.

They take good long swigs of beer and then madly dash out through the surf shouting. The water is so cold their balls shrivel and each boy immediately wants to sprint right back out of the water but that would be chickenshit hey. Peadar mills his long arms and zooms out through the brooding black walls and catches a swell and jumps up on his board and instantly falls off backwards which sends Niall into hysterics but then a wave dumps Niall too and he gets rolled good, sand in his nose and eyes and everything. As he surfaces desperate for air Peadar's board flies by his head like a ten-foot arrow and misses him by maybe two inches. Niall doesn't see it. He staggers up to the beach and sits down heavily, feeling sick. Peadar retrieves Niall's board and heads out again. As he waits for a wave he searches for Niall whom he sees huddled pale on the beach. Chickenshit. Then Peadar notices someone walking fast dark against the dark dune line at the very back of the beach. Then he turns to check the wave which is coming fast and then he turns back to see who that was at the back of the beach but as he does so he sees the water beneath him go pale as ice as a huge white shape slides by endlessly inches away from his face.

19.

It's a shark and Peadar is scared shitless. He grabs his board so hard his fingers go as white as the shark. He forgets the wave coming. The wave hits and he gets rolled. He holds onto the board as hard as he can he even wraps his legs around the end of it desperately. He tries to yell *shark* to Niall but it's too late he's underwater and he gags. He tries to keep his eyes open but there's sand and kelp in his eyes and his mouth and he gags. The wave smashes him against the bottom and his shoulder drags against the rocks and shells. He is gagging and choking. He rolls and rolls in the rocks. Sand in his mouth. Can't breathe. O god o god. The board smashes against his head o god can't brea where's th suddenly his head is above water and his lungs drag air in savagely along with sand and he chokes and a wave hits him in the face and knocks him underwater again he loses his board o god o god his foot touches bottom and he scrabbles desperately to get purchase and then his left arm is almost pulled *off* and he screams with terror o god! o god! and yanks his arm back as hard as he can but he is yanked right out of the water onto the beach screaming and kicking and punching and Niall is screaming and waves are crashing everywhere but Michael the cop has a relentless grip on Peadar's arm and he hauls the boy out of the hungry ocean yelling hey hey it's okay you're okay I got you I got you it's okay and then Peadar is choking and vomiting on the beach and Niall is crying and Michael is saying breathe breathe breathe all right there we go all right okay it's okay it's all right just breathe just breathe okay all right I gotta go I gotta go.

20.

Michael runs up the beach after the man with the coat. Across the sand toward the dunes. Last I saw he was cutting along the dune line. He'd hit the river and have to turn east. I'll cut through the bushes there and cut him off. He tries to run as quietly as he can but now he is cutting through salal and alder and fern and blackberry and salmonberry and the plants slap and grab at him. His knees hurt and his back hurts and the surge of adrenaline that rose when he hauled Peadar onto the beach away from the shark is ebbing. That was a huge shark. Have to remember that. Tell Cedar. Post signs. Huh huh huh he runs. Thinks of Sara and the girls. Don't think. Do. Move. Where is he? Stay cool. Move smoothly. No sudden motion. At the riverbank Michael stops and melds himself into the shadows and listens for anything that isn't river. Far away he hears the metallic clanking of the picnic tables being folded up on the football field. Hears nighthawks overhead. Wind sighing through spruce. He makes himself breathe evenly and listen to each sound individually trying to pick up any dissonance. That's the river. That's the surf. That's the wind. A rustling in the woods behind him. He tenses; and a raccoon waddles past toward the river. All right. Think. He's on foot. He doesn't know I saw him. Or does he? If he saw me with the boys on the beach. Shit. Shit. Okay. Think. He's either in the woods here or he's on the river path toward town. He has no reason to hide here if he didn't see me on the beach. Therefore he's on the path. Okay. Go slow. Quiet. Michael eases out of the shadows and walks along the path as quietly as he can possibly go which is pretty quiet. The river is loud. Where the path bends he slips into the woods for a moment to scout ahead. Still no moon. He tries to remember if there is a moonrise tonight or not. Suddenly a line from one of the books he reads to the girls at night pops into his mind: *goodnight stars goodnight air goodnight noises everywhere* and he smiles thinking how many hundreds of times he has said those words and then suddenly the icy barrel of a pistol is in his right ear and a calm voice is in his left ear: *don't move don't make a sound don't be a hero.*

21.

Anna Christie humming walks home with her two daughters and Sara humming walks home with her three daughters one the size of a bird inside her and No Horses looks around for Owen but as she rises from the bench to find him George Christie the old logger opens his mouth and out comes his cheerful growl.

Well, kid, here's the thing. Here's my idea. I'll plop her down on the table and you can study her from every old angle whichaway. Here's what I figger: we go into business together. I'll get ya wood and you cut her. I know where the good wood is and you know what to do with it to make it all arty and stuff. You're good at that. Everybody says so. I don't know jack about art but I like your stuff. It's not half bad. We can sell it to city people and stuff. Architects and retireds and that sort. They like fancy statues and art and stuff. We'll go fifty fifty you and me. Your problem economic wise is that you can carve the stuff but you are no good at getting it and selling it. My problem is that alls I know is wood.

I need the money is all. I don't know art. I know wood. That I know. I know wood good. So whatya say, we partners? We'll need a business name. You figger that. You're smart. Hell, this'll be fun. I know where there's walnut twice as thick as you, and ironwood, and yellow cedar, and the biggest old hemlocks you ever saw. I know those trees. I known 'em fifty years or more. They're good trees, most of 'em. Some are bad apples same as people. Some are rotten but not many. This one old cedar now, he's the king of the woods, and could he talk he'd say hell, time for me to be some statues that'll send them girls of yours to college, George. That's what he'd say. I listen to the old buggers, you know. I ain't religious but there's a lotta stuff in the woods nobody knows hardly at all. So whatya say, we partners or what?

Let me sleep on that one, George, says Nora. I like that idea very much but let me think her over, as my friend George Christie would say.

All right, kid, he says. All right. Well, I gotta go. I aint young enough to be up so late.

Night, George.

Night, kid.

Nora goes looking for Owen and finds him sprawled on a table in the middle of the field staring at the stars.

Working hard, Mr. Cooney.

I am that, Mrs. Cooney.

Got any room on that table for me?

Plenty of room right here on me, girl. Climb up.

Which she does and folds herself into him like a creek into a hill.

People will wonder what we're doing on the table, she muffles into his neck.

And just what would you like to do on the table? he says into her hair.

O no, she says laughing. Her breath a hot hole in his neck. No no. Let's go kiss our boy. There's a boy I know needs to be kissed way more than his daddy does.

22.

Michael the cop and the guy in the coat walk silently north through the dark woods to the river. Michael walks in front of the guy. For a little while the guy keeps the pistol in Michael's ear while they walk and then he holds it against Michael's neck while they walk but it's too hard to walk fast that way so he tells Michael to put his hands behind his head and walk fast along the path and if you do anything weird or try anything weird or say a word I'll put a bullet through your brain. Stay on the path. Just walk. Don't say anything. They walk and walk. Pretty soon Michael hears the river. He tries to stay calm and not think of the girls or anything. He tries to figure out the lay of the land. He ponders the gun. He considers that if the guy put it in his right ear it must be in his right hand. He listens to the guy's footsteps to hear if the guy is wearing boots or sneakers or what. He tries to gauge the guy's pace and wind, to hear if he's puffing or what. He tries to remember the guy from the time he saw him pressed against Kristi in the trailer in Trailer Town. Tall? Fat? He wants to talk to the guy to get him talking so he can figure him out but this guy is ratcheted pretty tight. Not a time to take a chance. Stay calm. They walk. It's dark.

Where's your car? says the guy.

By the boat ramp.

If it's not there I'll put a bullet through your brain.

It's there.

No more talk.

When they get to the river they don't take the walking path but instead continue right down to the riverbank where there's a little sandy rocky shelf. The guy makes Michael walk ahead of him along the shelf. East. The river is a little low but it's still fast and it's still pretty loud especially when you are right on the edge of it. They pick their way along the rocks. Michael is so alert that he's calm. He sees and smells and hears every sight and scent and sound there is. The guy's feet are quiet on the rocks. If he fires the gun down here no one will hear it. That's murder though. He a murder guy? Now they are on the riverbank below the parking lot and Michael pauses by the rickety little wooden stairs up to the parking lot. Up, says the guy. Michael starts to turn to look at the guy but the guy sidesteps deftly and puts the pistol barrel in Michael's left ear this time and says, Don't turn around again or I'll put a bullet in your brain. Go up the stairs slowly and walk toward your car. If there's someone there just say hi like normal and then get in the car. I'm right behind you. If you try anything weird I'll blow your head off. Go. Michael goes.

23.

Everyone is gone now from the football field and most of the tables are folded up and the grill is cold and the parking lot is empty except for one truck: Department of Public Works. You can just make out the DPW logo if you squint a bit—the heron, the salmonberry flower, the serpentine blue river winding through both. Behind the truck Cedar methodically packs small white sandwich boxes into larger boxes and then stacks the larger boxes in the truck. Each small box contains sliced grilled beef and a handful of salmonberries and a bag of potato chips. Each large box contains ten small boxes. There are ten large boxes. When all the large boxes are loaded into the truck Cedar starts loading large white jugs into the truck. Each jug contains ale from the barrels of ale that Stella brought from the pub. There are ten jugs. When the jugs are all packed Cedar takes one last walk around the perimeter of the field, checking for lost jackets and children, purses, smoldering embers, sleeping teenagers, live wires, confused older citizens, litter, shoes, whatever. Then he quarters the field and quarters it again, covering every square yard with his feet or his eyes, and when he is satisfied that matters are being left as shipshape as possible after such a civic bacchanal he climbs into his truck and begins his deliveries. He leaves one box at the doctor's house. He leaves two boxes at the adult center. He leaves three boxes at the homeless shelter. He leaves four boxes at the union hall where he knows full well the old loggers and sailors and fishermen and millworkers congregate too proud to visit the homeless shelter. He leaves seven jugs of ale at the union hall also, lining them up on the broad wooden railing of the hall so the first guy there in the morning will see them and be delighted. He drives up into the hills and leaves one jug of ale on Declan's porch. Driving back down he notices that the stars have faded. He leaves one jug of ale on Owen and Nora's porch. He notices that the night has changed from black to blue. In his truck he sits for a moment and looks at the last jug of ale. Your village priest, now, he'd sure enjoy that, he thinks, and he starts up the truck and swings toward the church but on the way he passes the old hotel and he grins and turns his truck toward the old cemetery by the beach where the old nun is buried and so as the first tender tentative tendrilled sunlight peers over the hills to the east there's Cedar on his knees by the old nun's grave carefully pouring the ale into her grass where it fizzes and foams for a moment and then disappears into the moist welcoming earth.

24.

Suddenly Cedar is very tired. He drives home. Home is a small house by the river. On the spot where he was fished from the river long ago. The house is round and made of cedar. Logs he found fallen in the woods. Hauled with a horse. Planed and notched and pitched. A house as round as an owl. All around it in green rows and colorful circles are plants from apples to zinnias. To the north, facing the river, a wooden chair for watching the river. To the east, attached to the house like a cheerful glassy goiter, a tiny greenhouse. To the west, a tiny yard fenced by cropped blackberry bushes in which grow a hundred potted saplings of trees from alder to willow. To the south, a tiny gazebo greenroofed with grapevines. In the gazebo three chairs. In the house three chairs. Windows everywhere of every shape and size. In the door a circular window the size of a face. Drawings and paintings everywhere covering every inch that is not window. No books whatsoever. On the mantel over the fireplace an osprey skeleton. No rugs nor carpets. In the kitchen three coffee cups. No music nor musical instruments. In the mudroom three sets of boots: hip, knee, hiking. No clutter whatsoever. In the cabinet three plates. No mirrors anywhere. In the bedroom three framed and mounted photographs. On the desk three paintbrushes in three sizes. One photograph is of Maple Head and her family on the beach late in the day late in summer, everyone disheveled and grinning. In the bureau three pairs of socks. The second photograph is of Cedar and Worried Man seated beaming at the rickety table in front of the Department of Public Works. In the desk three small machines: camera, binoculars, pistol. The third photograph is of a young soldier, broad of chest and brief of height, smoking a cigarette, shirtless, dusty, smiling, his helmet tipped back, standing by a campfire, legs splayed, utterly relaxed, rifle casually teetered on his shoulder, insouciant and childish, handsome and frightened, ancient and doomed.

25.

Michael the cop gets in the car and the guy with the gun slips into the back seat. Michael feels the cold barrel of the pistol at the base of his skull.

Start the car, says the guy.

Michael starts the car.

Drive slowly along the river road.

Where are we going?

Don't talk.

The dispatcher will call me.

Answer her normally. Don't do anything stupid. Figure it out.

Michael drives along the river road. His headlights pick out deer, raccoons, possum, once a coyote, green eyes gleaming like flashlights. He doesn't say anything and the guy doesn't say anything. The fir and cedar and alder and cottonwood trees make a dark tunnel through which the police car passes humming.

The guy takes the gun barrel off Michael's neck but Michael can still feel the guy leaning against his seat.

The dispatcher calls with a complaint of kids drinking on the beach and Michael says he will check it out. The dispatcher calls back a minute later to say don't bother because the kids went away.

Okay, Lizzie, says Michael.

Pause.

Where are you, Mike? says the dispatcher. You near the beach?

The guy in the back seat puts the gun barrel to Michael's neck again.

Just cruising, Lizzie.

Pause.

Could you get to the beach, Mike? Maybe check out those kids?

The guy pokes the gun barrel hard into Michael's neck.

I think I better just keep cruising, Liz. Maybe Jimmy can cover that for me, okay?

Pause.

If you say so, Mike, says the dispatcher.

Thanks.

Say hey to Sara.

I will, Liz.

And Mike—congratulations on the baby.

Thanks.

Bet it's a girl.

Bet it's a boy, says Michael.

The guy in the back seat pokes the gun barrel hard in Michael's neck again.

I better go, Lizzie, says Michael carefully. See you tomorrow.

You coming by here to file your report?

I'll get to that tomorrow, okay?

You tell me if I can help when the baby comes, Mike.

I'll do that. Gotta go now, Lizzie.

Okay. Night.

Night.

Where the river road intersects the road into town the guy scrunches down in the back seat for a minute but as soon as they are back into the tunnel of trees along the river the gun barrel is back against Michael's neck, colder than ever. The road begins to rise a little as they start up into the hills. The river is louder.

I have to piss, says Michael.

No, says the guy. Keep moving.

Not much gas left, says Michael.

You got enough.

Sun's coming up.

Quit talking. Quit fucking talking. I know cops. I know cop games. This is a game. No more talking, Mike, huh? You got a baby coming, Mike? You keep talking, you don't see the baby. Understand? Pretty simple. Don't play fucking games with me. I know all this stuff. You think you're the law. You think you can tell everybody what to do. You're not the law. I'm the law. I'm the law now. And I say drive. Got that, Mike? Answer me, Mike. Fucking answer me.

Yes, says Michael, and the car hums along under the brooding trees.

26.

The dispatcher's name is not Liz. The dispatcher's name is Ellen. She thinks fast. When Michael called her Liz the first time she grabbed a pencil and wrote down every word he said after that. She wrote the words so hard on her note pad that the page below bore the shadows of the words. When Michael's radio disconnects she immediately calls the other patrol car. Tonight the other car is a rookie named Jimmy. He doesn't answer. She runs down the hall of the police station as fast as she can go shouting for help. The night officer is a burly man named Roger. He is at the main desk. He comes flying out from behind the main desk in about a tenth of a second. Ellen tells him what happened. Roger checks the call list to see where Mike has been tonight. Ellen's hands shake. They run back to her phone board and she calls the other car again. This time Jimmy answers. She hands the phone to Roger. Her voice shakes. Jimmy starts explaining where he's been but Roger cuts him off sharp and tells him to cruise loose and find Mike.

We don't know where he is but we suspect he is not in control of the vehicle. We suspect an armed kidnapper. We're not sure if Michael is driver or passenger. Approach with caution. Don't be a hero. If you see him call me. Do not attempt to apprehend. Am I clear? Do not attempt to apprehend. Meanwhile I'll get as many cars out there as I can. Okay?

Jimmy says okay.

I did the best I could, says Ellen. I tried to keep him on the phone as long as I could so he could give me a code word or something. I could tell something was wrong. Not just the name. His voice was too careful. I could tell. I could *tell*. I did the best I could.

You did great, Ellen, says Roger, looking down at her over the tops of his spectacles. You did great.

For some reason he sees her like he has never seen her before, a brave small round woman in her middle years who takes an immense quiet pride in her work and does it well. All those hours alone at night by the phone talking to voices in the dark, he thinks. All those nights. You did great, Ellen, he says again, and reaches for the phone to call cars from nearby towns as he can but his hands are shaking now too and she picks up the phone and dials for him.

27.

Declan shoves off just before dawn and when the sun reaches the *Plover* he and the man with hours to live are two miles at sea. The man is strapped into his wheelchair in the stern and the wheelchair is strapped down also. Declan keeps a loose hand on the wheel. The man turns his head this way and that, looking and looking. Declan points out a pair of sea lions also going west. The man can't stop smiling even with the wet morning air whipping through him like he is made of paper. Declan points out whales, kelp forests, jaegers chasing gulls, a place where the top of an undersea mountain is only ten feet from the surface. The man asks a million questions. Declan gets the fishing gear ready. The man asks can he fish a little. Declan says how we gonna do that if you can't hardly use your hands? The man says maybe you can tie a line to my chair and when the chair shakes I'll yell. What if you get yanked overboard, says Declan. Then at least I can say I caught a fish once in my life, says the man, grinning. All right then, says Declan, and he sets a line. They fish for halibut for a while. A fish gets on his line and the man tries to yell but he can't hardly use his voice anymore either but Declan is watching him sharp from the bow and he gets to the stern right quick and hauls up a gleaming furious thing maybe a yard long wriggling and wrestling like a child in church. That's a chinook salmon, says Declan. What a stunning creature, says the man quietly. I'll clean and ice him for ya, says Declan. I don't think that will be necessary, Declan, to be honest, says the man, and Declan says o yeh, right, so he works the salmon off the hook and gets ready to throw it back but then turns and hands it to the man who holds it reverently grinning for a moment, all that wild silvery rubbery energy in his shaking hands, and then he hands it back to Declan who drops it back in the water. The fish holds there by the boat for a split second, stunned, and then with a flick and a shiver it vanishes into the green depths faster than you can blink.

28.

My garden faces south, as you see, says the doctor to Stella. They are sitting on his deck eating pears and drinking coffee. I calculate that the southern exposure is worth about twenty minutes of extra light over the course of the growing season here, which sometimes seems to be about twenty minutes long.

Stella grins.

Mostly it's garlic but there are some peculiar visitors there many of which have arrived on their own, says the doctor.

Windblow, says Stella.

I beg your pardon? says the doctor.

Windblow, that's when seeds drift in on the wind. A lot of plants issue seeds light enough to ride the wind.

The doctor leans back in his chair, delighted at the word.

You are a botanist, I see, he says.

O, I love plants, says Stella. That's what I'd really like to do, be a gardener. I used to want to run an orchard or a tree farm but I ended up with the bar.

You still want to run a tree farm?

I'd like to try. I'm not getting any younger. But I'd have to sell the bar for a profit and find a piece of land. Has to be just the right land too, with good drainage and southern exposure.

How much land would you need? asks the doctor.

Couple acres at least. I'd plant lots of fruit trees. Pears and plums and cherries. And I'd plant spruce too. It grows fast and I could sell them for Christmas trees. And grape vines. I always thought grapes would grow here but no one's ever tried. You have to plant them on the lee side of the hills and you'd need gravelly soil but there are some places here you could do it. I've seen some land I'd plant in vines. Some of that O Donnell land would be good vineyard, I bet.

You've really thought about this, says the doctor.

I have a lot of time to myself behind the bar, says Stella.

How did you come to buy the bar? says the doctor.

Windblow, says Stella, with a tight smile.

I see, says the doctor, who does see. One thing he has learned in his practice is to hear what his patients don't say; which is, he has often thought, more telling than their tales. He cuts another pear.

29.

After they stop to kiss their boy Owen and Nora walk home along the river and for no reason whatsoever Nora takes off running and she flies along the tide flat all the way to where the Mink River empties with a sigh into the ocean and when she gets there she doesn't stop but just dives right in like a slim knife. The river is black and braided and impatient. In two strokes she is across the river and standing in the brush on the other side. The world is silent except for the mutter of the river. Then to her astonishment she sees another runner arrive suddenly on the other bank of the river, popping out of the brush like a ghost. She can't make out who it is. The other runner steps waist-deep into the river and she tenses. The river hums and grumbles.

Sweet mother of Jesus, says the man in the river, I think my *balls* are frozen, that's the last time I ever pull a John the Baptist, and Nora bursts out laughing, the whole scene is so funny, him standing there wet to the waist, his hands out like a preacher, his long face grinning, and she's soaked, her legs quivering from her sprinting, the new sun poking like an insistent hungry calf at the cottonwoods crowding the riverbank, and she laughs aloud and holds out her hand and he takes a step toward her with his hand outstretched too like in the movies and the river pounces just as he steps into a deep hole he did not of course see and he disappears with a great splash and the river pours over him greedily and she grabs his hair and he scrambles up the other bank and they collapse into the bushes laughing and spluttering and then suddenly kissing as the sun vaults over the fringe of the trees.

30.

Maple Head is up before dawn. Worried Man should be up too but she lets him sleep. She looks down at him for a minute after she showers. He sleeps with his mouth open and his long white hair all tangled among the pillows. She slips into the kitchen and makes coffee. She packed for her trip the night before and a little green rucksack and ash walking stick wait by the door. She watches the sun rise from the porch. It hints at itself first and then announces itself melodramatically and finally arrives brilliant and searing between two young pine trees like two green fingers pinching fire. From the porch she can see a sliver of the river. She has seen this river from this porch for more than forty years. It may be that she spent more time on the porch than in the house. She nursed No Horses here in a wooden rocking chair and she read a thousand books here and spent thousands of hours listening. Whenever she needed to talk with a student from school she would do so on the porch; parents of students she met at the kitchen table or in her classroom. Sometimes the porch was fogged over completely in the morning and she would bundle up and watch the wind melt the fog away. At such times the birds declined to sing. The fog always retreated southeast. Sometimes she came out on the porch to get away from something sour in the house. Sometimes she felt the house was her husband's and the porch was hers. He had many ideas for the repair and renovation of the porch but she generally declined them. In summers sometimes she slept on the porch on a little foldaway bed. Above her the limitless seas of the stars. Sometimes she felt that the porch was a sort of boat. She never tired of the view: north to the river, east to the sandy hills that rose into small ragged mountains, west to the basalt cliffs brooding over the ocean. On very quiet nights she could hear the yelping of sea lions in the coves below the cliffs, and quizzical owls in the deep ravines the loggers never reached, where grew ancient hemlock jungles as thick as dreams. When the wind came from the west it bore the salt of the sea and the mossy shaggy dignity of the hemlocks. They smelled like grandfathers, she said once to her husband, who never forgot anything she said to him, and often turned her remarks this way and that in his mind long afterward, looking at them from different angles, wondering.

31.

The guy with the gun in the back seat of Michael the cop's car is no dope and he has no intention of shooting a cop unless he has to. But he also has no intention of going to jail. He's been in jail, twice, neither time very long but neither time very pleasant either. Once was the county jail and once was the state correctional facility. The county jail was essentially a workhouse and the state correctional facility was essentially a hell hole. The first time was for theft and the second time was for grand theft. Most definitely he is not going back to jail, no matter what. Most definitely he is getting into the next county and then he will figure it out from there. He knows that each county sees jurisdiction of suspects differently. He's read some law. He is no dope. Plus he knows a guy who knows a guy. High time to start over, he thinks. Past time. It's not like I have anything here to hold me. The kid isn't even my kid. No way she's my kid. She'll figure things out. She's smart, that kid. Her mother's a useless drunk but the kid's got brains. Five years on the county dollar and then she's eighteen. And she'll be a looker. She'll get by. Nothing to worry about.

But he finds himself sour thinking about Kristi alone.

Take that dirt road there on the right, he says to Michael.

They drive along the rutted road deeper into the woods.

Life in prison for killing a cop, says Michael quietly.

Shut your mouth, says the guy.

It's not like she's really my kid, he thinks.

Now that left turn.

What happened happened, he thinks. Things happen.

They pass a clearing where a wooden shack is falling down and Michael realizes where they are, in the old logging tract near the headwaters of the Mink. The shack was the cook house and after the timber company went belly up the shack burned when some drunk kids tried to light the old stove.

Now another left.

The county line, Michael realizes.

Now along the ridge.

Michael tries to slow down infinitesimally but the guy is watching him like a hawk and he pokes the gun in Michael's neck again and Michael speeds back up to thirty-five. He hears the guy roll his window down and feels the sudden air. The ridge was clear-cut eight years ago and the new spruce there is only head high and Michael has the odd sensation of driving through a crowd of green nodding people peering at the car. The county line is about a mile down this road. Michael thinks of everything he could possibly do. He could slam on the brakes and grab for the gun. He could swerve suddenly and grab for the gun. He looks in his rearview mirror and sees the guy looking out the window and he tenses his shoulders to swerve the car but just then there is a terrific crash as Moses the crow sails headfirst through the open left rear passenger window and smashes into the guy's face and the gun explodes and blows out the right front window and the car skids wildly and smashes into the wall of young spruces and there is a blizzard of feathers and glass and spruce needles and then a dense silence broken only by the chirruping of wrens.

32.

Worried Man was pouring coffee when he smelled fear so foul and immediate that he dropped the pot and scalded his hand. He grabbed the kitchen counter with both hands and felt for the fear. His hand seared with pain and his stomach lurched from the stench of fear. A man in a car. Two men. A nodding line of young trees. He felt the two men like two braided screams in his head.

May …

But she was already there, leading him to the sink and running cold water over his hand.

Two men in a car, whispered Worried Man.

Where are they?

Not far …

Bad?

Bad.

I'll call Cedar.

But Cedar's phone rang and rang and the Department of Public Works phone rang and rang and when Maple Head called the police department it was Ellen who answered, still on duty, unable to go home for fear of what was happening to Michael, and when Ellen heard that Worried Man had felt the two men in his head she began to sob.

Just then Owen drove up with Cedar to collect Worried Man for the mountain.

Okay, said Cedar calmly when Maple Head explained. Okay. We need eyes aloft. We'll send Moses.

Which is how Moses was aloft in the shimmering dawn; and how he swam up and up and up like a hawk until he could see the town below him like a buckle on a belt; and saw cars of every hue and shape humming and coughing through field and forest and lane; and saw finally on the eastern ridge a police car heading steadily south through the young green saplings sprouting like the tallest possible grass; and decided, no one ever knew why, not to speed back to Owen but to bank down toward the car; and how as he sped down along the ridge he saw Michael's grim face, and the hunch of the brooding shadowed passenger, and the blue glint of a gun; and how he folded his wings tight to his body, and curled his long leathery legs, and stooped wild and joyous and violent as a falcon, falling like a fist out of the new sun, falling toward the back window of the car like a bullet, all caution flown, filled with reckless joy, his last thoughts of the old nun who had one day found him fallen in the leaves, a moaning in the mud, a helpless gaggle of mewling bones.

33.

Just as Moses smashed into the man with the brown coat Daniel woke with a start. He lay there in the fragile light and stared lidded at the sparkling ocean stretching away from the long windows. His thoughts were blue and murky. He had been dreaming of his mother rocking him and he could hear the creak creak creak of her chair in his head. He rolled over to go back to the dream but his casts clanked and his knees woke up snarling and the dream slid away all raggedy like tattered cloth.

He sat up and rubbed his eyes and worked himself into his chair and wheeled out onto the deck. Gulls and terns were wheeling over the shimmering water and he could see cormorants diving in the surf and emerging suddenly with wriggling fish in their beaks.

Kristi came out in her pajamas and wrapped in a blanket and sat crosslegged on the deck. They both looked to the corner where the man who sold boxes and containers would usually be but the corner was gapingly empty.

He was the nicest guy, said Daniel quietly.

Yes.

What was his name?

I never asked, said Kristi.

The doctor knows.

Let's not know, said Kristi.

They stared out to sea but there were no boats visible, only the wheeling white birds and the diving black birds and the glimmering sea like a million shards of glass.

I'm going home today, said Daniel.

Today?

Yes.

Are your folks home?

No. My mom went camping with my grandmother and my dad is taking my grandfather to the mountain.

Why is your grandpa going to the mountain?

Sort of a science project. My gramma says it's a spiritual quest.

Is he religious?

Not like anyone else.

Isn't he kind of old to be climbing mountains?

I guess. He's tough for an old man though.

How are you going to get home? says Kristi.

I'm going to wheel home in this thing.

All the way up the hill?

Yup.

Alone?

Yup, says Daniel.

Can … you do that?

Yup, says Daniel.

I mean, is it okay with the doctor? Can you leave without his permission?

I don't know, says Daniel. I have to, though. It's time.

They sit silently some more and then Daniel says with his voice shaking just a little bit although he has taken deep breaths so it won't shake, Will you come with me?

Well, says Kristi, but she's facing the ocean and he can't see her face so he can't tell if she's saying *Well* as in *maybe* or *Well* as in *no*.

I could sure use some help, he says.

I doubt that, she says.

They watch the white birds wheeling and diving into the ocean and Daniel notices how they wheel smoothly until they see something promising and then they just plummet headlong.

Yes, I'll go, says Kristi. I'll go. We'll go. But first we have to do something about your hair. It's all tangled together. Did you wash it last night? Because it's all wild. It's all jungly. Usually it's in three braids, right? By color? My hair's not as thick as yours. Yours is to die for. Mine is all straw and spider strands. We better get some breakfast. We better talk to the doctor. Do you think he should come with us? It'd be fun if we went alone. I could push you. If you want. But I don't know. I guess I'm a little nervous. About going out there. But you'll be with me. We'll be together. And it's not far, right? Just up and over the hill? It'll be an adventure. Like a voyage. Like going to sea.

Like going to sea, says Daniel, and they look at the sea again, the birds whirling and diving into the glittering blue glass.

V

1.

Sometimes something changes you forever and often it's the smallest thing, a thing you wouldn't think would be able to carry such momentous weight, but it's like playground teeter-totters, those exquisitely balanced splintery pine planks with a laughing or screaming child at each end, where the slightest change in weight to one end tips everything all the way; and what tipped the doctor into a new life just happened a minute ago.

He was standing at his kitchen counter, having peeled and halved and quartered a pear for breakfast, and he had stepped to the left, to the sink, to rinse his hands, and dry his hands on a towel, and lift his coffee cup, and glance out the window—no reason really, just a casual look to see what's out there, a man might flick a million such glances in a lifetime—and he saw two boys walking toward the ocean.

Perhaps they were brothers. They seemed to be. Something in their faces, their squarish jaws, the set of their shoulders, the similar surf of their dark hair. They walked slowly. One was older by three or four years. Maybe he was thirteen. The younger boy was maybe nine. The older boy led the younger by the hand. The younger boy was cheerful and bubbling, peering everywhere with delight and amazement, chattering back to the wheeling terns overhead. The older boy didn't speak. He seemed intent on their destination, whatever it was. But he wasn't impatient, and he held his brother's hand gently. He didn't haul or pull or yank or command him; his hand was only a rudder for his brother's heedless ship. And the younger brother let himself be led with the most extraordinary faith and dignity and trust. His face shone. To him no harm could apply, no wound be inflicted, no seed of despair darkly flower, as long as his brother held him by the hand with such palpable patient love.

The boys walked slowly hand in hand to the corner and turned it and vanished, the younger one cawing like a crow now; but the doctor stood at the sink like a stone.

2.

Billy and May and Cedar carried Michael back to town in the Department of Public Works truck. He was unconscious. He bled on Maple Head's jacket. No one said anything. They took him to the doctor's house. The doctor was still standing at his sink. He ran out when he saw the truck. Cedar carried Michael into the office. He bled on Cedar's shirt. His feet dangled over the edge of the examining table. His shoes were lost. His socks were blue. He bled on the table. One sock had a hole in the heel. Worried Man called the police department. At the police department Ellen the dispatcher cried and called Michael's wife Sara. The doctor examined Michael. Worried Man called the hospital. Sara and her daughters ran out of their house and ran down the street to the doctor's house. Maple Head went out to wait for them. Concussion, said the doctor to Cedar, who wrote it down. Fracture of the collarbone. Fracture of the right elbow. Fracture of the right wrist. Deep cut over right eye approximately one inch long. That'll need stitches. Fractured right kneecap. Fracture left ankle, high. No other fractures evident. Help me get his clothes off. Cedar helps take Michael's shirt off. Worried Man waits by the phone. Sara's daughters arrive at the doctor's house. The young one is sobbing. Bruised sternum, says the doctor to Cedar. Sara runs up. *Major* bruises to the sternum. No other injuries evident, says the doctor. Boy, is that a bruised sternum. His chest is going to be sore for months.

Owen pulls up in his truck with the guy who used to have the gun. The guy was alive and unconscious and tied hand and foot with a thousand loops of fine wire from Owen's shop. The doctor examines him also. Six fractures. Cedar takes notes.

Sara, says the doctor, Michael is going to be fine. Do you hear me? All these injuries will heal fairly quickly and he will be fine. He will be back hale and happy. Do you hear me? All will be well and all manner of things will be well, Sara.

3.

Declan turns the engine off and the boat rocks quietly for a few minutes. The guy in the wheelchair has his eyes closed. Declan stares at the guy's face. Man, he lost another ten pounds in the last hour, he thinks, guy's going to fade away completely and there'll be nothing left but a wheelchair with a pile of dust in it.

Declan, says the guy softly.

Yuh.

I think my time has come.

The boat sifts against the sea and gulls wheel silently.

You want me to …?

Yes, Declan, I do. I would be very grateful if you would assist me in this matter.

His voice sifting down below even where whispers live.

Declan unbuckles the guy and lifts him out of the chair and stands him up. Feels like the guy weighs about twenty pounds, he thinks. Guy weighs what that chinook weighed.

The guy feels everything on his face, the wild holy world, the salt and the wet wind and the wheel of the birds, the hot sweet fingers of the sun, and then he stops thinking, he loses thought, he sifts down below where thoughts are, the last images in his mind as his lights go dim are his children when they were very small, the squirm and wrestle and tumult of them, the very last picture in his mind is them tumbling on a brilliant wooden floor, and then he's gone, and Declan is holding what used to be a man.

Very slowly Declan folds the guy back into the wheelchair and buckles him in again and sits quietly looking at the guy for a while. Then he lifts the chair onto the gunwale and scrinches it down to the water, holding on with both hands and bracing his feet against the slats. The guy's eyes are closed and he's smiling a little. His hair floats out around his head. Declan opens his hands and the guy and his chair sink endlessly into the green depths faster and quieter than you could ever imagine. The sea makes a little blurping sound as it drinks the guy and then there's no sound except the boat sifting against the water.

I don't know any prayers, says Declan out loud, startling the gulls, but if I knew any prayers, or thought they did any good, I'd say one for you. But I don't know any prayers, and I don't think they do any good. *You* did good, though. Amen.

He stands there at the gunwale another minute and then steps into the little cabin and starts the engine and turns the boat around and heads back to shore. He sets two halibut lines. He eats a sandwich. He sees a gray whale, two jaegers, a little whirlpool filled with sneakers and tampons and fishing floats, and what sure looks like the kind of little albatross that lives on Hawaii. Then, without any sort of momentous ceremony, he hauls in the halibut lines and turns the boat around and sets course straight west for where the sun goes when it falls over the rim of the world, and he stretches out for a nap in the stern, and the boat slowly putters into the endless ocean. The gulls follow, wheeling in huge circles.

4.

Grace and Stella are in the corner of the bar where fat buttery bars of sunlight hang out every time it is sunny which is, as Grace says, it's sunny like twice a year, you don't want to miss summer here, it's a great weekend.

The rest of the year is a fecking hell hole, says Grace, but she is smiling.

We can get this signed today with McCann, says Stella. You sure you want this?

Yup, says Grace.

And Declan is cool?

Yup. The land is in both our names and we agreed to make it pay however we could so we can take care of the boys. Dec wants them to go to college.

You don't want to go to college?

Nope. I got things to do. I got ideas. I don't want to study other people's ideas.

It's hard not to drink the profits, as if there are any profits, says Stella very quietly. Believe me I know. Believe me.

I believe you, says Grace, not smiling. I got ideas about me and drinking not being the closest of companions any more.

And the hours are long and you'll have trouble. Drunks, distributors skipping on bills, broken glass, sudden inspections, demand outstripping supply, supply outstripping demand. Whatever you think running a place like this will be, it isn't. It's like being a den mother for idiots, and there's a smell of stale beer and old grease that never quits. And the bathroom is always a mess, and no one will clean it for you, no matter how much people offer to clean it for you, they never actually get around to it, not that I am bitter or anything. And sometimes the field mice come in when it's cold.

You're being too persuasive, says Grace.

Got to be honest.

I'll be honest in return, says Grace. I got one word for you. Mud. You are buying a lotta mud. It's deep and evil and it smells like shit. It's always cold and windy even in summer. There's coyotes. There's skunk cabbage in the ravine and in March when the skunk cabbage flowers open it smells like shit more than it usually smells like shit. For every lovely day when goldfinches are surfing on the thistles and a falcon zooms by and you hear sea lions in the cove down below, there are a hundred days when it's cold and wet and muddy and it smells like shit. Also there's at least one huge cougar up there somewhere. Any questions?

They stare at each other for a moment, two sturdy flinty roiling fearful brave women, Grace with her chopped hair beginning to assume some sort of shape again, Stella with a cold face and the most gentle eyes you ever saw, and then they burst out laughing.

This is nuts, says Stella. Let's go for it.

Jesus, a vineyard and a tree farm and a nursery, you got balls, says Grace.

No, I got a bank loan, says Stella. And look who's talking. I could never make this pay more than enough just to keep me slaving away at it. Hope you make it work.

It'll work, says Grace. I got ideas. I got a lot of ideas.

5.

Moses didn't die but he lost both wings, shattered to tatters, and he lost a lot of blood, and he was unconscious for a couple of days, dreaming dark corvidian dreams, but then he woke, murmuring, and he and Owen are in Other Repair this morning, contemplating wings. Moses standing on the old football helmet, Owen sitting at the workbench, goggles on. Smell of paint, cedar, maple, fir, alder, varnish, cigars, tears, sweat, rubber, oil, sawn metal, burnt gasoline, smoked fish, sawdust, old newspapers, woodsmoke, footballs, turpentine, apples, ink, crow.

I'm thinking steel, says Owen. We could pull that off. Superlight steel with hinges that I design to work off your chest muscles. Your shoulders, so to speak, are still there, so you have the engineering to make this work. I had a good talk with the doctor and there's a lot we can do with implants. It's kind of an engineering problem.

I don't know, says Moses.

Look at these sketches, here, see, if I use your rotator cuffs, and figure it out with wires, I could make a pair of wings that would work. No way they would be as good as the originals but they would be functional. I *think* they would be functional. At least they would be cosmetic. Glossy black paint. We can get Nora to engrave them maybe. What say?

I don't know, says Moses.

You don't want new wings? .

I don't know.

Or wood, says Owen. What if George and Nora found some superlight wood, like balsa, and we made a set of wooden wings? Or you could have several pairs for various occasions. Like suits of clothes. Linen wings, paper wings, wooden wings, steel wings. Or you can have wings made from all sorts of feathers. Not just crow feathers but hey, osprey feathers! Heron feathers! Wouldn't that be cool? You could wear whatever wings you wanted in the morning. Be an osprey for a day. Boy, *that* would freak out the ospreys, eh? Or wings in different *sizes*, wouldn't that be cool? Like huge wings for summer, when you can be a kite. We'll take you out on the beach and fly you, wouldn't that be cool? And different colors. You can have bright orange wings for Oregon State University football Saturdays, hey?

I don't know, says Moses. I think maybe wings are a thing of the past for me.

What?

I find that I don't actually want new wings.

You don't want to fly anymore?

It's not that I don't want to fly, says Moses slowly, it's that I don't want to try to fly the way I flew. Does that make sense? I was one sort of creature and now I am another sort of creature, and I find that I am curious about the new creature. I've never seen the world steadily from this angle, from the pedestrian point of view, and it's sort of interesting *not* to have a bird's-eye view, you know? Everything is flatter. Everything is at an oblique angle. There are a *lot* more corners. It's a different geometry. Previously I perched, but now I walk. Yet I am aware that there may come a time when I mourn flight. I am aware of prospective sadness. But at the moment I am filled with curiosity. I would almost rather that you designed some sort of conveyance or vehicle for ground transport. Also I suspect that I will have to get comfortable with riding on shoulders and in the seats of cars. Perhaps a small seat belt is the engineering problem we should be contemplating.

Owen takes his goggles off and stares at the bird.

You asked, says Moses.

You are a most unusual creature, Moses.

I don't know. We are all unusual by definition, isn't that so?

Thank you for saving Michael.

I don't know that I saved Michael. He is a professional and very likely would have found a way to extricate himself from the situation.

Perhaps.

Perhaps.

Why *did* you do that?

I don't know, Owen. It was the strangest thing. I was very happy. It just seemed like the thing to do. I didn't think about it. I just did a barrel roll and went for it. It felt great to fall like a falcon. I have long wondered what it would be like to fall like a fist from the sky, accumulating great energy, and now I know.

Owen stares, smiling. The radio burbles a baseball game from someplace far away where the trees are bedraggled and desperate for water. Outside the shop the wind tacks to starboard and the change roils the smells inside the shop, so that the smells of sawn wood muscle out the oil and turpentine and newspaper and apples and ink. For a moment the smells of pine and alder wrestle with each other and then alder totally wins the day.

6.

The doctor's house is arranged in such a way that it huddles under the sandy hill like a baby asleep under the maternal jaw; to get to the ocean you go up, through a path splitting the jaw, and then down a precipitous rickety creaking groaning splintery staircase of weathered alder, or you go take the long way down the sandy path and all the way around the huddle of the hill.

Kristi and Daniel contemplate their options.

Down looks easier, says Kristi.

Up's quicker.

You in a hurry?

Let's go up. If you push and I pull we can do it.

But maneuvering a boy, age twelve, not slight, all those bicycled muscles still weightily there, in his wheelchair, not light, up an incline, is no easy task, and very soon, pants Kristi, we are not, going to, make it, hey, hey, hold up! Brake!

Daniel would say something witty but he's exhausted.

I got an idea, says Kristi after a minute. How about we get as far as the top of the stairs in the chair, and then I put you on that sled there?

For indeed huddled in a pile of old stuff under the lip of the hill there is a rusty sled, as well as half a small refrigerator, old shingles, a pickaxe, and what looks like it was once a weed whacker.

And I surf down the stairs? says Daniel. Whoa. Tempting.

Be easier than bumping the chair down step by step. There's a lot of steps.

Let's do it.

When they get to the top of the hill the wind says *hey!* and their eyes water with the salt and insistence of it. Kristi helps Daniel out of the chair and onto the sled. Daniel braces his legs against the ancient steering apparatus and pretends it doesn't hurt his knees. I better strap you in just in case, says Kristi, and she ropes him to the sled in various and intricate ways. They start laughing and cannot easily stop. Ready when you are, captain, says Daniel. Aye aye sir, says Kristi. She sits on the step behind him and wraps the ends of the ropes around her wrists and very gently pushes the sled down one step with her feet, taking exquisite caution not to bump or jostle him. She is staring into his hair from this angle. All that hair. Carefully braided this morning red black brown. She hauls back on the ropes like reins. She's stronger than she looks and in this way they descend step by step, as slowly as they can go. There are fifty steps. After a while they count out loud. The wind whips. At the bottom of the stairs the sand invites them gently down to the sea. Kristi reverses rigging and pulls the sled. Like a ship, says Daniel. She stops at the high-tide line but he says, let's go in. She doesn't say, but it's cold! and she doesn't stop to take off her sneakers or roll up her pants but just forges into the gentle surf face-first pulling him. The sled slides into the sea. Kristi doesn't say, but your casts! and neither does Daniel. She gets waist-deep and stops and lets go the tension in the ropes and Daniel floats there grinning. Both of them are soaked. It's the sunniest day there ever was in the whole history of the world. Daniel thinks of sea lions swimming through caves at the bottom of the sea. Kristi does not think, how are we going to get back up to the house? Neither of them says a word for a really really long time and the sun is friendly and nutritious and the sled rollicks and a gang of terns goes by all whirry and curious.

7.

What the hell, kid, says George Christie to No Horses, let's do it, what say, you got a real nose for wood and I know wood, and you know what to do with it, we could make a bundle, or hell, we could make enough not to starve anyways, and we both got mouths to feed, what do you say? Jump right in here with yes, kid, because I ain't getting younger and this is a one-time offer, a bo-freaking-nanza, you in, what say? We'll do her for a year to start. Special lines of stuff made from cypress, hewn from hemlock, elicited from alder, sculpted from spruce, polished from pine, seceded from cedar, hell, I'm writin' the catalogue copy as I go here, kid, you taking notes? Because there's a lot of tourists will come, kid. A lot of people will come through here in the years to come. They'll be starving for what we got here. We don't have jack shit here, we think, all we got is rain and drunks and garbage fish, and there's no more huge trees and huge salmon fish, so we got exactly nothing, that's what you're

thinking, I know, but I got a vision, kid, I see the future, when people
are sick and tired of electric shit and plastic shit and pressing buttons
to make everything go on and off, and being stuck inside houses and
offices and cars, you mark my words, people will come here just to
breathe, just to get rained on for a change, just to hear a real river, just
to smell real mud, just to see a real fishing boat going out to catch real
fish, trust me, people will come a long way just to see something made
out of real wood by a real person with a real knife, and that would be
you, kid, and there will be people desperate to buy something real, and
hold it, they'll be saying to each other you remember that time we went
to the coast and the sun sneaked outta the rain and we ate fish that was
caught there and drank beer that was brewed there, remember that?
wasn't that a great time? that's what they'll say, kid, as they're running
their hands over your carving of A Old Logger, hell, there's your first
line of product, the most amazing carvings of handsome burly colorful
old bastards who all look eerily like old George Christie, what say, kid,
you in?

Yes, George, says Nora, grinning. Yep. Yup. Count me in. You got to
quit being so shy, George. You want to speak up once in a while or no
one will ever know what you're thinking.

8.

Worried Man in his office in the Department of Public Works goes
over and over and over and over and over the equipment, feeling that
if he misses one tiny thing, one infinitesimal niggling shy ignorable
detail, it will of course be the Crucial Thing, the ephemeral bolt or
screw that secretly holds the everything together, and the whole idea
will collapse and shrivel and fail, and he will be an idiot, and Cedar
will be disappointed, and that will be a great shame. It turns out, he
thinks to himself, that even after all these years, even after all the times
I certainly disappointed him, that I *hate* disappointing him. Isn't that
interesting? And how many ephemeral screws hold everything together
anyway? What if little tiny screws are what actually holds the universe
together? If you had a big enough magnet could you find them? And
what size screwdriver would fit those screws?

Boots, gloves, socks, wool underwear, sweaters, hats, sunglasses. Tent, tent stakes, sleeping bags, blankets. Ice axes, crampons, rope, more rope, carabiners, skis, ice screws, ice saw, pickets, belay loops, snowshoes, shovel, knives, iodine tablets, matches, more matches. Waterproof match cases. Maps. Batteries. Compasses. Flashlights. Headlamps. First-aid kit. Wristwatches. Ham radio. Toothbrushes. Toothpaste. Toilet paper. Notebooks. Camera. Film for camera. Dried berries. Dried elk jerky. Dried salmon sticks. Walnuts, almonds, pine nuts, peanuts. Water. No beer. Aspirin. Whistles. The whistles make him think of Maple Head again and he smiles and winces.

Owen and Cedar drive up in Owen's truck. For some reason no one feels like talking. They load the truck, Owen doing most of the work.

If ye have faith as a grain of mustard seed, ye shall say unto this mountain, remove hence to yonder place, and it shall remove, says Worried Man.

Matthew, chapter seventeen, says Cedar. We're off, says Owen, and off they go, over rills and hills, creeks and rivers, streams and rivulets, swamps and springs, hamlets and villages, towns and cities, sprawl and suburb, and then up, through Marmot and Salmon and Wildwood and Brightwood, unto the mountain. As they rattle over the Salmon River bridge, just past Rhododendron, the mountain leaps out from behind a curtain of vaulting fir trees. It looks cold and stern and brilliant. It looks like something from another galaxy. It has angles and corners and faces and gleaming ravines. It looks like no living thing has ever been on or near or around or over it since the day it was born millions of years ago. Whosoever toucheth the mountain shall surely be put to death, thinks Worried Man. Exodus.

Past Government Camp, up to Timberline.

They unload in front of the lodge. Owen helps them with their packs. He and Cedar glance at each other sideways and Owen gives him twice as much to carry. A raven requests character references. Worried Man stares at the mountain. Chipmunks chitter. They review the plan—Pacific Crest trail to the northwest side, easy ascent past the last straggling junipers, camp, slow steady ascent over next three days, assess progress afternoon second day, examining terrain for caves, cautiously exploring caves if practicable, descend back to trail after five days maximum, etc. There are tiny butterflies in the aster flowers. They review signal plans and flags. There is a dusty grasshopper flexing on a rock. They review emergency procedures and contingencies. There are a dozen headlong bees among the pale bones of fallen alpine firs. They synchronize watches. The raven again inquires. They shake hands all round. Juncos and nutcrackers flare and flitter. Worried Man kisses Owen on his rough cheek and says *a chara,* take care of everyone. Ants sprint across seas of moss. Owen watches as the entire Department of Public Works strolls brisk and grinning up the dusty trail. The gnarled tough juniper trees bask and wait.

9.

Maple Head and No Horses walk upriver through the trees. Alder thicket and spruce copse. A flutter of grouse. Up and up and up. Hemlocks. They find a tiny creek neither of them have ever seen before and pause there for lunch. Wading in the creek poking for crawdads, staring at the water striders, listening for ouzels.

Dippers, we are supposed to call them now, says Maple Head.

Never, says Nora. Ouzels forever. Coolest word ever.

Up and up and up. The hills get steeper and steeper. In the afternoon they stop talking and walk along panting a little. On a particularly steep trail they hold hands.

Late in the afternoon, much more tired than they thought they would be, Maple Head suggests gently that they call it a day, and they find a dense copse of spruce to sleep in, with a springy floor that feels ten feet deep in needles, and they have a light supper, and make a tiny fire, and both of them figure they will have a thorough talk, but they are both asleep moments after they eat, and not even dawn trying to stick its fingers into the eye of the spruce thicket wakes them. Finally chickarees do, three of them, chittering loud and long.

Probably never seen beautiful women before, says Maple Head. We'll be legends in the chickaree world.

Up and up and up, through rills of hills, always along the river, which gets thinner and thinner. Another night's sleep, this one in a lovely little grassy meadow, the stars as uncountable and incalculable and miraculous as either of them have ever seen and both of them are star gawkers. For an hour they count shooting stars.

The next morning, though, neither of them feels like walking. It isn't that they're sore, although they're sore. It's just so clear and crisp and warm and perfect a spot in the world that leaving seems silly. They sprawl in the grass and talk. The river is a few feet away and now it's lean enough that you could hop across easy as pie. They drink from it, leaning their faces in like deer. Tiny fish flicker. Nora puts her head under like she did when she was a child and opens her eyes to see the fish startle past and the cold crystal water slides over and into her skin. They talk some more. They talk about how they don't talk as much as they should. They talk about old boyfriends. They talk about food and wood and kids and legs. They talk about the dark snow falling on Nora. They hold each other and rock gently. They run out of words. They rock and rock. Far far below they can just see a sliver of surf where the ocean is beseeching the land. The slender river burbles and murmurs. Maple Head's tears slide silently into her daughter's hair. They rock and rock. Then Nora sits up straight very quietly, looking at the river, and Maple Head sees it too: an ouzel flying in the river, bobbing up to the surface every few feet and then sliding back under. They sit rapt. The ouzel pops up on the bank after a few minutes and shivers and shimmers and the water flies green and gold back into the river and the bird pops back down but this time not into the water but into a beautifully hidden nest hole under a tuft of the meadow like a cowlick over the river. There's a pause thin as a pin and then both women burst out laughing and the ouzel sticks its head out of the hole in amazement.

10.

Dawn on the mountain is bright and silent. The colors are white and blue. Everything has a shining edge to it. Billy sits against an enormous ice-rimed rock that looks like a boat with spars and mizzenmast and yardarm and everything. He boils water for coffee. For three days there has been nothing but ice and sky. No trees or bushes or flowers or even a sturdy nutty little mat of plants hiding from the wind. Not even lichen or moss. Ungreen, disgreen, greennot. There is white and there is blue. The primary colors. Blue made white and white melted to allow all the others. That's how it must have happened. He and Cedar had made their way through green and blue, up through those last scraggly junipers and fingery asters, and yellow, those last tough little butterflies, into long hours of dust and ash, slogging through it like brown and gray snow, and then up into the ice fields, as high as they could get, and they have wandered and poked, searched and squinted, for days. Now Cedar checks through their equipment and plots the day. You start here and I start there, he says. Flare if there's a problem. We should stay together but our time grows short. I'll take the upper and you take this lower stretch. First priority, caves. If we find likely candidates, flare the other guy. Second goal: anything unusual, bones, fauna, petroglyphs. Utmost caution. Helmets. Walking sticks. Matches. Sunglasses. Ice axes. Flashlights. Headlamps. First-aid kits. Camera. Film for camera. A photographic record of phenomena is just as good as or better than eyewitness accounts. Flare at noon to attest safety. No time to meet for lunch. I calculate that we will have nine hours maximum for light and we had better make the most of them. More coffee? We can leave the fire banked. We'll want it this evening. Ready? Ready. Stay calm. Don't be a hero. This is great. This is fun. Can you believe this is happening? Me neither. Who would have thunk it? All these years. Ready? Ready. Flare at noon. Flare if any trouble whatsoever. Camera loaded. Deep breath. Let's go.

11.

Billy in the kingdom of the ice. He picks his way carefully and cautiously, angling northwest; Cedar went northeast. Ceremonial handshake as they parted. My oldest and dearest friend. Hope to see him again. Born from the rush of the river. Rushes, Moses. Where has the time gone? Eternity is in love with the productions of time. Blake. Time in its motley colors. It has color as well as speed and pace. Of course there are blue times and gray times, black times and golden times, times of red rage, time with russet edges, etc. Time held me green and dying though I sang in my chains like the sea. Dylan Thomas. Should write this down. Be a great project. Measure color spectra over time duration in coordination with perception of same. Owen can make a machine. Also examine perceived color of time in concert with reported emotional state: nostalgia, sentimentality, melancholy, romance, frustration, etc. Public Work. Imagine the report! Colored filters, film spools. Spoor of time.

This line of thought reminds him what he is supposed to be looking for and just as he realizes this, he sees, by heavens, a cave, the slice of its opening hidden so exquisitely from view by ice and stone that only someone standing right here, at exactly this angle, slightly below and to the west of it, can see how that lip of rimed rock is essentially a door, permanently flung open. He clambers up carefully and cautiously, using his stick, making sure of every step. The opening is essentially exactly his size, tall and thin. He turns on his headlamp. Thinks about firing a flare for Cedar but his curiosity is electric and insistent. He steps inside. His pack clunks against the opening. The cave is dry and silent. Flashlight … on. The cave is deep and spacious. A thin ashen dust on the floor. No bones to be seen. No footprints that he can see. Animals at this elevation would be rare but not unknown—eagles, marmots, ravens, ptarmigan.

You think so? says a voice from the sifting darkness at the end of the cave. I don't think so.

Billy is so startled he actually jumps, his pack jingling, and cracks his helmet against the roof of the cave.

Cedar? he says.

No.

Who are you?

A *very* good question.

Silence. Billy can hear his own heart thammering and thrumming. He suddenly has to pee. This is *not* happening, he thinks. His mind is all scrambly. How could there be a *person* in a cave that seemed so remote no human being had ever in a million years even laid eyes on the *door*?

Another excellent question, says the voice.

How can you *hear* me?

Don't be afraid, says the voice.

How did you get here?

A *third* excellent question.

Is this a dream? Am I dead?

You're not dreaming, technically, and you're not dead, yet, says the voice. But we need to talk about that. There are some things we need to talk about, so here I am. I have been sent, that's probably the best way to explain it. Why don't you sit down and we can get started? Don't worry about Cedar. He's safe. He will come looking for you in about an hour, because you didn't send up a flare when you found the cave, as you agreed to do, but that decision actually works out for the best, because it gives us a chance to talk. Would you like something to eat?

12.

The young she-bear is away up in the hills near the meadow where Maple Head and No Horses are holding each other and laughing and laughing. The bear had smelled them before she heard them and now she sees them, holding each other and rocking slightly like slender trees in great winds. The bear's two cubs trundle along behind her in ragged parade order, fascinated by bees and berries. By now the cubs have names in the dark tongue of bears. The smallest is called smallest and the largest is called eats snakes. These are their very first names. Bears wear many names over the course of their lives, sometimes carrying several at once. Names having to do with lust are forbidden by ancient custom. There have been bears in these hills for four million years. Bears remember everything having to do with bears. Bears love eating more than remembering stories about bears but it is a near thing. One time a small bear killed a wolverine in an argument about an elk calf and that story was told for seven thousand years, mothers telling it to their cubs in the cold dark places where they prepared to sleep through the winter. There are stories of white bears and blue bears and bears with stars and moons on their chests. There are stories of bears who swam in the sea and bears who could learn the languages of other animals and a bear who could climb even the thinnest trees even when she was very old. There was a bear who killed a whale trapped at low tide in the mouth of the river, that was a story told for many years, and a bear who would eat only fawns, and a bear who would eat only fish, and a bear who destroyed any horse he ever found, and a bear born without rear legs who lived on berries and nuts and never left the meadow where he was born, and bears who climbed trees to eat the eggs of eagles, and a bear who clambered onto a log in the river just to see what would happen and the river carried him out through the surf and he went away into the sea and was never seen again. That is the story of the bear who went into the sun, a story every bear hears while young. Bears do not tell stories about animals other than bears. By ancient custom all stories about other animals are told through the manner in which they affect the lives of bears. So that cougars, for example, who are called deereaters in the dark tongue of bears, figure greatly in the stories of bears, but always through stories of bears who fought them, or outwitted them, or tricked them into leaping on dark bushes they had mistaken for bears, or ate their tails, or lost an eye to their razor fingers, or imitated their yowling so successfully that they would come bounding toward romance and find instead a bee's nest, which is a story that happened to a bear who once lived not far from where Maple Head and No Horses are still laughing at the ouzel, who is still wondering what to make of this new liquid noise in the world.

13.

What are you? says Worried Man.

Incredibly, a *fourth* excellent question, says the voice. And you didn't say you wanted something to eat, so let us turn to the matters at hand. First of all, as you may suspect, I have awkward news.

Are you an angel?

Technically, no, says the voice. And I am not here to tell you that you are dead, or about to die. You are *not* about to die. Let's get that out of the way. People are always so paranoid about death. However, you will be entering the seventh stage very soon.

What?

I have been sent to commend your efforts thus far, says the voice. Your kindness, especially—*very* impressive. Plaudits, high marks. If this was a test you would have scored very well. My sincere congratulations.

Believe me, not everyone earns plaudits. I would applaud if I could do so. And your humor especially really helped your grade. Kindness is first, of course, but you'd be surprised how much humor weighs. Also curiosity. If only people knew. Although perhaps they do.

Billy sits. His pack jingles. A puff of ancient dust arises and hangs in the air for an instant like incense.

You sound ... Welsh, says Billy.

No no, says the voice. Much as I admire the Welsh. A tough little people. Mountain fastnesses. No empire will ever conquer the Welsh. I shouldn't tell you that, but it's probably evident to any sensible observer after many thousands of years. But we digress. I have been sent to tell you that you are about to have a massive stroke, which will damage your body permanently, as it were, but leave you lucid, if speechless. In short you keep your head but lose your voice and body. This will seem like a blow but it's a gift. I am afraid I cannot explain further. Your task in your time remaining is to discover the nature and character of the gift, and then use it to the best of your considerable ability.

How much time will I have left?

No no, says the voice, I am not authorized to tell you that sort of thing, and indeed I have no idea. I am a ... messenger. Not everyone is allowed a messenger before the seventh stage. I am not sure you understand what a compliment this is. There are only a few messengers. I can understand you are rattled by the message, but really, as you people say, it could be worse. I could be delivering the message that you have *completed* the seventh stage. Not many people get that message either. One did in your town recently, a woman. A great compliment too, that message. Very few people are applauded at the end of the race, as it were. It's hard to explain.

Wouldn't it be easier, says Billy, if I just died now? I mean, my family will have to care for me, and that will be such hard work. I'm sure you can empathize. I wouldn't want to inflict that on them. I think I'd rather die now. Or maybe you can give me a couple of weeks to wrap up my affairs? Or a month? A month would be great. I can get a *lot* done in a month. You'd be surprised. But less is good. Less is fine. I am good with less. Three weeks? That's a good compromise. I say four, you say two, meet you in the middle.

When a man knows he is to be hanged in a fortnight, says the voice, it concentrates his mind wonderfully. A man from Britain said that, very pithy man he was, too. Still is. It's hard to explain. But we digress. I am not authorized to negotiate, and I have another message to deliver. Your daughter has been lifted from a great darkness. There is a very great work before her. So those are the two messages I have been sent to deliver. Our time is finished. Are you ready?

Not at all, says Worried Man.

Would you like a moment to prepare?

Can I ask a question?

Maybe one.

What about time? What is it, where is it, can it be found?

That's three questions. Four, really.

Please? I spent years on this. Most of my life.

Is maith an scealai an aimsir, time is a storyteller, says the voice, isn't that what your son-in-law says? He is wiser than he knows, that young man. But time is more than a storyteller. Storytellers are something else altogether. I am not authorized to explain further. It's impossible to explain. Languages are not yet equipped. They have so much more to learn. Languages will ... expand. There will come a time when languages are sentient themselves. I suppose I shouldn't say these things but I must say it is a pleasure to *use* language. Such a supple and musical device. I can see why you enjoy it so. But we digress. It's time.

I have an idea, says Billy. Why don't we discuss this? We are both intelligent beings, if being is the right word for you, and I think I have a workable solution to our dilemma. You have been sent to deliver a message. I have come here on a mission, as it were. But my mission is unfinished, and as you say yourself I am granted a messenger out of respect, let's say, for previous effort. So what say we compromise? I suggest a thorough but workable paralysis, one that pushes me to the seventh stage, as you say, but leaves me capable of ... research.

I am not ...

Yes, authorized, I know. But how about paralysis only of the lower body?

I cannot think that would meet the terms of the assignment, says the voice.

Okay, says Billy. Whole body, but leave me head and arms.

I don't think …

Hands?

Well … one hand.

One hand it is. Head and one hand, then. Agreed. Which hand?

Your choice.

Let's go lefty. A new frontier. And if I am keeping my head I really should be left with my voice, yes? You could change it if you want. Could we go an octave lower? That would startle May. It'd be funny.

I am not authorized …

But time marches on, says Billy briskly, and I am sure you have a great deal to do with your time. I can only imagine the press of your duties, the messages to be delivered, the crucial importance of every passing instant. And I am sure I have kept you longer than you intended. Garrulity—it's a problem for me. May says so, and May has never been wrong.

Well …

But inside Billy roils, he shivers. No body! No more making love to May! No walking! No holding babies like footballs! No kneeling or sprawling or scuttling or shambling or ambling or shuffling or sprinting! No canter and no gallop! No dancing with May ever again in the velvet dark of the Department of Public Works with a bottle of wine waiting on the shelf! No throwing footballs to the boy on the beach and prancing about like a stork on acid when Danno makes an unbelievable spectacular diving catch flying face-first into the surf and emerges soaked and triumphant holding the ball like a dripping golden trophy and the boy and his grandfather laugh so hard their cheeks and stomachs ache for days! No wrapping his arms like tree trunks around the lean grin of his sweet swift daughter and muttering stories into the thicket of her hair! No puttering around in the shop with Owen trying to make real from steel the ideas hatched in his hoary head! No more shaking Cedar's hard hand like a slab of wood! No cupping May's left breast in his right hand as they fall asleep mumbling and smelling like salt and honey!

Time, says the voice. You are a deft negotiator. Permission has been granted. Remember that kindness is first. I would recommend that you lie flat now so that you don't crack your head.

Billy is suddenly exhausted. He stretches out, staring at the ceiling of the cave. Stalactites hang from the roof, stalagmites grow from the floor. C is for ceiling and G is for ground. We are aware of the quicksilver nature of time. The rushing of the waters. Time is a storyteller. Time is a . . .

14.

Cedar, walking northeast and steadily uphill on a diagonal, sees one cave slit after another and marks them carefully on a map he draws to scale in his notebook. He numbers the caves, giving them all NE prefixes to distinguish them from the caves Billy has no doubt identified on the northwest side of the scarp: NE1, NE2, NE2.5 (a tiny one), etc. He pokes into the ones he can get to without undue strain. Some are mere cracks, without depth beyond the gape of their opening; others narrow immediately upon entrance; others bend back upon themselves; one (NE8) makes an immediate right turn and opens to a sort of window in the mountain. Lovely sculpture, thinks Cedar. Cave design, there's a life's study. Forces of geology at work in fissure. Nature of stone under duress. Effect of climate and weather. Index of temporary inhabitants. Comparison of conditions by amount of sunlight captured by mouth of cave. Does cave structure reflect orientation? Do temporary inhabitants prefer south-facing caves? I have not seen hide nor hair of any inhabitant in these caves. Too cold. No food at this elevation. No prospect of food, no reason to be here. Except if you are on a goose chase looking for unimaginably huge spools of what might appear to be film of some sort. As if such a thing would ever in this life be possible. Maybe I shouldn't have humored him. Maybe a real friend would have long ago said, Billy, this is nuts, could we get back to fences and water supply and piping and ditch dredging and building a jetty? But no: *sure*, we can climb a huge mountain at our age. *Sure* we might find immense spools of used time. *Sure* such a discovery would create a stir unlike any other in the history of human beings and change the nature of human consciousness. *Sure* it makes sense that two obscure public works employees from an obscure town on the Oregon coast would be the guys to make such a discovery. No, we don't have anything better to do with our dwindling time and infinitesimal savings than parade off to a mountain and probably have heart attacks and freeze to death and be found decades later by intrepid mountaineers half our age. Headlong pursuit of the most ridiculous speculation in the history of the world: *excellent* idea! I am *all* for it! What an *idiot* I am! What an idiot *he* is! Where *is* that idiot?

15.

The doctor in his study reading. First light. There was a man in the land of Uz, whose name was Job, he reads. The ocean below his window is a swirl of mist. And that man was perfect and upright, and he eschewed evil. Ebb tide, the doctor notes. What? says Job, shall we receive good at the hand of God, and shall we not receive evil? The three clocks in his study murmur together. Wrath killeth the foolish man, and envy slayeth the silly one. He removes his spectacles and examines them patiently and opens a drawer and takes out a tiny pristine towel and cleans his glasses thoroughly and folds the towel and puts it back exactly as it was. Despise not thou the chastening of the One: for he maketh sore, and bindeth up, he woundeth, and his hands make whole. The first cormorant of the day whirs heavily over the house. Now my days are swifter than a post: they flee away, they are passed away as the swift ships, as the eagle that hasteth to the prey. The mist over the sea is shredded and the face of the ocean revealed. Man that is born of a woman is of few days, and full of trouble. A parade of pelicans sets forth, somehow flapping and cruising in unison, how do they *do* that? He cometh forth like a flower, and is cut down: he fleeth also as a shadow, and continueth not. The first heron of the day lands in the surf and conducts sand-crab research. I have said to the worm, Thou art my mother, and my sister. The heron changes tactics and takes up the one-legged ballet stance. How long will ye vex my soul, and break me in pieces with words? Question, writes the doctor in his daybook: how long on average does a heron wait to make a play? The light shall shine upon thy ways, and he shall save the humble person, and he shall deliver the island of the innocent, and it is delivered by the pureness of thine hands. And what, continues the doctor in his neat crisp handwriting, does a heron *think* about while waiting? God speaketh, yet man perceiveth it not. Or is the heron keyed to a terrific pitch of attentiveness? In a dream, in a vision of the night, when deep sleep falleth upon men, in slumberings upon the bed, then he openeth the ears of men. And how *do* they manage to stand for so long on one leg? Behold, God is great, and we know him not, neither can the number of his years be searched out, for he maketh small the drops of water, they pour down rain according to the vapour thereof, which the clouds do drop and distil upon man abundantly. By now the morning mist is dissolved, and the ocean laid bare in its roiling majesty, and upon it are boats and the animals of the skin of the sea, and in the distance leviathan; gray whales, thinks the doctor, noting that they are heading south earlier than usual. Hear attentively the noise of his voice, and the sound that goeth out of his mouth, he thundereth marvellously with his voice; great things doeth he, which we cannot comprehend. He checks his notebooks for whale migration dates for the last ten years. Fair weather cometh out of the north, and a terrible majesty. A quiet voice comes to the doctor from the kitchen, and the sheer surprise of another voice in the house, and the gentle salt of the voice, and the realization whose voice it is, causes him to pause in his labors, and he lifteth up his head, his spectacles glinting. Hast thou entered into the springs of the sea? He puts down his pen, and closes his notebook, but does not shelve it properly among its numbered predecessors, and he rises to his feet, and stands at the window, and bows his head, and turneth to leave; but as he passes under the lintel of his study, he opens his mouth, and out therefrom issues his voice, saying, I would love a cup of tea, Stella, thank you.

16.

Cedar checks his watch and has a sinking feeling in his stomach. He had a heart attack, the old goat, and he died, and he's frozen stiff.

Bastard. No flare. Shit. He works back across the ice field to the northwest sector and slowly and steadily works his way back and forth across the field of caves. Shit. Finds bootprints, enters cave, finds Billy supine and unconscious. Shit. Medical training, United States Army. No broken bones. No dislocation of neck or spine. Pulse normal. No apparent injury or trauma. Smelling salts. Billy wanders awake. Croaks unintelligibly and then grins. Flexes left hand. Grins again.

What are you smiling about, you old goat?

Billy tries to explain but his mouth isn't working right.

You aren't making a whole lot of sense, as usual.

Yes.

Can you sit up?

No.

Did you fall?

No.

Heart attack?

Stoke, says Billy, working away at the *s* for a bit. Stork.

Does anything work?

Head. Hand.

Any pain?

No.

I'll carry you out.

Yes.

Let's get down to the lodge and I will call Owen.

Yes.

I got you, Billy.

Yes. Good.

I'm going to tie your hands around my neck, okay?

Yes.

It's a long way down. Stop me if you are hurting.

Yes.

We'll go slow but we'll get there.

Yes.

I owe you a rescue, eh?

No no.

You'll be okay. You'll be all right. We'll find a way through this, Billy. The doctor will know. All right. Here we go. You ready?

Yes.

What are you grinning about?

Time, says Billy distinctly.

You're in shock, says Cedar.

Seventh, says Billy.

Pipe down and rest.

Yes. Yes.

Cedar, who has terrific peripheral vision still, notices and doesn't notice the startling depth of the cave as he hoists Billy to his feet and wraps him around his back; and later he will wonder if he saw or dreamed or wished to see a glint of metal in the rear of the cave, some kind of silvery flash, as if some big machine was huddled there; or an immense spool of some kind, as May would quietly say one afternoon, neither of them saying anything about it again, but both thinking about it more than they would ever admit.

17.

Down and down and down through an afternoon the color of bobcats and new footballs and fresh-sawn wood. Not golden but buttery. Faintly the simmer of surf. Down and down they come, Nora first, Maple Head putting her hand on her daughter's shoulder sometimes in steep passages. That bony shoulder like a wing. Tucked against me when she nursed. When she ran her shoulders flexed faster than they eye could see. My girl in flight.

Past the little copse where the chickarees came out to chitter and stare. Pausing for tea and cookies.

There are doors and windows everywhere, Mom, says Nora. I see that. I see that. I didn't see that.

If the doors of perception were cleansed, says Maple Head,

We would see everything as it is, infinite, says Nora. Dad says that all the time. He says a lot of things all the time. He spends all his time saying lots of things. That's William Blake, isn't it? What's the deal with Dad and William Blake?

He's wiser than he knows, your dad. Let's not tell him that.

What happens when this comes again?

Maybe it won't.

Probably it will.

Probably it will.

Will you walk with me then?

As long as I can walk and long after that too.

There's no medicine, is there?

Just the doors and windows.

Did you…?

Sometimes. Sometimes. Sometimes we had no money and no prospect of ever having money and that wears and eats at you. Sometimes we were ill and hungry and the rain was relentless and I couldn't see any way we would ever get out. Love doesn't save anybody. But I found doors and windows. I think maybe they are always there and we don't see them too well. This is why people invent religions, to map doors and windows maybe. Maybe that's what art is in the end. Who knows. But they're there. Consider the fowls of the air. Consider the water ouzel. This is one of those things that maybe the more you talk about it the more stupid it sounds, but there are a lot of things like that. You are like that for me. I can't explain more than a jot of how I feel about you but as long as there is a you I have joy in my bones. The fact that there was a you is a joy beyond calculation. It hurt when you were born and it hurts still. Let me keep my hand on your shoulder the rest of the way home. I think my hand is hungry for your shoulder.

Down and down and down and once they find a whole thicket of thimbleberries crammed with waxwings so eager and ravenous and foolish and gluttonous that they can hardly lumber off when Maple Head and Nora approach.

They look like little stuffed couches, don't they? says Nora, and they burst out laughing again.

18.

Declan dozing on the bow in the broad calm light thinks sleepily of sails and the lovely windy words of the craft of enslaving air. Yardarms and lugsails, gaffs and rigs, jibs and booms, luff and clew and tack. Boats buffeted by breezes. Westering winds. He'd always been interested in boats and ships from before he could remember—he vividly remembers his father hammering him for not paying attention to the work at hand because he was staring out at the vast barges and timber rafts and tankers that loomed on the horizon, not to mention the occasional skidding scudding sloops and yachts and daily slogging chugging fishing boats bristling with lines. *Nothing half so much worth doing as simply messing about in boats,* that was the line from one of the books Grace used to read aloud at night when they were little, tucked up in their rooms in the attic, the fragile plaster wall between them, her bed against one side of the wall and his on the other and her voice coming through the little hole he punched through, the size of a dime, the hole he surreptitiously enlarged week by week, and eventually added a little screen in it, like a confessional! said Grace with delight after she'd endured her first confession, mortified because she had nothing to confess, Declan magnanimously lending her some of his sins, a small theft, a mink trap that killed a pregnant grouse, a silence as a boy was bullied at school. Jesus, the books she read through that screen! There must have been *hundreds.* And he'd never read one back to her, not one. What *did* I do for my sister, exactly, other than rag her relentless every day for six thousand days? The one girl. We thought she was spoiled but maybe it was the other way around. The Boys, we hated that, the three of us labeled genderically, mom and dad never said the Girl, did they, but maybe it was harder for Grace, eh? Then mom bags us and there's no one there but Red Hugh hard of head and hand. Ach, the poor old bastard, an apt and suitable death, pierced by a wooden spear. Like the Tuatha. Jesus, what a clan. Good that I leave. Maybe it's best I leave. She can find her own way. Maybe without me everyone has more room to grow. Like trees in the woods. Speaking of trees, O Donnell me lad, isn't there a stepping-hole for an emergency mast on this ship, and didn't you and wharf rat Nicholas lay in not one but two whippet spars for just this sort of eventuality? Aye, captain, we did. Look lively then, boy! And scrounge around for a mainsail while you are down in the hold. Aye, captain! Right away, sir!

19.

Of course Owen made Worried Man a most amazing and unusual robochair, using the wheelchair the doctor had loaned Danny. He and Dan and Moses disappeared into Other Repair for days on end and there was a continual clanking and whirring of crowbars and sanders and fan belts and compressors and the wailing of many machines shaping a new thing that had never been in the world before.

*Any*one can make a wheelchair, said Owen, but *we* will make something else.

And when they came out, Owen and Daniel and Moses, after six days of very nearly round the clock labor, and buckled Billy into his new electric body, there was wonderment and merriment everywhere, on every face tears, in every mouth laughter. Cedar laughed so hard he nearly choked and Owen had to bang him on the back a while until he got clear, and No Horses laughed so hard she had the hiccups until dinner. Silvery it was, the robosuit, a sort of mobile metal parka, something like a race-car and suit of armor all at once, with a panel of buttons for the left hand by which everything was controlled, speed and cornering and even shiftable gears for hills and bad road conditions. It had heating and air-conditioning functions, a storage area for interesting things found along the journey, a sort of extendable mechanical arm on the right side for exploration, and subtle mirrors set all around so the occupant could easily see with a glance in all directions. It even had evacuation piping, in case the occupant was caught short, and an ejection apparatus, in case of emergencies. It had spare wheels cunningly set into the main body of the body, it had spare batteries, it had night lights fore and aft, and it would have had a radio antenna, said Daniel, if we thought you wanted to hear music all day, but we figured you didn't. Do you like it, gramp? Is it okay? I love it, Daniel, said Billy quietly, and his face shone also. Will you and Owen help me into it? If you hold it steady there Owen can perhaps hoist these old bones. I am more grateful than I can easily say, Owen. You are a prince among men. I am blessed and graced to have you as a son. The day Nora fell in love with you, that was a good day. This button operates the arm? And this button opens and closes the fingers? Can I make a fist? If I touch someone do they get an electric shock? Imagine the possibilities.

20.

Final project, says Maple Head to her class. In the last fifteen minutes of class today, write down some things you believe in that don't make sense. Write an essay, but don't worry about coherence and shape and narrative style. Just make notes. Play with words and ideas. Are there things that you believe with all your heart that don't make the slightest sense, if you examine them in the cold light of day? Try to use corners of your brains you don't usually visit, and take this seriously, don't be giving me flip essays about chipmunks and Oregon State football. Stop and think for a moment, about your family, your people, organizations, civic and religious and cultural entities, about core beliefs, about things you really and truly care about, and then write from your heart. Again I ask you to take this seriously, and try to just pour down substantive thought. Don't worry about coherence and shape and clarity, for once, just write freely. But be honest. We will not be reading these aloud in class, only I will read them, in private, so you don't have to pose and wear your usual masks. I'll give you one example, which you cannot use, and then off we go. For example: friendship. Does friendship really make sense? If, in the end, those who know you best are exactly those who can deliver you the most pain, who know your weak points and flaws and can with exquisite accuracy find and irritate those sore places, then why bother to get close to people? Similarly marriage, does marriage make any real sense in a world of serial infatuation, a world in which evolutionarily the distribution and dissemination of genes is better aided and abetted by a deliberate refusal to commit to monogamous relationships?

That's two examples, Mrs. M, says a boy named Blink. So we can't write about marriage either?

You married, Blinky?

Not anymore, Mrs. M, which gets a general giggle.

Well, then.

But Blink is stuck on thinking about marriage, and he figures he'll take a flyer on it in his fifteen minutes, because it turns out he is a majorly serious student of the marriage he sees up close and personal, which is his mom and dad, who have a tumultuous but interesting marriage, as far as he can tell, although the range of his experience with marriages is thin, whereas as far as he can tell his mom and dad are the only people in the history of the extended Blink clan to actually get married or stay married; here and there an aunt dove into marriage but quicksprinted right out, like one time, this was his Auntie Antonia, her marriage lasted three days, and ever after she talked of it as a crucifixion followed by three days in the tomb followed by a miraculous resurrection.

As my mother says Marriage doesn't make any sense whatsoever and is clearly an agreement between two fools for the Perpetuation of a foolish race, writes Blink. However, I believe that Marriage has its uses and utilities. However, it is a good example of a thing that makes some Sense but not much. Most of the time Marriage appears to be a Difficulty because the parties involved come from different planets and have to find common or overlapping Orbits. This seems mostly unworkable in the Personal Sphere just as it is in the Astronautical Sphere as we have seen recently in class. Observationally I speculate that arguing about Money and making humorous remarks is the key to Marriage. In conclusion Marriage does not make sense but I believe in it because I have seen it applied to real-world Problems and its curious Effects are something to be studied very carefully in the future by careful scholars. Further study is called for perhaps by the Government or a Married Committee or the Department of Public Works.

Time! says Maple Head. Pencils down. Pass your papers up your row to the front please. Ladies and gentlemen, I thank you. Away you go! Off! Away!

21.

Sara is on her knees in the garden and Michael is in a wheelchair at the edge of the garden and the girls are running around the house the younger trying to hit the older with a water balloon and the older sister is staying tauntingly just exactly out of her sister's flinging range which she, the older girl, knows to within the whisper of a whisker of a wren. Sara plants garlic, beans, carrots, tomato starts, broccoli starts, and, experimentally, eggplant. Second crop, she thinks. Second chance. She finishes the last row and mills through the whole patch again for weed seed and finally calls it a day and leans back against Michael's chair. He runs his hands through her hair. Fingers her ears. Lord, woman, he says, even your ears are attractive. She snorts. Were I not at the moment somewhat incapacitated, he says, bending down to murmur this in her ear, I'd carry you inside the house and lock the doors and remove every thread of your clothing and make those ears burn, yes I would. She giggles. I'd rub everything I got against one ear and then an hour later start on the other, he whispers, and now she's laughing, and he keeps murmuring cheerfully about how he will eventually end up rubbing against the exquisite sensual foothills of her extraordinary ankles, and this is such a peculiar phrase that she laughs so hard her cheeks and stomach hurt, and she stands up, laughing, to stretch her stomach, and as she turns around and reaches out a hand to touch his face her water breaks.

For an instant she thinks she laughed so hard she actually really and truly peed her pants although she's wearing her ancient cotton gardening dress that used to be blue but long ago became soil-colored as Michael says, but then her uterus contracts with a mighty and mindbending clench and she realizes *o my god o my god here she comes*, and she says *Michael the baby!* and his face flickers joy and fear and thrill and shame that he is helpless, all at the same time, she sees all this flash across his face, and he says calmly professionally husbandly, okay, okay, all right, if you can get to the house I'll get to the window and you hand me the phone and you get to the bed, and she says *too late o god!* and she crouches down and grabs the handles of his wheelchair as another contraction roars in *o god o god* and the baby wrenches inside her and gets ready to see the sun. Michael shouts for the girls but they think he is just barking some dad imprecation and they keep running. The baby lurches. Michael cups Sara's face in his hands. *O god o god.* The baby small and slippery spurts toward the light and Sara's hands go white on the handles of the chair and Michael strokes her hair and murmurs, okay okay all right all right and minutes later the baby slides smoothly out of Sara onto the sweet soil at the edge of the garden. Sara kneels and picks her up and the tiny girl opens her eyes and they stare at each other for a long time. Michael is sobbing so hard his chair shivers. The two sisters, with that eerie sensory apparatus for shimmering moments that kids have, materialize silently and stare at their new sister. For a long moment the only sound anyone can hear is Michael crying quietly but then the baby says *mew?* and the sisters start giggling and all is well and all manner of things will be well.

Is that a girl? says the older sister.

Yes, love.

What's her name? says the younger sister.

Daddy wants to name her Albina.

Do you?

No. Her name is Mia Serina. That means my heart.

Hi Mia! say the sisters together in their voices high and sweet as birds. Hi Mia!

22.

Now a pub, thinks Grace, is not a bar, so drinking, all due respect to drinking, should not be the paramount activity in the pub. Talking is, right? Or even better, listening. So I have to arrange matters so that people listen to each other. While drinking. Maybe we should have smaller glasses. Or push all the chairs and tables closer so people overhear what people are saying and then they cannot resist saying hey. And there should be kids. Kids are a good sign. You can't get drunk when there's kids. And dogs. And maybe birds. Parrots? A heron? Jesus, can you have a pet heron? What if it gets into a fight? I can see me calling Michael about the heron starting a fistfight about who's the best football player ever. But sports teams, yes. Bowling. Baseball. Maybe we can have a fishing league. Dec could run that. And wine tastings with whatever Stella makes. People like stuff like that. Poker tournaments. Poetry readings. Plays. Hey, plays in the pub, yes. Write that down, Jesus, Grace, get organized. A board of trustees? Maybe we have Mass here sometimes? Language lessons? Get Owen to teach Irish? Woodcarving? Get Anna to sing opera songs at night. One night a month. With Michael maybe. Need piano player. Need piano. Music cools people out. Soothes the savage breast. Good food. Easy to make.

Sandwiches, soups. Open at noon for lunch. Close at midnight. No one stays in a bar after midnight except to drink. I should know. Movies? Movie night. Football games. Maybe old football games. Great games from the past. Film fest: every single time the Beavers hammered the poor bedraggled sorry ass Ducks. Yes. Guest speakers. Be the village green. Be the center of town. Be the heartbeat. Be more than a bar. Be a pub. Pubs are fun. Stop by for an hour. One pint is plenty. Be normal. Kids welcome all day and night. Lemonade. Jar of chocolate bars on the counter. Darts. No pool table. Pool tables breed fights. Windows open. Tables outside? Back deck? Peadar can build a deck. Build it around that huge spruce. No parking lot. So what. People who want to come here will come here. Be a destination. No cars by the windows. Look out at real things. Trees. Beach. Kids. Rain roaring in off ocean. Wood stove. Newspapers and magazines. Books. Bookshelves. Reading glasses available. Reading nooks. Great books. What are the great books? Jesus, did I ever read anything great? All those books through the wall to Declan. Jesus. Friendly proprietor. Tough but charming. Sober. Patrons cheerfully offer to buy owner drink and owner shakes head grinning and says not today, I take Tuesdays off. Change day as necessary. Or not during Lent. Not during March. Not during football season. Made a vow. Made a promise. Swore to high heaven. Yes. Made a vow. Promised management to lay off and see what happens. New world. New country. New drapes.

23.

In the county of Limerick in the west of Ireland there is a hill that swells like a breast from the skin of the soil. Between Baile Geagoge and Baile na hAbhann, says Owen to Daniel, that's the way my grandfather would say it when he tried to say where we were from.

Daniel stares at the small sea of the valley beneath them. Green squares like a quilt. Little rock walls that look like they have been there one million years.

More mud than grass eh, says Owen. Up we go, son. Just a bit more now. Your knees sore? Can I carry you now?

Yes please, says Daniel.

Just a bit more up through the trees, then.

This is so beautiful, dad.

It is that, Dan.

All the trees are up here on the hill, says Daniel.

Yeh, says Owen. Once there were trees all over the island thick as hair on the head of the king, but they were all cut down very long ago. A great shame. Mostly vast and epic oaks, they say. The old stories are full of forests that were all dark and mysterious and magic. Oak is still a holy wood here even though you hardly ever see an actual living oak, the poor things.

Daniel on Owen's back sees the little house in the trees first.

Dad.

Here we are now, son.

Can I walk now, please?

Can you? You all right?

Yes.

Sure?

Yes.

They hold hands on the mossy porch. The house crouches beneath the pines. It's dark among the thick arms of the trees. The wind seethes. There's a yellow light in the house. Owen knocks on the mossy door. Daniel's hand tightens in his father's hand. A shuffle comes to the door. Owen knocks again. The wind is stuffed with pine. The door opens and the yellow light wanders out curiously and Daniel finds himself staring at an old woman exactly as tall as he is. They stare at each other curiously before the woman notices that Daniel's hand is in another hand and her eyes sail up Owen's arm to his face. The wind stops to listen. *A mhàthair,* says Owen, *seo do mhic, an bhfuil cead againn teacht isteach?* Mother, here are your sons, may we come in?

24.

Worried Man here telling stories into the tape for my grandson Daniel. Now, boy, you have asked me time and time again about Cedar, and I have told you what I know, which isn't very much, how we met him by the river, and fished him out, and how he and I became the best of friends, and went into the public works business, and how eventually we did go to the holy mountain, with odd results, these things you know. But you have also asked me about Cedar and the war, and of that story there is not much to tell. He does not speak of it even to me or to your grandmother, and I know beyond a doubt that we are dear to him, and trusted, and at home in his heart. Some stories are not for everyone to tell, and that story is for you to hear from Cedar alone. All he has said to me is that being inside a war changed him utterly, that it wasn't one memorable event but many small moments that built up to be a mountain in him, and that he emerged from the war sworn to build rather than destroy. I think he would have been good at whatever he turned his mind and hands to. He would have been an excellent priest or mayor or mechanic or a thousand other things. Why he never married I do not know. How he feels about not having his own children I do not know. There are some things about even the people you love the best and deepest that you will never know. That's just how it is. Sometimes I will notice something that maybe means something but it's not for me to ask. He has a scar that circles right around his entire neck at the top of his chest, for example, a serious scar, like someone drew a scar with a thick pale marker, but how that happened and why I do not know. The ring finger on his right hand doesn't work, he has a deep fear of swamps, and whistles and sirens make him uncomfortable and irascible. Perhaps these things have to do with war. I do not know. Not even your grandmother knows, and she knows more about Cedar than anyone alive in the world at the moment. But I believe it is an error to wonder about what you do not know, at the expense of savoring the excellence of what you do know. No one works as hard as Cedar. No one cares more about the safety and cleanliness and health of this town and its beings of every species. No one has more creative ideas faster than Cedar. No one can build a fence faster and more thoroughly than Cedar. No one is as quick with his fists or as reluctant to be quick with his fists as Cedar. No one is as loyal as Cedar. No one likes salmonberries more than Cedar. No one can run as fast as Cedar, except, of course, your mother, who may be the fastest human being in the history of human beings, and human beings have been around for a very long time, even longer than me, and I am half a million years old. I have to finish studying the theory of evacuation piping now, so I will conclude this tape, but not before I say that *you* are the child of my heart, Daniel of the three-colored hair, prince of the sea.

25.

Getting Worried Man *out* of the robosuit at night was an adventure, and it took Maple Head a few nights to figure out the drill, but she got good at it right quick and could peel him like a banana and squirt him into the bed and have him naked and grinning between the sheets in less than twenty minutes. For the first few nights they made a game of it and set a stopwatch and laughed at the nuttiness of it all under the sadness of what amounted to a nearly complete loss of the body he used to have, but then one night in the dark came the moment both of them had secretly been dreading but in the end you have to sail straight into those moments or you are not really married at all.

What happened in the cave? she says.

There was a sort of … messenger, he says.

Tell me.

I don't know if it was real, May. Maybe I just had a stroke and dreamed the rest.

Tell me.

We were quartering the slope, and Cedar went east and I went west, and I found a cave that was sort of secretly cut into the mountain, you know? Something about it just seemed, I don't know … right. So I went in, and then there was a … voice. I didn't *see* anything, really, but the voice was so clear and articulate and strange. The voice said it had two messages to deliver, one that Nora was lifted from a great darkness because there was a great work before her, which it didn't explain what that work was, and the other was that I was about to have a major stroke and be paralyzed except for my brain. So I … negotiated.

You negotiated paralysis with a voice in a cave?

Well … yes.

Keep talking.

Believe me I know how weird this sounds.

Do you?

Long silence from his side of the bed.

I … I'm sorry I was so selfish, May. I'm so sorry.

Long silence from her side of the bed.

The whole thing was crazy, to go at all, he says. It was selfish.

Longer deeper silence.

It's like you have a thing in your head that you're absolutely sure you have to do or be, he says, and that shoves everything else out of the way, and you lose … proportion.

The day you left was the first day I ever felt like I didn't care anymore, she says, so quietly that he almost doesn't hear her but he does.

Silence as deep as a sea. Their hearts hammer quietly. Two owls in the firs behind the house whinny and burble. The first cold winds of winter stick exploratory fingers through the windows left open an inch. Two raccoon kits, on their own tonight for the first time ever, huddle on the fence and ponder independence and the fallen burst tomatoes in the garden.

What else happened in the cave?

I asked that not all of me be paralyzed.

And?

Request granted.

Don't tell me …

No, no, not that, he says, smiling in the dark. Tempting as it was. It's my left hand. Works like a charm. See?

Can't feel it.

Let me just walk it over these mountains here.

Foothills.

Mountains to me.

What happens if it walks south of the mountains?

Why don't I start it walking that way and see what happens?

26.

Kid, this is totally going to work out, says George Christie to Nora. They are in her studio and he is surreptitiously looking for a place to spit. Look at these order sheets, kid, sweet mother of Christ, there's fifty there easy, what did I tell ya, this is going to be easier'n making snot pie. I'd start with the alders was I you, that's an easy wood to get, and then move into the spruces and meanwhile I will haul ass and find more hemlock and such. Hell of a fine beast your hemlock but it's a bitch to yank it out of the ravines for which you need helicopters or teenagers or a real good horse. Horses are best. Teenagers are good but they eat more'n the horses do. These other woods I can get 'em in baby doses. Cherry and that sort of thing. Hazelnut, holly, white cedar. That's for the spindly shit people like. Magic arrows and dreamcatchers and boxes for necklaces and that sort of female stuff. It's a puzzle. People have their things though, is all. Yours looks to be what's inside wood. You with me here, kid? You taking notes? You catching the font of wisdom here? Because I ain't going to last forever, you know, one of these days old man hemlock is going to take revenge on old George for culling so many of the long green herd over the years, and that'll be fair and square. They'll find me out there wearing a big honking tree limb and staring blank at the stars and all the other trees'll be talking how they finally cut down the old guy. Fair enough. Worse ways to go. You with me here, kid?

27.

The days are shorter and the mornings colder and it's almost wet season. Grace starts a betting pool in the pub for the first day of the Rains. The priest takes All Souls Day. The doctor takes All Saints Day. Owen takes Halloween. Daniel takes Election Day. Worried Man takes November 28, William Blake's birthday. Kristi takes November 13, Robert Louis Stevenson's birthday, because she found a copy of *Kidnapped* in the doctor's house and thought it was the coolest book she ever read, period. Maple Head, pretending to be a pessimist, takes October 15, Saint Teresa of Avila's feast day, because Teresa was a tough bird who didn't take guff from anybody. Cedar takes October 26, feast day of Saint Evaristus, because how often do you get a chance to back a Jewish saint in a race? No Horses takes December 8, the day the Buddha achieved enlightenment, at about five in the morning. Michael the policeman tries to take all of November by eminent domain until he is hooted down and has to settle on the day after Election Day because that's the day every year he says when there is a perceptible rise in stupid general hope in the direction of the state and nation. Sara takes the day after that just to see her name next to Michael's name. Grace takes Veterans Day and silently marks the square for Declan. Moses reaches into the hat blind and pulls out October 27, which he discovers later is the birthday of Captain James Cook, who sailed right past Neawanaka in the old days, and indeed there is a story passed down among the crows of an enormous tall boat with huge white wings flying up the coast through the rain toward the country of the ice where ravens are kings, although there are a lot of stories about boats among crows, they have been noticing boats for thousands of years here. Nicholas, grinning shyly, agrees with Nora that the rains will not come until December, and is razzed so thoroughly that he flushes and forgets to pick a day. Niall and Peadar O Donnell, and George and Anna Christie and their eight children, and Timmy and Rachel, and Michael and Sara's three girls, they all get days in November, Stella cheerfully picking the dates out of the hat and refusing to choose a day herself no matter how much she is teased and razzed by the assemblage. At the end of the evening when everyone is putting coats on and shaking hands and settling tabs, she sits for a moment in a corner with the doctor and thinks about all the people who could have squares in the pool but don't and no one even thought to speak their names aloud: Red Hugh O Donnell, and the quiet man in the wheelchair who went with Dec on the *Plover*, and Nicholas' dad, and Kristi's dad, and the nun who died in the old hotel, and Grace's mother, and Rachel's baby, the inch who went to sea. On their souls our prayers, she thinks silently to herself. Amen to that, says the doctor aloud, his cigarette glowing in the dark. Amen to that, Stella.

28.

Later, wrapped in a shawl on the deck, Stella asks the doctor what was the hardest thing he ever had to do as a doctor? Technically, she says, I mean, medically, not emotionally, I can only imagine the hardest things you have had to encounter emotionally. I mean surgically, I guess. He is silent for a while, his cigarette glowing, the thirteenth and last of the day, the apostle Matthias. I sewed a man back into his skin, he says finally. Did I ever tell you about that? Circumstances had conspired to remove the man's skin from his chest, both anterior and posterior. He was, as it were, the nakedest of men. But circumstances had also conspired to put me in a position to address the problem immediately. The patient was thoroughly unconscious, and indeed he remained in a coma for several days after I sewed him back into his skin. I was lucky to have at that time an excellent assistant, who immediately coated the patient with a substance sufficient to fend off infection while I stitched the skin back together, and my assistant and I then slipped the skin back on the patient, a fairly arduous task. A little minor detail work here and there, and some patching, especially under the shoulders, and we were done. The only really noticeable scar was around the neck, that was unavoidable. I am not sure that such an operation had been done before. Probably it is now the surgical equivalent of child's play, but then we were quietly proud of our work. The patient, as I say, remained in a coma for several days, and by the time he awoke, healing had progressed at such a rate that he was aware only of tightness of fit here and there and a sagging sensation under his shoulders. He chalked this up to the same event that had caused his original difficulty, and my assistant and I did not see fit to explain overmuch. Nor did we have the time or leisure in that environment to attend to patients as we would have in other circumstances. This patient for example had experienced trauma such that he was a changed man ever after, and his physical appearance was the least of his concerns. His objective in life became something else altogether from what it had been before the event. A most remarkable case both medically and psychologically. Observing his behavior since that time has been an education of inestimable value. You might think that a man who had survived a traumatic event of that enormity, and suffered loss on what can only be accounted an epic scale, would retreat into some sort of emotional refuge, or erect sturdy defenses against any hint of pain, or decline any and all responsibility for other people for the rest of his life; but indeed the reverse was true, and his sense of responsibility grew so vast and thorough that I sometimes wonder if it has bred its own set of problems. A most remarkable case.

Do you stay in touch with him? asks Stella.

O yes, says the doctor. I see him twice a year professionally and more often in the social ramble. You know him. Small man, tough, firm-minded. Wants to make sure everyone in town is safe and secure. Considers the health and happiness of every resident his life's work, and quietly assumes responsibility under the aegis of a Department of Public Works, the definition of which he has successfully stretched like a new skin.

Cedar!

The doctor takes a long pull on Matthias.

That is what he has called himself ever since the war, yes. He took a new name when he got a new skin and I must say that the name has come to fit him beautifully. To be honest I cannot even remember the name he had when we were in the mountains during the war. That name died with the man he used to be.

29.

The day before the rains came Michael the policeman received the State of Oregon Above and Beyond Medal from the Governor of Oregon in a special ceremony in the school auditorium at noon to which the entire community was invited and after which an informal reception starring the Governor and the Superintendent of the Oregon State Police would be held in the pub. The Superintendent, a slight man with a limp and a dry wit that has much enlivened his long career in law enforcement in the state, begins the proceedings by noting that he himself was also like Michael once the entire de facto police department in a rural district but that his most famous arrest was that of wolverine that (a) had become a past master at robbing fur traps in the district and (b) was not supposed to exist, wolverine officially being extinct in the State of Oregon, but there it was, inarguable, furious, and not smelling exactly like a rose neither, said the Superintendent, to general laughter. The Governor addresses the assemblage after handing Michael the medal. There are some moments when we are tested to the very bottom of our souls, says the Governor, and those moments always arrive unexpectedly, and very often no one is there to witness them, and the decision to act comes from the deepest part of who we are, our truest selves; for this very deepest aspect of the soul we have only words that do not fit very well, but those are the words we have, and I use them here with humility and gratitude: character, courage, honor. I have been governor for eight years, says the Governor, and before that I spent many years in civil service, and I have seen much, and now that my own service is about to end, I can be frank about what is important, as opposed to what we say is important. Children are important, and serving each other is important, says the Governor, and everything else is not as important. We argue and debate and excoriate and demonize and send things to committee, says the Governor, and meanwhile children starve and are raped and endure illnesses a doctor could arrest in an instant. But for every night when I sat in my office with my head in my hands filled with despair at the way children were being mistreated in the state I had sworn to serve, says the Governor, there were always mornings when I heard about men like Michael. There are such astounding seeds of grace and courage in us, says the Governor, that you cannot, in the end, surrender to despair. That is what I have learned, above all other lessons, in my time, says the Governor, and that is why I present this medal to this man before all his friends and neighbors, and say publicly that we admire him and thank him, for his courage is, if we are honest with each other and using real words this afternoon, an act of love.

30.

Well, son, says Cedar to Nicholas, I've drawn up the papers for you to quietly take over the Department, *de facto* rather than *de jure*, *de jure* Worried Man and I will remain co-directors but we are getting old no question about it and it's time for someone young and strong and smart and ambitious to take over and bring new energy to the ancient enterprise, although you bet your butt I will be issuing advice hand over tea kettle.

Sir?

Nicholas, don't call me sir, it gives me peristalsis in the esophagus.

Cedar.

Nicholas.

I've decided to go to college.

Nicholas?

Oregon State University, sir. In Corvallis.

I know where it is, son.

To study marine biology.

Have you been admitted?

No, sir.

Nicholas, stop calling me sir, it's killing my bladder.

Cedar.

Did you apply?

Yes, sir.

And you have expectations of being accepted?

Yes, sir. I am the salutatorian of my senior class.

My salutatorianations.

Thank you, sir.

Nicholas, please stop calling me sir.

Sorry. Sir. Sorry.

Do you have any money for college?

I've applied for two scholarships and three grants. The prospects are good. I met with Mr. McCann at the bank and he helped me find funding sources.

Your father knows about this?

I told him last night.

Does he approve?

He was … startled. But he says I should shoot for the moon. He's … changed.

You're sure about this decision?

Yes.

Well. Well. I'm happy for you, Nicholas. College will be good for you. Launching pad for what you can become. And I understand that's an excellent university. Despite the football team.

Yes sir.

Damn my ancient and bleary eyes, Nicholas.

Sorry.

Can you work summers for the department?

I'd be thrilled if you would let me.

And you are enrolling in January, if they see fit to admit you?

September of next year.

Would you like to work here until then?

Very much so, s ... Cedar.

31.

George Christie writes and calls every single person he ever knew in the logging, timber, milling, wood processing, wood finishing, housing, marketing, and shipping businesses, not to mention every union rep and barkeep he ever knew of which there were a few, as he says, and he makes a contact list as long as yer other arm, as he says, of the people who express interest in buying or selling the extraordinary objects to be carved and shipped by what he and Nora have both begun to call Old Bastard Wood Products, and they make up a preliminary catalogue of selections, and interview woodshops large and small within a hundred miles to ascertain who might be able to handle subcontracted smaller pieces if such need ever comes to pass, and after brief consideration of nonprofit status they incorporate as a for-profit corporation, and then he says, as he and Nora are sitting on the deck of her studio, now here, kid, is when someone who is a human bean has to go meet the customers and shake their fins and nail down the orders, that's how it works, so we are going to have to hire a rep, you got any ideas?

And she says, yes, me.

No no, kid, says George, you're the talent.

I'll go.

Kid, you are not paying the closest attention to old George Christie, which you should. I ain't young but I ain't always stupid either.

I'm going to make the journey, George. I've been thinking about a journey I need to take alone, and here it is. I'll be gone about a month. I'll be sure there are plenty of carvings done before I go. You map out the itinerary for me and I'll go. I've never been over the mountains, George, and it's time. I've never gone anywhere just *because*. I'm going to wander with purpose. Trust me.

Well, I don't know, kid.

Really.
Really?
Your family …
My business, George. No offense.

32.

The doctor takes Worried Man out for their evening wander around town. Stella is taking a long long long hot shower after a long day digging post holes. The doctor is sitting on her porch smoking Labbaeus, the eleventh apostle, who was surnamed Thaddaeus. He watches a heron flap slowly and intently east to west, emerging from a dell in the hills and working slowly toward the sea. The sun is glorious but its heat is spent this late in the season. Down at the edge of the vineyard where the fence will go a coyote osmoses along the line of vegetation, waiting for something to bolt. The doctor counts three fishing boats on the horizon, all of them rigged for salmon. The sky fills gently with swifts, taking over from the swallows, who head home in a ragged gaggle, chaffing each other and doing somersaults. A vulture takes a last cruise on general principle and then folds up his tent and surfs down to the dairy farm where lately the vultures like to sit on the far fence at dusk giving the willies to the high school kids who come to make out as night falls. Sara and the girls are making supersoup, which is so dense with potatoes and turnips and rutabagas and onions and leeks that Michael says he could use it to plaster the tub haw haw. The priest is working on his sermon for All Souls Day, which started out as twenty pages of closely reasoned prose, which he cut to ten, and then to five, and then to two, and now he is smoking a cigar and contemplating the very real possibility that he will rise on that day of ancient prayer for the soul of the deceased, and approach the lectern, and adjust the microphone, and clear his throat, and say *wake up!*

33.

This is Daniel Cooney making a tape for the Oral History Project. I am twelve years old but will be thirteen tomorrow, on All Souls Day. This is my first tape. I am nervous. I hope to be a professional bicycle racer. This is my ambition. I think I can do it. My mother was a famous runner and my father says his side of the family was renowned in years past for relentless illogical activity, so I have the right genes. Also I want to be an ocean scientist. I am especially interested in sea lions, which are not lions. I used to want more than anything to leave this town but recently while recuperating from an accident I learned to appreciate the town in other ways. When I needed help a lot of people were immediately ready to help. This was a lesson for me. There are lessons everywhere, I guess. That is a lesson in itself. My father is Owen Cooney, a mechanic and repairman. My mother Nora Cooney is an artist who is starting a business with a family friend. Her real name is No Horses. My grandfather works for the town and my grandmother is a teacher. Because it is a small town I know almost everybody and they know me. Because the town is on the ocean it used to be a fishing town and a logging town also. But now those jobs are finished in their former form as our family friend George says. So as a town we are not sure what we will be. Some of us are afraid the town will die because everyone will have to leave to find work. Some other people think we will invent new ways to be a town. I am not sure about this and no one has asked me. I think we might become the bicycle-racing capital of the world, or maybe a place famous for studying sea lions. That could happen. My friend Kristi thinks that our town will become famous for storytelling. She says maybe we will build a storytelling factory and people will come to hear and buy and trade stories and there will be story festivals and contests and etc. That could happen. We do have a lot of stories here. As long as my grandfather is alive we have an endless supply of stories. His white name is William Mahon but his true name is Worried Man. This is ironic because he does not seem worried very much. There is a story there I am sure. My dad and I are building a boat for my grandfather. Not for the sea but for a tree. It is a tradition on my mother's side of the family that when someone dies he or she is placed in a boat and the boat is hoisted into a tree, usually a cedar but sometimes a hemlock. My grandfather also had an accident recently on Mount Hood and lost the use of most of his body except his head and hand. He says it was not an accident at all but I don't know what that means. My dad and I are working on the boat secretly. It is a gift for my grandfather. In a way it is his coffin. You want to be careful about how you present a coffin as a gift to the guy who will be using it eventually, says my father, but on the other hand you want to get it done before it's needed, he says, so we are quietly building it on the weekends and after school. We are using every wood that grows in or around the river, and then using stones from the sea as filigree. Also the priest has blessed the boat. We want to have everyone in town say a story or a prayer into it until it's crammed with stories and prayers for my grandfather. Our friend Moses has collected feathers and tufts of fur and small bones and things to put in the boat. My mother carved a heron into the prow. My grandmother put a book into a special cedar box near the stern that my father built especially for the book. I am not sure what the book is. My grandmother says she will tell me one of these days. My father says there's a huge amount we don't know about life and death, and, all things considered, having a really good boat to travel in seems like an excellent idea. This makes sense to me. Yesterday we cut words into the side of the boat. My dad did it in the language that his side of the family spoke for thousands of years: LIAM Ó MATHÚNA, A BHÁD, it says, which means WILLIAM MAHON, HIS BOAT. Thank you, the end.

34.

Moses, sitting on the football helmet at Other Repair, issues a speech as Owen planes planks. Human people, says Moses, think that stories have beginnings and middles and ends, but we crow people know that stories just wander on and on and change form and are reborn again and again. That is who they are. Stories are not only words, you know. Words are just the clothes that people drape on stories. When crows tell stories, stories tell us, do you know what I mean? That's just how it is with crow people. We have been playing with stories for a very long time. There are a lot of stories that haven't been told yet, did you know that? And some stories get lost and don't get told again for thousands of years. You find them sometimes all lonely. That's why we have wings, you know. To go find stories. There are some stories that only certain kinds of people can tell. For example the wolverine people, there are some stories only they know and if you try to tell one of those stories nothing comes out of your mouth. That's how dancing and singing were invented, you know, to try to jiggle the stories out. O, yes, a very long time ago. And there are stories that can be told only under water, and stories that can only be told far up in the sky. There are some goose stories that can only be told when you go over the top of a mountain. There are human stories like that too, of course. Some human stories you can only tell at night and some can only be told to children, isn't that so? There are caves south of here where there are human being stories scattered all over like pebbles on the beach. You wouldn't believe how many human stories there are. I have seen that cave, but I cannot tell those stories, Owen. Yet there they are, waiting for someone to come along and pick them up and tell them again. Because stories keep going and going. They are a sort of food, I think. But what do I know, Owen? I am only an old crow person who used to have wings.

Sitting on an old football helmet and chattering like a jay, says Owen.

Ah, the jay people, our cousins, a garrulous people, the jay people.

Look who's talking.

Exactly. Hey, is the game on the radio? Can I turn it on?

35.

The traditional annual All Saints Day Dinner at Maple Head and Worried Man's house. November 1, the ceremonial beginning of wet season, football season, remembering season, inside-the-house season, basketball season, soup-and-stew season. May and Billy and Nora and Owen and Daniel and Kristi and Cedar and Nicholas and Moses around the table. Grilled salmon, last tomatoes of the season, basil minced with garlic and oil, fresh steaming loaves of bread with Oregon State University logos punched into the crusts in honor of Nicholas being a College Boy. Gooseberry pies. Cheese from the other end of the county where Cedar knows a guy who trades milk and cheese for professional consultation as regards water-distribution systems. Ale from Grace's pub. Wines from a vineyard in the valleys to the east that Stella says is the kind of wine that will more and more be made here in the future including God help us all in Neawanaka at what will someday be famous as Stella Maris Vineyards you mark my words. Trails and tendrils and threads and webs and weaves of talk. The Department of Public Works. Early planning for the town picnic. College football. How to ascertain the gender of a new heron without having your eyes pecked out by that terrifying blade of a beak. Legendary train stations around these United States and the possibilities of Nora visiting, for example, the train station in Mississippi where W. C. Handy invented the blues probably late in the afternoon. The nun who died gently in the hotel: three stories that she liked to tell Moses, having to do with sunder, thunder, and plunder. A disquisition on the gooseberry and its application to the physics of time travel. Disquisition: evacuation systems and robosuits. Q: if a man sailed directly west into the ocean from Neawanaka, on, say, a small fishing boat, which country would he strike first? Q: if a woman wished to publish a book crammed to the gills with stories of Neawanaka, would the better title be *Further Annals of Neawanaka,* or *Sisaxai Stories*? Sea lions: their anatomy, life cycle, and primary role in story sagas among aboriginal peoples of the central Oregon coast. The Great Hunger in Ireland, 1845-1852, and its rippling effects on the descendants of the survivors. Argument: the order in which berries ripen on the central Oregon coast, from salmonberries in May through gooseberries in October. Subargument: salalberries—watery weak-ass excuses for fruit or subtle glorious treasures? Kristi not only smiles for the first time that No Horses has ever noticed but she also actually no kidding bursts out laughing when Owen and Billy and Daniel have a contest to see who can sound the most like a chuffing huffing enormous arrogant male sea lion hauled up on the beach crowing about his harem and challenging any and all local dogs to battle. Cedar does the dishes with Nicholas after Cedar begs Maple Head to *please* find something *decent* on the radio for the oppressed kitchen *slaves* who cannot *bear* to listen one more *second* to this classical *crap* droning out of the radio and she tells him to stuff it but then finds a station playing nothing but the Beach Boys, *yes!* Coffee and pie. Owen spreads a map on the table for Nora. Nicholas wheels Billy out to the deck for a cigar. Kiss the joy as it flies, says Billy quietly. Blake, you know. Yes sir, says Nicholas. Kristi holding Moses in her lap in the corner as Daniel halfheartedly does his math homework. Maple Head builds a fire.

36.

At four in the morning, on All Souls Day, the Day of the Dead, the second of November, the priest winning the betting pool, seven drops of water fell from the sky, headlong, pell-mell, sliding from the brooding mist, and then seventy, and then the gentle deluge, a whisper of wet, a thorough and persistent pittering on leaf mold and newt knuckle, web and wood, tent and vent, house and mouse, the rain splittering the sea, soaking boats, rinsing streets, fluffing owls and wetting towels, sliding along power lines and dripping from eaves, rivuleting and braiding and weaving tiny lines in the thirsty earth, darkening the trunks of trees, jewelling the strands of spiders, sliding along clotheslines, moistening the infinitesimal dust in rain gauges. The rain gags a thrush chick who opened her mouth because the rain sounds like her mama. A rushing rivulet saves a shrew who is about to be snagged by a snake. New trout, having never seen rain on the river, rise eagerly to ripples on the Mink. Some windows close against the moist and some open for the music. Rain slips and slides along hawsers and chains and ropes and cables and gladdens the cells of mosses and weighs down the wings of moths. It maketh the willow shiver its fingers and thrums on doors of dens in the fens. It falls on hats and cats and trucks and ducks and cars and bars and clover and plover. It grayeth the sand on the beach and fills thousands of flowers to the brim. It thrills worms and depresses damselflies. Slides down every window rilling and murmuring. Wakes the ancient mud and mutter of the swamp, which has been cracked and hard for months. Falls gently on leeks and creeks and bills and rills and the last shriveled blackberries like tiny dried purple brains on the bristle of bushes. On the young bear trundling through a copse of oaks in the woods snorffling up acorns. On ferns and fawns, cubs and kits, sheds and redds. On salmon as long as your arm thrashing and roiling in the river. On roof and hoof, doe and hoe, fox and fence, duck and muck. On a slight man in a yellow slicker crouched by the river with his recording equipment all covered against the rain with plastic wrap from the grocery store and after he figures out how to get the plastic from making crinkling sounds when he turns the machine on he settles himself in a little bed of ferns and says to the crow huddled patiently in rain, okay, now, here we go, Oral History Project, what the rain says to the river as the wet season opens, project number … something or other … where's the fecking start button? … I can't see anything … can you see a green light? yes? is it on? damn my eyes … okay! there it is! it's working! rain and the river! here we go!

Thanks

Lodestars, compass points, emotional touchstones during the wrestling of this peculiar tale to paper:

The Complete Poetry & Prose of William Blake
The Horse's Mouth, by Joyce Cary
Sweet Thursday, by John Steinbeck
Cloudstreet, by Tim Winton
For the Time Being, by Annie Dillard
Nehalem Tillamook Tales (told by Clara Pearson)
The King James Bible
Hymns to the Silence, by Van Morrison
The Rising, by Bruce Springsteen
Third Symphony, by Henryk Gorecki
Tosca, by Giacomo Puccini

Thanks too to the fine writer and former logger Jim LeMonds of Castle Rock, Washington, for help with logging details; to Sara Ogle and Melissa Madenski of Neskowin for true stories of the coast that I have borrowed and jerryrigged; to the erudite editor and scholar Dave Hanson of Sheridan for natural history help in the Cheamhill River watershed; to the poet and scholar Isabel Stirling of the University of California at Berkeley for prompt and creative natural history assistance; to the fine poet Ger Killeen of Marylhurst University, for help with my Gaelic; to my friends Bob Antonelli and John Wironen and Ed Obermiller, all Catholic priests of the Congregation of Holy Cross at the University of Portland, for their help with Latin and Catholic ritual; to the fine writer and wonderful scholar Stephen Dow Beckham of Lewis and Clark College for Salish language details; to Jo Alexander, Micki Reaman, and Tom Booth at Oregon State University Press for wonderfully sharp eyes and for help with Tillamook stories; to Detective Jon Harrington of the Oregon State Police for help with police matters; to the salty cheerful Mark Jacobson for his help with automobile repair matters; to the wonderful writers David James Duncan of Montana and Robin Cody and Barry Lopez of Oregon for continuous laughter and tart honesty; and to the fine painter and electric soul Mary Miller Doyle, whose total belief in the people in these pages allowed these pages to be written over the course of some years. No Mary, no novel. The moral, then: it's all her fault, heh heh heh.

Brian Doyle